UnknowN
Museums
of Upstate New York

To Harriet,

Chuck D'Imperio

Trolley Museum of New York, Kingston

UNKNOWN MUSEUMS

of Upstate New York

A GUIDE TO 50 TREASURES

CHUCK D'IMPERIO

SYRACUSE UNIVERSITY PRESS

∞ The paper used in this publication meets the minimum requirements
of the American National Standard for Information Sciences—Permanence
of Paper for Printed Library Materials, ANSI Z39.48-1992.

All photographs appearing in this volume are courtesy of the author.

For a listing of books published and distributed by Syracuse University Press,
visit www.SyracuseUniversityPress.syr.edu.

ISBN: 978-0-8156-1028-1 (paper)   978-0-8156-5248-9 (e-book)

Library of Congress Cataloging-in-Publication Data
D'Imperio, Chuck.
Unknown museums of Upstate New York : a guide to 50 treasures / Chuck D'Imperio.
pages cm
ISBN 978-0-8156-1028-1 (pbk. : alk. paper) 1. Museums—New York (State)—Upstate
New York—Guidebooks. 2. Upstate New York (N.Y.)—Guidebooks. I. Title.
AM12.N4D56 2013
069.025747'1—dc23 2013023850

Manufactured in the United States of America

"...Their actions were nothing short of heroic."

I had the unforgettable experience of traveling thousands of miles around Upstate New York while researching and visiting all fifty museums mentioned in this book. My journey came to an end, for the most part, at the close of the summer of 2011. I then set out to turn all of that research, and all of those experiences, into the book you now have in your hands.

Sadly, at the end of that summer Mother Nature reared her fierce head, and she was not in a good mood. First Hurricane Irene, and then, just two weeks later, Tropical Storm Lee, delivered a devastating one-two punch to the region. Both disasters carried with them billion-dollar price tags. The devastation was almost indescribable. It presented Upstate New York's museums with their greatest challenge in recorded history. Over 80% of the Empire State was listed as a "disaster area" one time or another in September and October of 2011. Several of the museums in this book suffered severe damage.

I am happy to report that after two years, I have contacted all the storm-damaged museums, and almost all are back in operation. This is due in no small part to the tireless museum directors and volunteers who slogged through the fury of the storms, many times ignoring their own personal safety, to remove and secure priceless artifacts from the endangered museums. Their actions were nothing short of heroic.

Museums in Owego, Marlboro, Granville, Fleischmanns, and other communities were heavily impacted by the historic dual storm surge. They are included in this book.

They are up and running again, thank God. If you were ever going to visit one of these New York treasures, may I suggest that now would be a very good time to do so. They can use your help.

Having said all that, I must sadly report that one museum, originally to be a chapter in this book, received more damage from the flooding than any other.

I spent a wonderful afternoon with Ann Peconie, the director of the Walter Elwood Museum in Amsterdam. She gently guided me through the many floors of precious Mohawk Valley artifacts on a sunny day. It was a lovely museum, rich in its history. It was housed in Guy Park Manor, a splendid stone riverfront estate built in 1774 by the nephew of Sir William Johnson.

In August of 2011, Hurricane Irene zeroed in on this magnificent old place and savaged it. It ripped the ancient outer walls asunder, spilling priceless artifacts into the turgid waters of the Mohawk River. Many items were lost forever, many others damaged irreparably. The destruction to the Walter Elwood Museum was almost total.

There are plans to relocate what items they have salvaged to a newer location on higher ground. Guy Park Manor was a mortal casualty of the hurricane and is now but a mere memory.

Ann Peconie was one of the most dedicated and passionate museum directors of the many that I had the pleasure to interview for this book. I dedicate this book to her, her staff, and the spirit that she embodies on behalf of all museums who "keep New York's past alive for New York's future generations."

After much hard work by an army of supporters and volunteers it looks like her museum may just be on the way back. Before this book went to print I spoke with my friend Ann about the loss of her beautiful Guy Park Manor museum home and the destruction to her beloved museum. Her words are inspiring.

"It was unbelievable how the Museum members and supporters pulled together to help us get the collections out of the flood-ravaged building, Chuck," she told me. "We had people arriving from as far away as New York City and Syracuse that wanted to come and assist us in our time of need. Amsterdam residents young and old came out to do what they could to provide us assistance.

We are so excited after many long months of cleaning, sorting, and saving what we could of the damaged collections, to have finally found a new home in the former Noteworthy Complex and Sanford and Sons Carpet Mills at 100 Church Street in the heart of Amsterdam, on the bank of the historic Chuctanunda Creek where Amsterdam was truly born hundreds of years ago. We expect to open late spring or early summer of 2013."

As a tribute to the original Walter Elwood Museum in Amsterdam, I have included its entry as the final "In Memoriam" chapter in this book. It describes the original museum exactly as it was the beautiful, sunny day of my visit, just three weeks before it disappeared into the swirling Mohawk River. I do this both as a tribute and a warning.

Let none of us take these wonderful treasured museums for granted, for in an instant . . . they may be gone.

AUTHOR'S NOTES

This book is divided into general regions for simplicity of reference. Obviously, some counties fall into two or more areas; I have designated them as within the region where they are dominant geographically. For example, the city of Ilion (Remington Arms Museum) is clearly not in the Adirondack Park, but I have placed it in the Adirondacks/North Country section. Herkimer County (where Ilion is located) sprawls over more than 1,450 square miles, reaching deeply into the Adirondacks.

I have made every effort to include as much current information in this book as possible. As of the date of the book's printing (2013), all the contact information included is accurate. It is wise, however, when visiting these museums, as in all travel, to make advance contact with them to assess any change in hours, admission prices, location, or museum details.

CONTENTS

INTRODUCTION

> "Living is like tearing through a museum. Not until later do you
> really start absorbing what you saw, thinking about it, looking it up in
> a book, and remembering—because you can't take it in all at once."
> —AUDREY HEPBURN (1929–1993), actress,
> humanitarian

I remember the very first museum I ever visited. I was ten years old and my fifth grade class went on a field trip to the New York State Museum in Albany. This was when it was inside the mighty, multi-columned State Education Building across from the Capitol.

It was the first great, grand building I'd ever been in. The ceiling disappeared into the dark woody shadows of the towering rooms. The "clickety-clack" of our little hard-heel shoes reverberated off the tile floors and careened from wall to wall. Most of what we saw that day is forgotten, but a few items stand out even after a half-century.

I remember a diorama (everything was behind glass, safely out of reach of the sticky fingers of us kids) featuring an Iroquois longhouse. I recall the sad-faced Native Americans peering out of their animal skin parkas as faux snow glistened on the ground around them. Their eyes were so lifelike that I found myself waiting for them to blink at me and invite me into their dreamscape.

I remember military battle flags, dozens of them, hundreds of them. They lined a long hallway, and each was adorned with a different colored ribbon hanging from the staff. Our tour guide, a matronly woman with half-glasses on a chain and a handkerchief tucked into her ample bosom, intoned, "These battle flags are the proud banners of our *very* freedom." I remember she trilled the word "very" as if to give it its own power. Hers was a voice dipped in authority, and it rose effortlessly above the clickety-clack cacophony of the herd of elementary school children.

A giant mastodon skeleton stood guard in the center hallway of the museum. Our guide told us how the behemoth had been discovered in a nearby town called Cohoes. It was a large, scary, and, in a way, forlorn sight. The Cohoes Mastodon weighed ten thousand pounds when it was alive, we were told. I always remembered that figure. "Ten thousand pounds, boys and girls," our leader told us in an excited, dramatic tone. It was a figure that no fifth grader could comprehend, and that made the giant beast all the more mysterious in our eyes. Still, he looked a little lonely.

I had never seen a stuffed animal before my visit. I was wide-eyed at the lifelike deer, cougars, bears, and other animals all preserved in settings reflecting their natural New York State habitats. Dozens of birds were frozen in time peering out of bushes, perched on tree branches, and some even hanging by not-quite-invisible wires simulating their flights of fancy.

And I also remember Indian arrowheads. Thousands of them.

And that is pretty much it. But the overwhelming feeling that I took from that day in 1959 was a sense of having been someplace *important*. Someplace majestic, reverential. The chandeliers, the marble columns, the dark mahogany display cases, the professorial docent, the gloomy and mysterious exhibit rooms, the sad-faced Native Americans beckoning me into their longhouse. The cougar ready to pounce. The still-life robin feeding fake worms to her still-life babies.

It was magical.

My impression was that we were literally in the presence of history. And to our collective surprise, we little kids were allowed into this hallowed place to see what appeared to us to be "adult things." When we boarded our bus to return to our little town of Sidney, two hours from Albany, I could not get the images from my first museum visit out of my head.

As I was lulled into slumber by the rocking and rolling of the school bus navigating the dips and rolls of Route 7, my head was buzzing with vivid images. Of the Iroquois men returning from a hunt with food for the evening meal in the longhouse. Of the battle flags waving furiously overhead, above the charging U.S. soldiers running breakneck up San Juan Hill with Teddy Roosevelt. Of the hulking mastodon lumbering his way through the prehistoric muck of Cohoes looking for a place to hibernate for oh, say, a century. The lilting chorus of the Adirondack songbirds. The growling of the unseen mountain lions. My mind was a flashing slide show of sights, sounds, colors, and action, which, by the way, was almost the exact opposite of the reality of the dim, quiet, shadowy, and static museum.

The imagination of a ten year old has no boundary.

In the fifty years since that first introduction to a museum, I have been to dozens, perhaps hundreds of others. Art museums, natural history museums, military museums, science museums, wax museums, auto museums, and many others. Big and small ones. Great ones and odd ones. I have been to museums in the palaces of Europe and to museums in American garages. I have basked in the glow of da Vinci's *Mona Lisa* in Paris, and I have scratched my head at the world's largest ball of twine in Cawker City, Kansas.

The Unknown Museums of Upstate New York is the latest in a series of books I have authored about my native region. Since museums act as the best primers one can use to experience a place, I decided to seek out some of the most unusual museums in the region known to locals as simply "Upstate" (the word Upstate referring, basically, to everything up and out of New York City).

Surely everyone knows about the marquee museums of the region. The New York State Museum in Albany has hundreds of thousands of visitors a year (and it is free!). The Corning Museum of Glass is a tourist magnet of the Finger Lakes area. The Strong Museum of Play in Rochester is one of the most popular museums in the entire state. The Munson-Williams-Proctor Museum of Art in Utica is world-class, hosting works by O'Keefe, Dali, Picasso, Whistler, and Thomas Cole. The National Baseball Hall of Fame and Museum in Cooperstown, more than any other museum, certainly needs no introduction.

But what about the New York State Museum of Cheese? Or the National Bottle Museum? Or the Slate Museum? Or the D.I.R.T.

Museum? Ever heard of these? I didn't think so. But I visited them and forty-six others in my five-thousand-mile journey around the state seeking out these fascinating repositories of New York history. They are small, sometimes hard to find, and often overlooked by travelers passing by. Still, they have stories to tell, and great ones at that!

The most visited museum here is the Lucy Desi Museum in Jamestown, which welcomes forty thousand visitors or more annually to its multi-level home in the downtown business district. The least visited museum in this book is the Robert Louis Stevenson Cottage and Museum, with only five hundred visitors coming through the front door. A year! The "Number of Visitors Annually" listings for the museums give voice to the fact that these museums struggle mightily to stay vital. For example, if you see that the Iroquois Museum in Howes Cave receives about fifteen hundred visitors a year, you might say that is a pretty significant number. But once you factor in that most of these visitors, say fifty a day, visit during the summer tourist season, well, you can see that things are pretty quiet the rest of the year.

I hope this book changes all that.

These museums are *all* worth a visit. Surely not every one of them will interest all readers. When I started out my research for the book and mapping out my itinerary for fifty visits to fifty museums, I had no clue what awaited me.

I had no interest in fly-fishing, for example. Yet my afternoon at the Catskill Fly Fishing Museum in Livingston Manor was one of my favorite days of last year. I had played with a toy kazoo when I was a child, so I thought a visit to the Kazoo Museum in Eden would be a fun, yet brief, stop. I was there for hours. And I left with a new kazoo that I actually made! And it was like that over and over during my six-month journey around the state. (You'll notice I appear in a few of the museum photographs. I did this to show the various sizes of them, from big to small.)

I do not own a gun. In fact I don't think I've ever really fired one. Still, my visit to the Remington Arms Museum in Ilion gave me great insight into the history of guns, the romance involved with the pioneers and their gun, and the artistry that goes into creating these magnificent firearms. What do I know about stock car racing? Nothing. And yet my time at the

D.I.R.T. Museum in Weedsport was a fascinating three-hour look at what once was, and may again someday be, one of Upstate New York's most popular pastimes.

Some of the homes that have been turned into museums are among my favorites. To stand at the foot of the actual bed on which President U. S. Grant died at the Grant Cottage Museum in Wilton is a moving experience. At the mansion which houses the Seward House Museum in Auburn, I touched the carriage from which Secretary of State William Seward was thrown during a ride through Washington, D.C. Seward was in his sick bed recovering from his injuries sustained in this carriage accident on the night the conspirators came to kill him after Lincoln was shot at Ford's Theatre. The ancient Gomez Mill Museum in Marlboro has one of the most amazing histories of any home in the U.S. Of course, nobody knows about it. Maybe after they read about my visit to this awesome, understated Hudson Valley home they will be enlightened.

The museums in this book can be found in virtually every corner of the vast Upstate New York region. And though the thrust of this work is to shine the light on the museums themselves, if you follow the fifty subjects in the book you will have covered some pretty amazing locales. The largest city with a featured museum in this book is Albany, where the USS *Slater* Destroyer Escort Museum is located in the Hudson River at the foot of "Capitol Hill." Albany's population is approximately 100,000. The smallest community to host a featured museum in this book is Osceola, which is the home of the National Fiddlers Hall of Fame and Museum. The population of this North Country hamlet is about two hundred. Regardless, both the capital city's floating museum and the country hamlet's toe-tapping museum are both equally worth a visit.

Without a doubt, you have been to most of the communities featured in this book. But there is a chance you may never have had the pleasure to wander into Childs or Newark or Romulus or Vails Gate. They are tiny little map dots sprinkled across Upstate. I have been to them all and they were all fun.

People have asked me how much time I spent in these museums. Well, it varies. A half-hour would suffice at the Cherry Valley Museum. Maybe an hour at the Holland Land Office Museum in Batavia. One could easily spend a couple of hours at the Trolley Museum in Kingston or the Military Museum in Saratoga Springs. Several, including the Northeast Classic Car Museum in Norwich and the Lucy Desi Museum & Desilu Studios in Jamestown, require a significant investment of time.

Each entry features five different sections. The main body of the entry tells the history of the museum itself. I call the next section the "Wow Factor" section. When I visited each of the fifty museums, I asked the director or curator to tell me the one special item at the museum that causes visitors to pause, reflect, or even laugh. The one item that causes people to say, "Wow!" when they discover it. This section is my favorite, and the directors' choices are fascinating. The third section is called "The Take-Away," where I explain the significant reaction I had to each individual museum. I wrote this after my visit was complete, and here I try and give my own revelations of the museum. The number of annual visitors is also listed.

In the section I call "Up around the Bend," I tried to pick another place for the traveler to visit while at the museum. My intention here is to make a fulfilling experience out of a trip to the museum. Maybe there is another historic site, a famous restaurant, a nearby oddity, or even another museum you will find amusing or interesting nearby. I think you will find this an adventurous section.

I also list the "Nuts and Bolts" of each museum, giving the reader all the particulars (hours, location, directions, admission fee, website, etc.) about each museum. It is my hope that the readers of this book will become hungry to seek out all of the different entries, to slip this book into the glove compartment of their car and pull it out when they go on the road in Upstate.

The "From Here to There" feature is included so that you, the reader, may actually form your own itinerary when using this book in your travels. This segment allows you to visit the nearest museum to the one you are at, thereby creating a flow, an itinerary that will enhance your experience on the road.

It is important that we pause for a moment and reflect on the status of our museums in the present. These treasure troves are valuable repositories of our culture and heritage, and as such, there is an unwritten mandate that we keep these places sacred and available to future generations. That is not always easy.

In this time of uncertain economic fortunes, New York's more than 2,000 museums are collectively "holding their breaths." The money stream from above has withered to a trickle as grants, state and federal contributions, and public donations have diminished in the face of budget tightening. And the ripples go far and wide. Take, for example, school field trips. It is estimated that more than six million students annually avail themselves of the wonders of New York's museums. Sadly, in the face of harrowing school budget drawdowns, field trips to these museums are often the first thing to go. This frustrates educators and cheats the young students out of valuable, and many times initial, exposure to our museums. As personal economic woes worsen, deep (and even shallow) pocket donors become shy and fundraising efforts become more desperate.

Just under twenty thousand New Yorkers earn a living directly related to employment with our museums. As financial pressure increases, these jobs are reduced and more and more of the museums rely heavily on a passionate volunteer corps to keep the lights on and the doors open. Exhibits change less frequently, programs, forums, and discussion panels are eliminated, hours are shortened, and corners are cut. Gas prices rise, and fewer and fewer visitors pass through the turnstiles.

Yes, New York State museums, of all sizes, face mighty challenges. So what can we do?

The strongest remedy to our museum's woes is to get up, get out, and go visit.

The more visitors a museum can produce, the more the boards of directors of these museums will take notice. While many offer free admission or ask for a "goodwill donation," you can show your support by making a contribution on your way out the door. Every dollar you are able to drop into the box on the front desk of a museum means less stress when the heating bill comes, more funds to acquire that next "must have" historical item, or more dollars to spread around when an interactive children's program becomes available. Think of your museum donations as great seeds that will flourish and grow and help rebuild the health of the New York State museum family.

And that is the underlying purpose of this book. It was never my intention to have this be strictly a database of information about our state's museums. First of all, there are more than a thousand museums in New York City and Long Island alone that do not even fall under the purview of my main geographic focal point, Upstate New York. In our region the museums are for the most part in small and rural communities. They lack the luxury of having a potential nearby visitors' pool numbering in the millions like our fellow New Yorkers downstate do. A volunteer cadre or a local historical society runs many of these museums independently. To call their budgets "shoestring" would be a monument of understatement.

But they have great and wonderful historical riches to share and despite their unique financial challenges, the upstate museums bear their mission with dignity, pride, and enthusiasm. It is my hope that this random selection of fifty little-known museums in Upstate New York might be the catalyst that sparks a rejuvenation in the interest of our rural communities, in the myriad of personalities that have added so much to our culture over the last three hundred years, and shines the light on their rich and important contributions to our state and nation.

The research, travel, and writing of this book have been a real eye opener for me, and the one thing that I will always cherish is the time I have spent with the directors and curators of each museum. Fifty in all. They are passionate, sincere, hardworking, dedicated "keepers of the flame." They work on disappearing budgets and put an incredible amount of sweat equity into these great little beacons of history. Each museum has become an extension of the director whom I spoke with (and vice versa).

I should also point out that for doing my research it was necessary that I try and interview the directors of these museums. Visitors should be assured, though, that each of these places is fully staffed with knowledgeable and enthusiastic personnel who are all more than able to answer any and all questions you may have when visiting.

Ask Liz Callahan to describe the humongous water wheel at Hanford Mills Museum in East Meredith, and her eyes dance with excitement. Ask Deb Brundage what a cobblestone is, and she will act like a kid on Christmas morning as she weaves the tale of the Cobblestone Museum in Childs. Mention to Bonnie Hays how impressed you are with the magnificent woven tapestries hanging from the ceiling of the Alling Coverlet Museum in Palmyra, and she will get choked up. Ask Gary Moeller what his favorite display is at the National Bottle Museum in Ballston Spa, and he will excitedly direct you to the "privy exhibit" of old bottles found in ancient outhouses! Ask Judy Rapaport what the reaction is of visitors to the Safe Haven Museum in Oswego, and she will tell you that "not a few tears have been shed in this room."

All of these museums certainly deserve a visit from you.

New York State Regions

1,000 Islands/ Seaway

Greater Niagara

Finger Lakes

Chautauqua/ Allegany

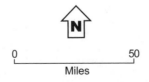

0 — 50
Miles

Syracuse University Cartographic Laboratory

1,000 Islands/
Seaway

Adirondacks/
North Country

Capital
District/
Saratoga

Central-
Leatherstocking

Catskills

Hudson
Valley

Region One

CHAUTAUQUA/ALLEGANY

Chautauqua, Allegany, and Cattaraugus Counties

1

AMERICAN MUSEUM OF CUTLERY
Cattaraugus, Cattaraugus County

*T*here is a certain small pocket of Western New York that is extremely hilly. As you drive west through Ellicottville, which hosts one of the state's largest ski resorts, you come to the small town of Cattaraugus in the county of the same name. Main Street is a steep hill, covered with old bricks. At the very top you will find the 1888 storefront home of the American Museum of Cutlery.

When the building was constructed, in 1851, it sold knives. After a fire destroyed the building, it was rebuilt in 1888 and it continued to sell knives.

Now it showcases them.

"We believe this is the only museum specifically dedicated to the history of edged tools in the entire Western Hemisphere not affiliated with any retailer or manufacturer," Patrick Cullen, founder and curator, told me. "We are chartered by the New York State Department of Education."

"Why Cattaraugus?" I asked.

"Believe it or not, western New York State and northwestern Pennsylvania had more than two hundred companies making knives, axes, and other cutting tools between 1850 and 1910. Our town is known as the country's first official railroad boomtown. The New York and Lake Erie Railroad (connecting the Hudson River with Lake Erie at nearby Dunkirk) was the longest railroad line in the world back then and Cattaraugus was the last difficult section to be completed. When the railroad announced it was changing course to traverse our local terrain, our population went from about twenty residents to nearly two thousand in a matter of a couple of weeks.

"After two long years of working railroad construction here, many of the workers decided to just stay here to live. Cattaraugus became an important center of commerce. Stage coach lines, cattle drives, we had it all. We even had a medical college! Numerous factories and small axe shops popped up like sprouts around the region," he said. "When the railroad line was completed in 1851, the Erie Canal was obsolete. And significant east-west commerce coursed right here through Cattaraugus."

The museum is certainly one of the smallest in this book. The old storefront looks much the same as it did when it opened in 1888. Tin ceilings, black and white floor tile patterns, gleaming old wood and glass display cases. Along the right side of the room is a long display case brimming with old knives (labeled "farrier," "butcher," "skinning," etc.). Some are displayed more prominently, like the ominous looking 1870 buffalo-skinning knife in its own case.

The tops of the walls are crowded with the stuffed heads of a wide assortment of animal heads (no doubt knifed to death). The left side of the room also has display cases featuring grinding tools and a separate display featuring the local company, Cattaraugus Cutlery Company.

"They made millions of knives here," Cullen told me. "The founder, J. B. F. Champlin, and his son started the business and later were joined by the Case brothers. They set up a company just out of town in Little Valley. Many immigrant craftsmen from Europe made up the work force, and their knives were the best in America. Admiral Byrd even ordered special knives from them to take on his South Pole expedition. Later the company would evolve into the W.R. Case and Son Cutlery Company. The company was eventually bought by Zippo lighters, and they have their big plant and headquarters just over the line in Bradford, Pennsylvania," he told me.

Other major knife companies still active in the Cattaraugus region are Cutco, Ontario, Queen, and Great Eastern.

"There is an interesting story about how the Case boys ended up in Cattaraugus," Cullen told me with a smile. "It may be just a story, but it is a good one. As it was told, they got caught selling horses to the infamous James Gang out in Nebraska and came to our remote hills to hide out from the law. Once here, they started making knives with their brother-in-law, who owned Cattaraugus Cutlery, and the rest is history," he laughed.

Wow Factor
When I asked Mr. Cullen what his wow factor would be he was stymied.

"I am so tempted to say the murder weapon," he said. "It is a very old, sinister looking dagger. A man in England named Corder killed a woman named Maria Marten in 1828 with it. This was no small murder case either," he continued. "Corder shot Maria, stabbed her, and then strangled her. He was hanged for his crime. I understand that he was dissected to see why he was so evil. Corder hid the knife in a wall, and it remained unfound for over a hundred years. Somehow, a U.S. soldier got his hands on it and it ended up in the States. I bought it twenty years ago from a rare book dealer along with a book about the murder case.

"I stumbled upon a photo of the dagger in a Metropolitan Museum of Art book and started doing some research, and by gosh, it turned out to be a Spanish dagger from the 1700's and most likely the murder weapon from 1828, since it was found in the wall in the home where the murder took place. The book was published at the time of the murder, and it illustrates the marks in her heart and ribs which match the cross sections of the knife we acquired and now have here at the museum."

"So how could that dagger not be the wow factor?" I asked the curator.

"Let's just say it is this." He was talking about a small exhibit in the front of the store.

The exhibit is titled "The World War II Knives of John Merritt." In the display case are knives, military items, and photos of a local Cattaraugus man whose heroics in the South Pacific in World War II are very much talked about in town.

"This guy is a real hero. He is the wow factor here, as far as I am concerned," Cullen said softly.

"He was a gunner in a Grumman TBF airplane and flew out of Bougainville in the Pacific with Pappy Boyington and Al Foss. The one small knife in the exhibit was made here and he kept it strapped to his ankle the entire war. He is still with us and is wonderful to talk to. This man made a difference and is what is best about the greatest generation. I know there are more knives with stories out there. We need them here in this museum. Anybody can display any old knife. This museum is about so much more."

The Take-Away
The American Museum of Cutlery is a perfect example of the little-known museums in Upstate New York that I wanted to research and include in this book. They are small, work on shoestring budgets, struggle to get their word out, and are usually the realization of a dream come true for the founder. The extensive knife and tool collection on display here is

basically the private collection of one man, Patrick Cullen, the founder. This is similar to Bob Kazmierski and his Wildlife Sports Museum and Marty Phelps and his Medina Toy Train Museum, both featured in this book. They, and others here, are the driving forces behind their museums and basically have put their passions and lifelong hobbies out there for the entire world to see.

And we are all better off because of it!

The thing I liked best about this museum is the marriage between the subject and the setting. The surroundings of the small storefront, the feel and the smell of it, all create a fantasy atmosphere that gently blends with reality. It is not a hard stretch to imagine you are transported, if only for a moment, back in time to a century ago and you are here in remote Cattaraugus and you're buying knives to put in your wagon and take back to the farm.

I thank Messrs. Cullen, Kazmierski, Phelps, and many others for providing my readers and me with such wonderful little windows into the past.

The Nuts and Bolts

The American Museum of Cutlery
9 Main Street
Cattaraugus, New York 14719
(716) 257-9813
Website: http://enchantedmountains.com/place/american-museum
-cutlery

• *Travel Suggestion*

Take Rt. 353 twenty miles north of Salamanca. On the drive to Cattaraugus you will go through Little Valley, the original home of Cattaraugus Cutlery Company (its large barn with the company name across the side can still be seen here).

• *Museum Hours*

Thursday through Sunday 1 p.m. to 4 p.m.
Tours by special appointment

- *Admission*
    Free

- *Number of Visitors Annually*
    1,500

Up around the Bend

While you are in a "cutlery state of mind" I would suggest you drive a half hour south of Cattaraugus to Bradford, Pennsylvania. Here you will find the state-of-the-art headquarters of Case knives and Zippo lighters (www .zippo.com). The facility is very large and very popular with tourists. You can't miss the building . . . it is topped with a large flip-top Zippo lighter and a large Case jackknife.

On a curious note, as you enter Cattaraugus from the south you will pass the 60,000 square foot Setterstix Company on your right (261 South Main Street). This is now one of the largest manufacturing plants in the region. And what do they make?

Sticks. Paper sticks. For everything from corn dogs to cotton swabs to lollipops. More than 17 billion paper sticks come out of this giant bright red factory annually!

From Here to There

The other museum in this book that is nearest to the American Cutlery Museum is the **Kazoo Museum** in Eden. It is thirty miles north of Cattaraugus.

2

Lucy Desi Museum and Desilu Studios

Jamestown, Chautauqua County

*E*verybody loves Lucy.

Lucille Ball was born in 1911 on Stewart Street in Jamestown, N.Y., but spent much of her youth in neighboring Celeron. Years after she passed away, her remains were moved from Forest Lawn Cemetery in Hollywood to her parents' family plot at Lake View Cemetery in Jamestown.

From the cradle to the grave, it appears that beloved Lucy has made the circle complete.

"People from all over the world come to our museums. Lucy is just so universal," said Susan Ewing, former Director of Group Sales at the Lucy Desi Center for Comedy. "They smile and whisper and laugh the whole way through."

The block-long museums are filled with Lucille Ball memorabilia, most of it, obviously, centered around her groundbreaking role on *I Love Lucy*. The Desilu Studios portion contains memorabilia from the television days: Emmy Awards, sets, costumes, props, scripts, etc. The Lucy Desi Museum chronicles the personal life of Lucille Ball and Desi Arnaz.

"She was quite a daring personality," Ewing told me. "She would have been accepted easily today, but back in the 1950s? No way," she laughed.

"Lucy owned studios, dared to negotiate contracts, and really succeeded in a Hollywood which was then very much a man's world. She even appeared pregnant on TV. Now that was daring," Ewing told me.

The museums are wonderful warrens of nostalgia. A rare video clip here, an awards case there, a fabulous designer gown worn by Lucy on

9

television over there, back there some signed scripts, and here an album of family photos. It is almost Lucy sensory overload.

"We do have a lot of material, that is for sure," the director said. "Her daughter Lucie has been a wonderful help to us at her mother's museum. While Lucie is not involved in the day-to-day activities here, she is always being called upon to answer some question for us or to identify people in old family photos. She has been great."

George Clooney once came through here. And Joan Rivers. And many of Lucy's former Hollywood friends and co-stars. "Keith Thibodeaux, who played Little Ricky on the TV show, has been here several times. Can you believe that he is now in his sixties?" Ewing asked.

Many of the celebrities (along with thousands of fans) pour into Jamestown for the annual Lucy Festivals. 2011 saw a massive outpouring of love for the centennial marking Lucy's birth.

Downtown Jamestown pays tribute to their favorite daughter with towering murals painted on the empty walls of buildings around town. A giant "Lucy Tasting Vitameatavegamin" on one wall. A massive "Speed It Up on the Assembly Line" image on the back of another large building. A big double "Lucy-Desi Postage Stamp" mural on the wall of the post office. It all really makes for a fun and interesting "kiss" to one of America's premier entertainers.

A trip to Lake View Cemetery is a must. Lucy's grave is one of the most visited final resting places in Upstate New York. The front of her gravestone is the large pink heart logo that opened her TV show each week.

Lucy's childhood home still stands at 59 Lucy Lane in Celeron, a suburb of Jamestown. It is now a private residence.

Wow Factor
"There are many," Ewing said, "but the car is a real show stopper. It is Lucy's personal 1972 Mercedes Benz. It is gold colored, has Lucy's initials on the door handles (LBM, for Lucille Ball Morton), and it was the last year the model was made with that particular grill. It must have been a real show stopper when she came down the street in this! It is a wow factor with a capital W," she told me.

The car fills a room by itself. Besides the Lucy connection, the car really adds a bit of old Hollywood style to the museum.

The Take-Away
Being a certified baby-boomer, I, of course, loved this place.

Nothing is overlooked here. There is a television set prepared to film the famous Vitameatavegamin commercial. The props and cue cards are all set for the tourists to reenact the famous segment. The museum videos your performance and your family and friends can squeal with delight as they watch you stumble through one of TV's most iconic scenes on an old 1950s style television set.

Nice touch.

I was amazed at the recreated rooms from the Ricardos' New York City apartment. The couch, the fireplace, the kitchen, the chairs and end tables, all just as I remembered them from TV. It's as if you expected Ricky to come barreling through the door any minute yelling, "Lucy! You got some 'splainin' to do!"

The Nuts and Bolts
Lucy Desi Museum and Desilu Studios (AKA: The Lucy Desi Center for Comedy)
2 West Third Street
Jamestown, New York 14701
Note: There are two building entrances: one for the "studio tour" and one for the museums. Both are on the same block.
(716) 484-0800 [(800) LUCY-FAN]
www.lucy-desi.com, www.lucycomedyfest.com

• *Travel Suggestion*
Exit I-86 at Jamestown and follow North Main Street (Rt. 60) south two miles to the museum. Within a few hundred feet of entering Jamestown, you will notice Lake View Cemetery on your left. This is where Lucy is buried. There are signs leading you to her grave.

Heading west, Jamestown is the largest and last city in this far corner of New York State.

• *Museum Hours*
Monday through Saturday 10 a.m. to 5 p.m.
Sunday 11 a.m. to 4 p.m.

• *Admission (includes both Museum and Studios)*
Adults: $15.00
Senior (60+): $14.00
Youth (6–18): $10.00
Children 5 and Under: Free

• *Number of Visitors Annually*
40,000

Up around the Bend
Jamestown is located at the southern end of Chautauqua Lake. After touring the Lucy Desi Museum and Desilu Studios I would suggest a leisurely

drive up the west side of the lake to the internationally famous Chautauqua Institution.

This resort and educational center was founded as a playground for the rich and famous in 1874. Speakers of world renown (including presidents, kings, best-selling authors, and celebrities) have been appearing here since the beginning. But it is the architecture that really stuns here. The whole Chautauqua Institution community is on the National Register of Historic Places. The buildings reflect the glory of the Gilded Age and are in pristine condition (most buildings and residences are privately owned). The backdrop of the lake makes this one of the prettiest residential districts in America. Dine at the famous Athenaeum Hotel, with its sweeping double verandas and high-ceilinged ballrooms. The hotel, built in 1881, is the largest wooden structure east of the Mississippi River.

From Here to There
The other museum in this book nearest to the Lucy Desi Museum is the **American Cutlery Museum** in Cattaraugus. It is thirty-five miles northwest of Jamestown.

OTHER MUSEUMS TO
EXPLORE IN REGION ONE

Westfield: "The McClurg Museum has been the home of The Chautauqua County Historical Society (CCHS) since 1951. CCHS was founded in 1883, making it one of the oldest historical societies in western New York State." (716)-326-2977, www.mcclurgmuseum.org.

Bemus Point: Bemus Point & Chautauqua Lake Museum. "Memorabilia, photos, genealogy information for the Town of Ellery, Bemus Point, & Chautauqua Lake." Open all year by appointment. (716)-386-2274.

Lily Dale: Lily Dale Museum (located inside the Lily Dale Assembly). "An 1890 one-room school house is now home to the Lily Dale Museum. The museum is located at the corner of Library Street and East Street across from the Healing Temple." (716)-595-8721.

Alfred: The Alfred Historical Society and Terra Cotta Museum. "This historic building was erected in 1892 by a local terra cotta and roofing shingle company. The entire building is made of their products. When Alfred University vied for the land the building sat on, a public fundraising effort allowed the building to be saved and moved to a new location."

Salamanca: The Seneca–Iroquois National Museum. "A Western New York museum dedicated to telling a rich story of Native American history in the region. Tours, exhibits, displays, and a gift shop which features handmade and artisan quality items." (716) 945-1738, www.senecamuseum.org.

Region Two

GREATER NIAGARA

Erie, Niagara, Orleans, Genesee, and Wyoming Counties

3

HOLLAND LAND OFFICE MUSEUM
Batavia, Genesee County

A gallows? Or a gibbet? Either way, you know it's going to hurt.

The Holland Land Office Museum is a wonderful showcase for the history of the roots of Western New York.

"Remember, Chuck, the Holland Land Office in Batavia is the actual birthplace of Western New York," museum director Jeff Donahue told me. "Genesee County is the mother of all counties. It all started right here. This is where millions of acres were divvied up into farms, villages, and counties."

The office was the place where the Dutch landowners carved out the wilderness of Western New York, using the primitive surveying tools of the day, including chains, spikes, links, etc. Many of these original tools are on display at the museum.

The surveyor and manager of the Batavia office was Joseph Ellicott, a legendary pioneer of the region who was called the single most powerful person in Upstate New York for the first two decades of the nineteenth century. He answered to only one man: his manager Paolo Busti in Philadelphia.

"Yes, Ellicott and 150 surveyors were responsible for surveying over three million acres in approximately two years," Donahue told me. "Their influence was incredible."

The museum building is striking. It is made of limestone (several previous patent offices, made of wood and not affiliated with the Holland Land office, burned to the ground taking their records with them). Its four great columns have been a distinctive Batavia landmark for more than

two centuries. Two impressive 1834 U.S.–Mexican War cannon "guard" the entranceway.

The museum has several rooms, each detailing a specific period or segment of life in the region: from farming, to clothing, to culture. Many of the pieces on display are truly historic one-of-a-kinds. Brigadier Gen. Eli Parker, a famous Seneca who served in the Civil War and helped draft the terms of surrender at Appomattox, is a native to this region. His armchair, in which he sat while doing much of his writing, is on display here.

Charles Franklin Rand, who was the very first volunteer in the Union cause for the Civil War, was a Batavia native. Although he was "the first to answer Lincoln's call," Rand's Medal of Honor was awarded to him for his courageous actions during combat at Blackburn's Ford, Virginia. Captain Rand is buried in Arlington Cemetery. His Medal of Honor is on display at the museum.

Now, back to the hangman's gibbet.

"First of all, the difference between a gibbet and a gallows is quite profound," the director told me. "If you are executed by gibbet, you stand on a platform and a noose is placed around your neck, and then a counter-weight is dropped and the gibbet pulls the noose upward, leaving you dangling with a broken neck. Of course on a gallows, you drop through a hole in the floor and die the same way."

So why is this lovely man telling me these gruesome things with a hint of delight in his voice?

Because they have a gibbet. At the museum.

It is located in the back of the museum, housed in its own room. "The school kids love this room. They are always attracted to the macabre, and this does not disappoint." The room, a recent add-on, protects the gibbet from the elements and the prying fingers of the little ones. It towers above the visitors (it is behind a glass wall) and is original in every way.

"Even the rope noose you see there was used in an actual hanging," he whispered with pride.

Wow Factor

Well, the wow factor isn't on display quite yet, because it is the museum's newest acquisition. But it will be soon.

"One thing we have always looked for is an actual admission ticket to a hanging held here in Batavia. Since Batavia was the county seat, they used to be held right around the corner from the museum building, and were quite popular," Donohue told me. "Recently, a neighboring museum told us they had acquired an actual ticket to a public hanging in Batavia and asked us if we would we like to have it. Before I could hardly put the phone down, several other museum directors and I went over and got it. It is magnificent."

And does the ticket actually name the "star of the show"?

"Oh, yes," the director went on. "It is dated May 4, 1866. The hanging of Levy Mayhew took place at 1:00 p.m. He was convicted of murder as part of a love triangle that ended violently. Plus the ticket is signed by the then-sheriff of Genesee County, Parley Upton. It's a good story, and I am sure it will be the wow factor when we get it properly displayed at the museum."

The Take-Away

This is an excellent museum. There is much to see of interest here. Of course, everybody makes a beeline right to the gibbet room. But don't forget to wander the little park around the left side of the building. Here is a tall monument to government survey office manager Paolo Busti, with his profile featured on the front of it. The park is well manicured with wild flowers and landscaping. Tonawanda Creek flows lazily along behind the museum, and an attractive footbridge takes pedestrians to the other side. Signage tells of the commemoration in 2012 of the two hundredth anniversary of the War of 1812 with the planting of a garden here. Batavia was an important refugee center for those fleeing the attacking British in the Buffalo, Lewiston, and Black Rock areas.

The museum is located on the busy main street of Batavia, but the addition of the little park offers it an aura of placidness amongst the commercial ado surrounding it.

The Nuts and Bolts
Holland Land Office Museum
131 West Main Street
Batavia, New York 14020
(585) 343-4727
www.HollandLandOffice.com

• *Travel Suggestion*
Batavia is located right off the New York State Thruway, Exit 48.

• *Museum Hours*
Tuesday through Friday 10 a.m. to 4 p.m.
Saturday 10 a.m. to 2 p.m.

• *Admission (Suggested donations)*
Family: $5.00
Adults: $2.00
Child/Student: $1.00

• *Number of Visitors Annually*
2,500

Up around the Bend

For an interesting view of history circa 1971, drive ten miles south of Batavia on Rt. 98. This brings you to the small town of Attica. Here you will find the super-maximum prison that was the sight of the most famous prison riot in American penal history. In front of the towering prison walls is a memorial to the ten guards who lost their lives during the riot. It is grim and sobering, but interesting nonetheless.

From Here to There

The other museum in this book that is nearest to the Holland Land Office Museum is the **Jell-O Museum** in LeRoy. It is ten miles due east of Batavia.

4

COBBLESTONE MUSEUM
Childs, Orleans County

*W*hat *is* a cobblestone, anyway?

"A cobblestone is a rounded stone you can fit in the palm of your hand," Deborah Brundage, the executive director of the museum, told me.

Childs is just a four-corners crossroads two miles north of Albion, N.Y. Believe it or not, it is the heart of "cobblestone country."

"We are in a glacially perfect spot for these precious cobblestones," Brundage told me. "In fact, within a 75-mile radius of Rochester, you will find ninety percent of all existing cobblestone buildings still standing in the whole country."

Cobblestones are pretty little items, and they make for a visually stunning article to use to construct a building.

"Remember," Brundage told me, "only the four to six inches of the exposed exterior are made of cobblestones. The structures themselves are made out of what we call "rubble walls." That means the builder would use whatever items he could find to actually build the building, and then would face the structure with these beautiful, graceful stones."

The main building (of the several in this "Historic Cobblestone District") is the 1834 Cobblestone Church. It is the oldest cobblestone building in North America. And it is stunning.

The exterior of the church is a gentle, quilt-like array of shiny, round cobblestones. Thousands of them. *Tens of thousands* of them.

"They are sturdy, aren't they?" Brundage asked me. "They have withstood every imaginable natural obstacle thrown their way. From rain to

heat to incredibly hard winters, over the last nearly two centuries. And yet look at them," she sighed.

They were beautiful.

The inside of the church is awesome. The high ceilings give the structure a feeling of being in something like a "prairie cathedral." All of the old contraptions are here. The short, numbered private pew doors. The *trompe-l'oeil* painting behind the altar giving the room a sense of being twice as large as it really is. The old faux paintings on the pews and altar. (You can even see where the "artist" signed his name some fifteen decades ago: "Jay.")

The heating apparatus for the church is like nothing I have ever seen before. A potbelly stove sits on each side of the church. Their separate smokestacks spider out from the stoves, soar over the heads of the congregation (radiating heat) and then join in front of the altar, where they then disappear skyward through the ceiling in a single chimney. Believe me. You have to see it to believe it.

There is no shortage of light in the church, either. Massive original forty-pane windows permit sunlight to virtually flood the entire building.

In fact, the only windowless room is the church's original bathroom, which is located in a front closet for emergency purposes. You can look in and see the rough rubble walls which made up the unfinished interior walls, as compared to the finely crafted six inches of shiny cobblestones which dress the outside.

Above the pews is a grand choir loft, with a shiny reed organ.

"Up there are a couple of my favorite items in the whole place," Brundage excitedly told me. "Look," she pointed. "That little curtain running across the bottom of the loft is there so the men in the pews couldn't look up and be shocked at the sight of a lady's ankle," she laughed. "And see that screen next to the organ?" she inquired. "Well, remember in those days it was a pump organ. So rather than watch some old organist pump feverishly away while playing the hymns for the congregation, a young lad would sit, hidden by the screen, and do the pumping for the organist. You never saw the "blow boy," she laughed.

Next door is the cobblestone parsonage (1836). It is an amazing house filled with antique items. Many of them are original. Kitchen gadgets, furniture, china and silverware, a two-person vacuum cleaner (!), a sausage stuffer, a moustache cup, a clothes iron that actually held *hot coals in it*, and much more all add up to a fascinating look at life in Western New York in the mid-1800s.

In this house hangs the portrait of the woman who actually coined the still-used Universalist moniker: "The Church of the Good Shepherd." Also Horace Greeley, the famous reformer, politician, and journalist, once held title to this house.

Another small building in the Cobblestone Historic District is the 1849 one-room schoolhouse.

"Notice all the common-sense techniques they used in the 'old days,'" Brundage showed me. "The floor of the classroom is ramped up eight inches so the older kids in the back could see the teacher over the heads of the other pupils. The youngest kids sat in the smaller desks in the center row. The globe was on a pulley system so the teacher could lower it when instructing the kids on geography and then raise it up to the ceiling (and out of harm's way) when not in use," she said. "The outhouses in the back are all original, as are the blackboards and slate boards."

Another prominent item is a 1930s-style radio sitting on its own shelf above the teacher's desk.

"We have records showing that the kids in this school went out and sold Jell-O to raise money to buy their very own classroom radio," she said proudly. "They were just so practical in those days," she told me. "Notice that the little kids' desks are the only ones without ink wells," she said. "The younger ones didn't have the fine motor skills to use pen and ink until they were a little older."

Even the cloakroom had separate hooks for each student to hang up their most precious items: their boots, their ice skates, and their lunch boxes.

Wow Factor

"That's easy," Brundage told me.

We walked back to the parsonage and entered the main parlor. The room is set up as if the family was mourning the passing of a relative. At the head of the room is a casket.

Kind of.

"They called this a 'cooler,'" she told me. "Inside this finely crafted wooden box is a metal container holding the deceased's body in a metal holder. They then packed the whole thing in ice to keep it 'fresh.' The top was then lowered and mourners would pass by and peer at the face of the dearly departed thorough this glass-covered hole," she said, pointing to the head of the casket. "Notice the drip valves to drain the water at each corner, too" she said quietly. "Usually, nobody has ever seen one of these before."

Never seen it? I have never even *heard* of it before.

The Take-Away

While there are other types of museums similar to the ones found in this book scattered around the country, the sheer uniqueness of the Cobblestone Museum is the take-away from a visit here. There is simply no other place that can claim to be such a rare one-of-a-kind spot as this, both in its natural significance (cobblestones) and in its historic impact (the number of existing buildings made from them). This is a fascinating place!

The Nuts and Bolts
The Cobblestone Society Museum
14389 Ridge Road West
Corners of Rts. 98 and 104
Albion, New York 14411
(585) 589-9013
www.CobblestoneMuseum.org

• *Travel Suggestion*
Exit the New York Thruway at the Batavia Exit (48) and travel north on Rt. 98. The museum is just two miles north of Albion. At the corners of 98 and 104 you will see the small "campus" of buildings that make up the property. Park behind the church and you will be able to leisurely stroll among all of the buildings.

• *Museum Hours*
June 23 through Labor Day: Sunday 1 to 5 p.m.; Tuesday through Saturday 11 to 5 p.m.
September and October: Sunday 1 p.m. to 5 p.m.
Group tours by appointment.
    You are advised to call before visiting, as hours may change without notice.
    The historic Cobblestone Church is available for weddings, regardless of denomination.

• *Admission*
Adults: $8.00
Seniors and AAA Members: $6.00
Children: $3.00
All tours are guided tours.

• *Number of Visitors Annually*
Around 1,000

Up around the Bend
Albion is just two miles down the road from Childs (in fact, the Cobblestone Museum, though in Childs, actually has an Albion mailing address). Albion is rich in history and has one of the most gorgeous courthouse squares in Upstate New York. The majestic courthouse is surrounded by stunning churches on all sides. Interestingly, one of the churches was built by millionaire George Pullman, the railroad car magnate. Before he built the church in Albion in 1894, Pullman actually *worshipped at the Cobblestone Church*!

From Here to There
The other museum in this book that is nearest to the Cobblestone Museum is the **Medina Railroad and Toy Train Museum** in Medina. It is ten miles west of Childs.

KAZOO MUSEUM
Eden, Erie County

*I*t's just a step up from an empty box of Chiclets and a step down from a piece of wax paper draped over a comb.

"Yes, the kazoo is classified as a mirliton. This is a musical instrument whose origin is obscure. Or, to be more specific, a kazoo is a membranophone, an instrument that makes a sound through a stretched membrane," said Karen Smith, the museum's curator.

"Huh?"

"Our kazoos make a unique noise, like kids who used to blow hard through a box of Chiclets or a wax-papered comb. A trilling humming sound. But we have refined the art of the membranophone here at the Kazoo Museum."

Kazoos are fun. There is no denying it. Smith handed me a classic #D19 standard unit and what did I do? Well, first I looked around, a little embarrassed. But then? What the heck. I put the thing up to my lips and blew with all my heart. I hummed "Yankee Doodle Dandy" and was red-faced when I finished.

"See. Everybody does that," she laughed.

The Kazoo Museum has roots in Eden going back to about 1916. Novelty makers Emil Soberg and Michael McIntyre arrived and began making wooden kazoos. Soon they urged Harry Richardson, a stove and furnace parts manufacturer, to use pieces of his scrap metal to make a new version. Within a year they were producing more than 1,000 kazoos a week.

An American icon was born.

"All of these machines are original," Smith told me as we walked through the factory. A single motor runs all of the eighteen huge presses. The intricate spider web of pulleys and belts is amazing to watch when in action.

"Everything you see in here is original to the beginning of the factory," she said.

Each press station has a single, often infinitesimal job in the construction of a kazoo. One shears the tin, another crimps the edges, another stamps the kazoo logo on it, and another places the membrane across the hole.

"They once used cat gut and animal entrails for the music-making membrane," Smith told me. "Thank God we have progressed to a mylar resonator."

There are only four parts to any kazoo: the top, bottom, resonator, and caplet (which holds the membrane). No glue, no nails, no welding. Just four parts to make a joyful little toy that has amused generations for more than a century.

"We have a whole history of kazoos in these cases," she told me as we inched between the glass cases. "The first kazoos were sold from a Sears catalog in 1893. They were sixty cents each." Inside the cases were kazoo cars, kazoo planes, kazoo people, and kazoo musical instruments (slide trombones, trumpets, etc.). There is even a kazoo ear of corn! They have colored kazoos for weddings and Valentines Day, etc. Red, white, and blue ones for the Fourth of July. A 24-karat gold kazoo that sells for $18.99. The array is limitless.

"We even have some kazoo whiskey bottles," she said as she pointed to a collection of specialty liquor kazoos that were made in 1933 to celebrate the end of Prohibition.

The tour of the factory is very interesting, especially when the belts and pulleys and motors are all in action. "Yes, this place really comes alive," she said.

Wow Factor

The *pièce de résistance* of the museum comes at the very end.

"We let people actually make their very own kazoo," Smith told me as we approached a large contraption that clearly was as old as the building itself.

"Here, you try it," she prodded.

It was great. I took two simple pieces of metal, placed them on the machine, and then pulled a giant lever that compressed the two pieces together, as one. Next I jammed the caplets down over the hole and then placed the nylon membrane (resonator) over the hole.

"Go ahead, give it a try," she chuckled.

I looked around once more and then again lifted my very own kazoo to my lips and gave out with a hearty reprise of "Yankee Doodle Dandy."

No ten-year old ever had more fun making a kazoo than I did that day at the museum.

The Take-Away

The Kazoo Museum ends with a videotape of the NBC Nightly News program from 2008. Reporter Roger O'Neil came to do a story on kazoos for their segment called "What Works." It is a funny video to watch. And I thought I recognized someone in it.

"Yes, that's me," Smith smiled. "And those children in the video are my grandchildren."

She also told me that John F. Kennedy, Jr. once came here to buy some kazoos.

Watching this old place come alive gives the whole factory a sense of Willie Wonka-ness. The contraptions whiz and wheeze and the belts spin madly and the motor sputters and snorts. It is quite magical.

The employees of the Kazoo Museum factory are clients of SASI (Suburban Adult Services, Inc.). This organization mentors adults with physical or mental disabilities. Some have been working here for decades. Seeing them all at work gives this whole manufacturing midway a noble sense of purpose and heart. SASI has been the sole owner of the Eden facility since 2007.

Smith runs the gift shop in the front of the factory, The Kazoo Boutique, as a separate entity. It is a gaily decorated, dazzling shop filled with trinkets, toys, glass objects, candy, T-shirts, one-of-a-kind collectibles, books, high-end jewelry, and yes, kazoos.

The Nut and Bolts

The Kazoo Museum and Factory
8703 South Main
Eden, N.Y. 1405
Note: You can't miss it. There is a giant kazoo on the roof!
(716) 992-3960
www.edenkazoo.com

• *Travel Suggestion*

Take Exit 57A off the New York State Thruway (Eden/Angola). Eden is about twenty miles south of Buffalo.

• *Museum Hours*

Sunday and Monday: Closed
Tuesday through Saturday 10 a.m. to 5 p.m.

• *Admission*
Self-guided tours are free.
(There is a nominal fee for making your own kazoo.)

• *Number of Visitors Annually*
1,500

Up around the Bend
Travel west on Derby Road just five miles and you will come to Derby, N.Y. Here, on a cliff overlooking Lake Erie, you'll find "Graycliff," one of designer Frank Lloyd Wright's greatest residential masterpieces. It is open for tours (www.graycliffestate.org). On a clear day you can actually see the mist rising over Niagara Falls in the distance.

From Here to There
The other museum in this book that is nearest to the Kazoo Museum is the **American Cutlery Museum** in Cattaraugus. It is thirty miles south of Eden.

6

JELL-O MUSEUM

LeRoy, Genesee County

"There's always room for. . . ."

Do I really have to finish that sentence?

The Jell-O Museum is a wondrous, fun, and very interesting museum dedicated to everybody's favorite jiggly dessert. The gelatinous concoction has been around for many years. In fact in 1845, Peter Cooper, the famous inventor of the steam-powered locomotive *Tom Thumb*, registered a patent for a savory gelatin.

The dessert as we know it really started to gel (pun intended) when in 1897, a LeRoy carpenter, Pearle Wait, added the first sweet flavors to the dish (strawberry, raspberry, orange, and lemon), and dubbed the product Jell-O. Still, they were barely able to give the stuff away. Wait's neighbor, Orator F. Woodward, bought the trademark from him in 1899 for $450. The rest is history.

In 1902, Woodward ran a single advertisement in the *Ladies Home Journal* and the new product took off. Within a few short years, Jell-O was being advertised as "America's Most Famous Dessert." Over the years, Jell-O became a pioneer in consumer advertising and their product became so popular that it became the generic term for any gelatin dessert.

"In the early days, Jell-O employed only the best, most famous illustrators for their magazine ads," Caroline Bolin told me. She is the manager of the Jell-O Museum gift shop. "Maxfield Parrish and Norman Rockwell, for example, both did many famous ads for Jell-O."

The museum is maybe the most colorful museum you will ever find. Jell-O was famous for its dramatic use of colors. "Actually," Bolin told me,

"we don't even refer to them as colors here. We refer to them as flavors. The most popular item in our gift shop is the Jell-O logo T-shirt. It comes in all six *flavors*," she remarked.

The exhibits tell of the birth of Jell-O from its humble beginnings in LeRoy to its present world-wide reputation. Many displays are hands-on. You can actually listen to famous radio and television advertisements from the old days, featuring such stars as Kate Smith, Lucille Ball, Andy Griffith, and Jack Benny. There is an old-timey feel to the museum, with its high ceilings, wainscoting, and country-store ambience.

I asked Bolin what was her favorite part of the Jell-O Museum.

"I just love the story of the Jell-O girl, which we tell in a large exhibit. Early on, the company decided to hire a real four-year-old girl (Elizabeth King) to be the product's 'mascot.' Later, they turned to artist Rose O'Neill to create one artistically," Bolin recalled. "Miss O'Neill was a world-famous artist, who invented the original wildly popular Kewpie Doll. To have a person of her stature, and a woman no less, doing the advertisements for Jell-O as early as 1912 was considered groundbreaking."

The museum is really a lot of fun. There is a play area for small children where they are allowed to draw ("re-create") old Jell-O ads, and can even pretend to make and sell Jell-O at a children's grocery store. Adults will be fascinated by the information panels (there is a lot of reading here, but all of it is interesting) and physical displays of Jell-O boxes, molds, recipe books, paintings, and more throughout.

Of course, one of the most memorable days in the history of the museum (and of LeRoy in general) was June 8, 2004. Comedian Bill Cosby, a Jell-O spokesman for more than thirty years, came to visit the museum. Hundreds crowded around the museum steps as he addressed the throng. "Isn't it funny? I was eating Jell-O long before I ever got paid for it," he shouted. The crowd roared.

Wow Factor
"Well, there are a lot of fun items here, but people just can't seem to get enough of the Jell-O brain," Bolin chuckled.

In 1969, a Canadian physician, Dr. Adrian Upton, reported that the contents of Jell-O were very similar to the makeup of the human brain. On March 17, 1993, technicians at St. Jerome Hospital in Batavia (N.Y.) confirmed that the brain waves emitted from a human are in fact similar to the frequency found in a bowl of jiggling Jell-O.

"So we have an exhibit on it that people just rush to. It shows a replica of a human brain (painted like green Jell-O). A panel tells the story of the brain/Jell-O connection. People laugh when they see it," she told me. "Most people who stand and look at this silly thing really do say 'wow.' But the tests results proved it: Jell-O does in fact have the same frequency of brain waves as a human brain!"

The Take-Away
There is no museum in Upstate New York quite like the Jell-O Museum. It is fun to walk through and look at all the red, green, and yellow (and more) little boxes that we have seen on our grocery store shelves for most of our lives. The facility is well lit and lends itself to an easy flow through and around the many exhibits. The gift shop is great. They have everything you can imagine with Jell-O on it. Look for the Jell-O pens. They

are perennial best sellers. Big fat writing pens with a simile of the jiggly dessert inside it.

I bought two. My kids love them.

The Nuts and Bolts

The Jell-O Museum
23 East Main Street
LeRoy, New York 14482
(585) 768-7433
www.jellogallery.com

• *Travel Suggestion*
Leave the New York State Thruway at Exit 47. Follow NY Rt. 19 south three miles.

• *Museum Hours*
April 1 through December 31: Monday to Saturday 10 a.m. to 4 p.m.; Sundays 1 p.m. to 4 p.m.
January 1 through March 31: Weekdays 10 a.m. to 4 p.m.

• *Admission*
Adults: $4.50
Children 6-11: $1.50

• *Number of Visitors Annually*
13,000

Up around the Bend

You do not have to go very far from the Jell-O Museum to hit another fascinating spot in LeRoy. In fact, just follow the "Jell-O Brick Road" (a path of red brick pavers) from the museum in the back to the big house in the front. This is the home of the LeRoy Historical Society, and it is terrific.

Built in the early 1800s, this Greek Revival beauty houses three full floors of local history, art, and artifacts. The LeRoy family lived here from 1822 to 1837. Here you will also find the fascinating story of Ingham

University, one of the first women's schools of higher education. The guided tours are especially interesting. One of the great highlights is entering an old-fashioned kitchen. All of the utensils, appliances, furniture, and more look like they could have been transported from your Grandma's old kitchen and placed here. Very interesting!

The LeRoy Historical Society and the LeRoy House can be accessed online through the Jell-O Museum. They share the same property along East Main Street.

From Here to There
The other museum in this book that is nearest to The Jell-O Museum is the **Holland Land Office Museum** in Batavia. It is seven miles west of LeRoy.

7

MEDINA RAILROAD
AND TOY TRAIN MUSEUM

Medina, Orleans County

*N*ow this is a museum that'll bring out the kid in everyone.

The toy train set on exhibit here is the longest HO-scale train layout in the U.S. It is over two hundred feet long and is almost impossible to take in on a single visit.

"Yes, this is the culmination of a six-decade collection of toy trains," said Marty Phelps, founder and director. "As you can see, there is a little bit of everything in it," he laughed.

And is he ever right.

From end to end, the train layout is precise in its depiction of America and American history. The trains are constantly running through the layout (six complete trains, up to 100 freight cars included, are running at any one time). As I wandered slowly along the panorama, I was taken back to a time, some fifty years ago, when my own train set was my pride and joy. The mountain ranges, the gorges, the forests with their fake, yet real-looking trees, the many villages and cities portrayed. Eye-popping is how I would describe it.

"We have hundreds of buildings and thousands of people doing all kinds of things in our layout," Phelps told me as he guided me around the set pointing out things that I had missed in my other two walkabouts. "Look over there," he said. "It is a replica of a Civil War battle being fought with an old 1860s train running through it. And over there is a busy Great Lakes dock."

The dock *was* busy, with miniature stevedores loading and unloading crates of goods along a way-too-real waterfront.

"And look at the ship. Does it look familiar?" he asked me.

I got within a couple of inches of the ship and read the name along the bow. *Edmund Fitzgerald.*

"That is a seven-foot-long scale model of the tragic *Edmund Fitzgerald*, of the song fame," he told me. "It was scratch built, all by hand, by a guy named Bill Hendrickson. He is 88 years old. That is a real wonder," Phelps said.

You could go crossed-eyed trying to discern all of the Lilliputian wonders arrayed in the layout. A full blown carnival with working bumper cars, Ferris wheels, and carousels. Farms with tractors and barns. An airport with all sorts of vintage aircraft. Factories with workers inside making all of the things that made America work at the turn of the twentieth century.

"The goal here is H.E.P.," Phelps told me. "That means History, Education, and Preservation. We must keep the heritage of the railroad days alive for our children and grandchildren."

Phelps not only built his dream, but lives it, too. Well, he lives *in it*.

"I lived near the railroads years ago and always wanted to open up a museum for toy trains. So I found this old 1905 depot here and fell in love with it. It is the largest standing wooden freight depot in America. I bought it. And I live upstairs in an apartment, so I am never too far away from my treasures," he smiled.

Trains are the centerpiece of this magical place, but there is a lot more to the museum than just toy trains. The walls are packed with railroad memorabilia, photos of nearly every American railroad, train schedules, commemorative plates, framed artwork, antique conductor hats from a hundred long-gone railroads, and dishes and chinaware from the ritzy private railroad cars of the rich and famous.

One collection is hard to miss. The entire, and I mean *entire*, perimeter of this giant building is lined with fire department helmets.

"You'd be hard pressed to name a community in New York that is not represented here," Phelps told me as he pointed out a helmet from my own hometown. "We have nearly five hundred different helmets on display here."

Fire helmets. Toy trains. Railroad uniforms. Whistles and bells. Like I said, this museum will bring out the kid in everyone.

Wow Factor

"Oh, that would be outside the museum," Phelps said as we walked out the side baggage door.

"Look at those beauties right there," he pointed.

Alongside the toy train museum, sitting on original tracks, are a series of majestic old trains. Real trains.

"Our train excursion rides are extremely popular," he told me. These are classic 1940s- and 1950s-era luxury trains that once rolled through Western New York. They have been refurbished to perfection and offer the very best in rail excursions."

"Our 1947 Budd passenger coaches are comfortable in all seasons. In the summer we open up the windows, and in the winter we turn on the heat."

"There are snack bars, restrooms, and even live entertainment on board. The excursions take you though miles of beautiful Western New York countryside and include stops at Erie Canal port towns including Middleport, Gasport, and Lockport. We have several winery excursions. We go out in the summer, of course, and even have a winter Polar Express ride for the kids. Thomas the Tank Engine visits here in May and we have Santa Train rides, too. But our Fall Foliage train rides are the most popular. As you can imagine, the scenery is spectacular that time of the year," Phelps said.

The Take-Away

I loved this museum. I spent three hours in it, wandering around inspecting the massive toy train layout, viewing the hundreds of train items on the walls and in the display cases, and listening. Yes, listening.

While I was there, several old railroaders came in for a visit. What a hoot to "eavesdrop" on them as they sought out memorabilia from their old employer (New York Central Railroad) and reminisced with Marty Phelps about their days "on the rails." It was great.

I bought hats, and coffee mugs, and T-shirts and toy trains for the kids, at the gift shop.

Of all the museums in this book, I can say honestly that this was one I really hated to leave.

It is a magical place.

The Nuts and Bolts

The Medina Railroad and Toy Train Museum
530 West Avenue
Medina, New York 14103
(585) 798-6106
www.RailroadMuseum.net

• *Travel Suggestion*

Leave the New York State Thruway at Exit 48A (Pembroke/Medina). Travel Rts. 77 and 63 north fifteen miles to Medina. If you see train tracks, you will see the museum!

- *Museum Hours*
    Tuesday through Sunday 11 a.m. to 5 p.m.
    (Museum opens at 9:30 a.m. on scheduled train ride days)

- *Admission*
    Adults: $7.00
    Seniors: $6.00
    Teens (13–18): $4.00
    Children (2–12): $3.00
    Children under 2: Free
    Note: Museum admission is included with all train rides.

- *Number of Visitors Annually*
    20,000

Up around the Bend

Medina is filled with history, and one could easily make an afternoon of it here. Some of it is quite significant. Other items in town are less significant historically, but are the most fun.

For example, visit St. John's Episcopal Church at 200 East Center Street. Odd, isn't it? Known far and wide as "The Church in the Middle of the Street," you'll have to go and see its unusual location to understand. After all, *Ripley's Believe It or Not* came here in the 1930s to see it for themselves! And this is most certainly an Erie Canal town. Just go down to 3699 Culvert Road and take a look.

The Erie Canal crosses overhead here, and this is the only place along the entire 360-mile Erie Canal where you can actually drive *under it*!

This is a cool town, a historic town, and yes, a fun place to spend an afternoon!

From Here to There

The other museum in this book that is nearest to the Railroad and Toy Train Museum is the **Cobblestone Museum** in Childs, N.Y. It is just four miles north of Medina.

OTHER MUSEUMS TO
EXPLORE IN REGION TWO

Buffalo: Steel Plant Museum. "Located in an old steel manufacturing district, this museum is dedicated to preserving the history of the now-gone heavy steel industry of Western New York. Many old steel companies were once thriving here, including Bethlehem Steel, Lackawanna Steel, U.S. Steel, and Republic Steel." (716) 821-9361, www.steelplantmuseum wny.org.

East Aurora: Elbert Hubbard Roycroft Museum. "The museum features artifacts and furniture from the Roycroft-inspired Arts and Crafts Movement." (716) 652-4735, www.aurorahistoricalsociety.com.

East Aurora: Millard Fillmore House and Museum. "President Millard Fillmore built this house for his bride, Abigail, in 1825. The house was later purchased, renovated, and moved to its present location by local benefactress Margaret E. Price, of Fisher-Price toys fame." (716) 652-4735, www.aurorahistoricalsociety.com.

North Tonawanda: Herschell Carrousel Factory Museum. "15,000 visitors a year go through this seven structure museum to see and ride the historic merry-go-rounds. The first carrousel was built by Allan Herschell here in 1916." (716) 693-1885, www.carrouselmuseum.org.

Region Three

THE FINGER LAKES

Monroe, Livingston, Steuben, Cayuga, Wayne, Ontario, Yates, Schuyler, Seneca, Tioga, Onondaga, Cortland, and Tompkins Counties

SEWARD HOUSE
HISTORIC MUSEUM
Auburn, Cayuga County

*W*hat a man. What a house!

William Henry Seward (1801–1872) was one of the towering American political figures of the mid-nineteenth century. He strode the highest halls of power in Albany and Washington, first as New York's twelfth governor and later as a U.S. senator from the Empire State. He also served as secretary of state under two presidents. His life was filled with triumph and drama.

"Mr. Seward's life reads like an exciting novel," Alexis Parsons told me. She is the Administrative Coordinator for the Seward House Museum.

"Many people forget that he was a target for assassination on the night Lincoln was killed. A small group of conspirators aimed to decimate the heads of power in Washington, and Seward was certainly one of them. In fact, Lewis Powell invaded his house on April 14, 1865. Powell attacked and seriously injured several male members of the household before fighting his way into Seward's bedroom, where he stabbed the secretary of state several times in the face and neck," she told me in gripping detail. "Of course, all of this is well documented in the museum," she said.

The Seward home in Auburn is about as magnificent as they get in this central part of the state. It really was much more the home of Frances Adeline Miller, whose father owned the house. She married Seward on October 20, 1824.

"She then lived here until she died," Parsons told me. "So if you add it all up, Frances was a resident of this house for nearly six decades."

The house is filled with priceless heirlooms, from tapestries to furniture to china to art.

"All of it was here when William H. Seward III passed away in 1951. By order of the Seward will, the house was then to be used as a museum. It really is an exquisite collection of Americana from an important period of U.S. history," she told me.

As I wandered the rooms, each one overflowing with Victoriana and personal Seward artifacts, I was struck in particular by the artwork.

"Yes, we are blessed," Parsons told me. "We have an original Thomas Cole painting that was commissioned for Mr. Seward himself. Also, we are so pleased to have four Emanuel Leutze paintings. Of course we all know him for his famous painting of George Washington crossing the Delaware, but we like the ones we have too," she said softly.

Among the Leutzes here is the iconic painting of the negotiations for the purchase of Alaska. "In it you can see Mr. Seward in a tense conversation with the Russian diplomat Eduard de Stoeckl. A giant globe is between them. This is the image used in most textbooks when the purchase of Alaska is discussed. We are so proud to have it here at Seward House," Parsons declared.

Among the other artists held in the Seward collection are several rare photographic images made by Civil War photographer Matthew Brady.

One of the most fascinating aspects of the museum comes from the fact that the Sewards were almost never together.

"Of course, Secretary Seward's position meant he had to travel extensively, and Mrs. Seward was perfectly happy to stay here in Auburn and raise their four children. Because of this, we have a voluminous collection of letters exchanged between William and Frances over the years. They are remarkable in that it is almost like reading a biography of their lives. We have learned so much about them, their family, this house, and the times they lived in, just from these many letters," Parsons said.

I asked her about Seward's reputation as a leading anti-slavery voice of the period.

"And his wife, too," she reminded me. "Frances was raised a Quaker and was heavily involved in the women's rights movement in neighboring Seneca Falls. And yes, this house was definitely used as a safe house on the Underground Railroad. We know this from her letters to her husband."

"How so?" I asked.

"In several letters, Mrs. Seward refers to 'passengers' who were visiting and staying down below in the kitchen. Of course the passengers were runaway slaves and the basement kitchen was a hiding place."

The kitchen is great. It is large and broad and appointed in much the way you would expect it to look in the mid-1850s. The exacting detail of the preservation of this home is astonishing.

"It really is a treasure," Parsons said, "and so were the Sewards."

Wow Factor

"I have always liked the clothing that belonged to the family," she told me. "We have a lot of it, and it is all amazing. Of the collection I would have to say my 'wow factor' would be just a certain pair of pants, a silk vest, some fancy embroidered stockings, and a little pair of shoes," she laughed.

In this mansion filled with glittering artifacts, I asked her why these few pieces of clothing were her favorites.

"Well, these were the exact clothes Mr. Seward was wearing when he was officially presented to the Royal Court in London in 1859."

The author Doris Kearns Goodwin spent some time at the museum doing research for her 2005 book *Team of Rivals: The Political Genius of Abraham Lincoln*. Mr. Seward was one of the 'team,' she said.

The Take-Away

This place is top notch all the way. It is a stunning 32-room mansion in pristine condition (the museum only uses fifteen of the rooms for displays). The grounds are gorgeously landscaped with gardens, patios, fountains, and statuary. It is almost sensory overload to walk from one room to another.

My lasting impression of the house was that of a single item. Seward's private carriage.

"Mr. Seward bought the carriage to travel around Washington in. He even put the Seward family crest on the doors," Parsons told me. "One day a door popped open and the driver stopped and got down to fix it. While he was on the ground the horse got spooked and charged away, with Mr. Seward still in the carriage. He was eventually thrown out and suffered serious injuries, which plagued him for the rest of his life. As he lay in his bed recuperating from a broken jaw, broken arm, and broken collarbone, the wicked Mr. Powell came in (under the guise of delivering medicine) on the night of President Lincoln's assassination and attempted to kill Seward. So this carriage really has a story to tell," she said.

Boy, does it ever.

The Nuts and Bolts

    Seward House Historic Museum
    33 South Street
    Auburn, New York 13021
    (315) 252-1283
    www.sewardhouse.org

• *Travel Suggestion*
    Leave the New York State Thruway at Exit 40 and travel south through Weedsport on Route 34 the ten miles to Auburn.

- *Museum Hours*
  March through December: Tuesday to Saturday 10 a.m. to 5 p.m.
  Memorial Day through Labor Day: open Sundays
  Tours go off on the hour. Last tour leaves at 4 p.m.

- *Admission*
  Adults: $8.00
  Discounts are given for seniors, AAA, and military.

- *Number of Visitors Annually*
  16,000

Up around the Bend
Fort Hill Cemetery (19 Fort Street) is less than a mile from the Seward home. Here, William, Frances, and others in their family are buried (Glen Haven Section). Harriet Tubman, also an Auburn resident and a friend of Seward's, is also buried here (West Lawn Section). The cemetery is beautifully maintained and well worth a visit.

From Here to There
The other museum in this book that is nearest to the Seward House is the **D.I.R.T Museum** in Weedsport. It is ten miles north of Auburn.

9

SIMS STORE MUSEUM
Camillus, Onondaga County

$\mathcal{T}$he Erie Canal is the gold standard of engineering achievements for the Empire State. And all along the canal route between Albany and Buffalo there are historical markers, museums, and remnants of the once-mighty "Marriage of the Waters." The Sims Store Museum is one of the best, and one of the oddest.

"These general stores were the lifeblood of the waterway," Liz Beebe, vice president of the museum, told me. The Sims Store is part of the Camillus Erie Canal Park.

The Sims Store is actually a re-creation of the store of the same name, which operated two miles up river. It was located at a strategic place along the canal where boats had to wait to enter the locks.

"Business was brisk," Mrs. Beebe, who was dressed in a flowing gingham gown and bonnet of the era, told me as we walked along the waterway and up to the store.

Inside, the building is broken up into several different sections. In the area of the ground floor we find a replica of the general store with all of its old-time goods on display. There are foodstuffs, hardware, clothing, toys, and other items. "You really could get almost anything at these places," she told me.

I asked her where she acquired many of the hundreds of antique items on display.

"When we set up the museum, we tried to channel our interpretation of an old general store after the buildings at Old Sturbridge Village in Massachusetts. And once the word got out about the Sims Store, people would

just stop in and donate items to us. The local folks have been extremely supportive of the store," she said.

In the rear of the ground floor are many displays, dioramas, photographs, and scale models of the canal and life along it. Upstairs you'll find three more large rooms in which the story of the building of the canal is told, plus displays of the workingman's tools and surveying equipment.

The outside grounds of the museum are quite beautiful. Mrs. Beebe and I strolled along the canal as she described many of the outdoor items treasured here at the museum. One of the last buoy boats used on the canal is here, as well some original canal directional buoys. This boat, Buoy Boat 159, would cruise the canal looking for kerosene buoys that had gone out. It could check on thirty lanterns a day. It was built in 1930 and refurbished in 1953.

Clearly, the centerpiece of the museum's possessions is located in the back of the museum. "These are actual lock gates from the old Erie Canal," Beebe told me as she pointed to two large, dark contraptions standing under a wooden canopy. "They are the only ones left," she said.

They found these canal gates (called "doors") buried in the muck of the canal bed. They measure eighteen feet tall and 110 feet long, and were made out of a single piece of wood.

"It took them three months to dig them out of the bottom of the canal," she told me as she rubbed her hands over the rough wooden surface. "They were from the Gere's Lock #50, a couple of miles up. It was quite a chore, I guess," she laughed.

Quite a chore, indeed. Right behind the massive canal doors is a huge original Sulky Derrick Stump Puller. Any stump, or an old canal door stuck in six feet of mud for a century, certainly would have stood no chance against this towering, powerful "yanking machine."

Wow Factor

Mrs. Beebe was truly perplexed trying to come up with her favorite wow moment at the museum. Like almost every other museum official I have spoken with for this book, her reply was the usual "there are just so many." So rather than stew over the question, she asked if she could make a phone call.

"Well, I just spoke with my husband and he said to take you upstairs and show you the large wall mural," she said. Her husband, by the way, is Dr. David Beebe, the president of the Camillus Canal Society.

The mural is really big and really awesome. It depicts life on this section of the canal in the 1800s. It was painted by Weedsport native Dawn Jordan, one of Upstate New York's most famous muralists. Her work is seen all over the region, and she specializes in Erie Canal murals.

"We are so proud of this mural," Ms. Beebe said. "It really captures the beauty and importance of our little canal. Its size is unusual for an indoor mural. It is nine feet tall by nineteen feet long. And of course it is a wonderful depiction of our aqueduct."

"Your aqueduct?"

"Yes, just a mile down the canal our organization has just recently completed the restoration of the Nine Mile Creek Aqueduct. It is the only working aqueduct along the canal today. You really must go down and see it," she insisted.

I did. And it was incredible.

Canal aqueducts were built to carry canal boats over water that was too difficult to navigate. This one features a four-arch towpath that crosses the Nine Mile Creek from thirty feet above it. It was built in 1841. The stonework is beautiful and the restoration is really something to see. In 2009, the aqueduct was reopened to boat travel for the first time in nearly a century. The museum shows the progress of the construction and restoration in dramatic color aerial photographs. It is a short walk down the path from the Sims Store. It was listed on the National Registry of Historic Places in 1976.

The Nine Mile Creek Aqueduct is also part of the Camillus Erie Canal Park.

The Take-Away

I must say, with Mrs. Liz Beebe as my guide, my visit to the Sims Store Museum was as close to stepping through the looking glass as I got in researching this book. She was a delightful and well-versed volunteer who obviously loved this place. Dressed in her old-fashioned garb and speaking in slow country mannerisms, she made me feel as if I had been transported back into an old postcard of the store. She was great.

The museum site is lovely. The canal lazes right past the front door of the museum. Across the water are several boats docked at a mini-harbor. There are three excursion boats that take visitors out on cruises during the summer season. The *Ontario* and the *Camillus* make short narrated rides along the canal way. The classic *Iroquois* takes guests on a leisurely dinner cruise and actually crosses the Nine Mile Creek Aqueduct.

I was here in early summer to research the Sims Store for this book. It was beautiful. I can only imagine that a trip here in autumn would be stunning.

As I said my good-byes to Mrs. Beebe, she gave me a hug and stood and waved farewell to me from the front porch of the store. As I looked at this little lady in her old-fashioned cap and granny gown smiling in the summer sun at me, I got a feeling that maybe I didn't want to leave after all.

The sepia-toned postcard that is the actual Sims Store Museum kind of made me feel like I really belonged there.

The Nuts and Bolts

The Sims Store Museum
Erie Canal Park
5750 Devoe Road
Camillus, New York 13031
(315) 488-3409
www.eriecanalcamillus.com

• *Travel Suggestion*
From the New York State Thruway take Exit 39 and follow signs to
690 East toward Syracuse for about 3 miles. The road splits. Take the
right fork (Exit 6), following an overhead sign that reads "Auburn/
Lakeland 695 to Route 5 West." Continue west about four miles and
take the exit marked Camillus/Warners. Just before the exit there is a
large green sign for the Erie Canal Park.

• *Park and Museum Hours*
Summer Hours
Thursday 12 p.m. to 4 p.m.
Saturday 11 a.m. to 3 p.m.
Sunday 1 p.m. to 5 p.m.
Winter Hours
Saturday 11 a.m. to 3 p.m.
Narrated Canal Cruises
Summer only, Sundays 1 p.m. to 5 p.m.
Dinner Cruises
Wednesdays and Thursdays 6:30 p.m. and 8:15 p.m. (Reservations
are required.)

• *Admission*
Free

• *Number of Visitors Annually*
12,000

Up around the Bend

There could be no better time to visit this museum than at the end of August. The Great New York State Fair is a 12-day Empire Extravaganza and it happens right over the hill in neighboring Geddes. It started in 1841, making it the oldest state fair in the U.S. It easily attracts a million visitors a year. It has great midways, top name entertainment, a full pageant of exciting rides and thrills, and several huge exposition barns. The food at the fair is outstanding. It features many New York State regional delicacies like chicken riggies (Utica), hot wings (Buffalo), spiedies (Binghamton) and more. For dessert, grab a half-moon cookie: they began at the Hemstrought Bakery in Utica.

The Fair (www.nysfair.org) is less than a ten-minute drive from the canal museum.

From Here to There

The other museum in this book that is nearest to the Sims Store Museum is the **Salt Museum** in Liverpool. It is thirteen miles northeast of Camillus.

10

CENTRAL NEW YORK
LIVING HISTORY CENTER

Cortland, Cortland County

*T*alk about ambition!

The CNY Living History Center encompasses *three* different museums, all with unique stories tied to this geographically central area.

"More than 1,000 people came through our opening weekend," said Chief Operations Officer Doreen Bates. "And what a sentimental day that was," she laughed. "It was at 1:00 p.m., June 8, 2012: exactly thirty-five years *to the minute* from when the last Brockway truck rolled off the line here at the Cortland factory."

"Yes, it took us a while, but when the doors finally opened we were ready to go," said Chip Jermy, president of the Homeville Museum.

The Homeville Museum originated as the private collection of local resident Ken Eaton, a passionate and well-respected collector of militariana, railroad memorabilia, and local history.

"Ken was an amazing man. I knew him for many years," Jermy told me. "He was a lifelong collector, and each item was significant. Many had stories attached. Everything he had was documented, labeled, mounted, framed, and researched. He literally turned his entire house into a museum. People would come from far and wide to see his collection, which numbered well into the thousands of items. He had an extremely extensive collection of model trains and military items. Teachers would bring their students on field trips so that they could experience these items up close.

"Oh, and you couldn't miss Ken's house, either. He had an actual Army tank out in the back yard. We now have that tank here at the museum, and it definitely gets people's attention," he laughed.

"Visitors to the Homeville Museum Collection have always walked away amazed at what they have seen. After Ken died in 2006, his collection was carefully placed into storage for several years until it was put on permanent display when the Living History Center opened in 2012.

"I am most grateful for everyone who has continued to keep Ken's vision alive, and for the great facility we have here."

"We were very lucky to get this big old building," Hugh Riehlman, president of the center's board, told me. "It was once one of Cortland's biggest general stores. It was owned by A.B. Brown. He was kind of like a Sam Walton who never left town," he laughed. "When it closed, there were suddenly 20,000 square feet of prime empty space ready to be used. An angel named Peter Grimm stepped in and donated the funds to buy the property. And here we are."

Riehlman took me into a large adjoining barn to view "Museum #2."

The Tractors of Yesteryear Museum ("TOY's," as the staff refer to it) is an extensive collection of agricultural equipment (mainly tractors) dating back nearly a century. There are rows and rows of them standing stoically under the ancient rafters of the lower section of the barn.

"TOY's is really unique to our area," Riehlman told me, using the abbreviated name for the museum. "In here we have one of the most complete collections of tractors in the state." The brand names are certainly familiar, even to a "non-farm boy" like me. But these machines are old. Standing fender to fender are John Deeres, Farmalls, Allis Chalmerses, International Harvesters, and more. All several decades old. And then, of course, there are names that I didn't recognize.

"This here is a 1961 Minneapolis Moline tractor," Riehlman said as he rubbed his hand over a dark colored workhorse. "This is one of the only tractors you will find that was the color brown," he said. "And here is one that is real rare. It's a 1937 McCormick Deering. It is one of less than three thousand ever made. Very rare," he said softly.

Clearly there is a story to tell about his oldest tractor. A 1918 Fordson Model F.

"This was a product of Henry Ford but not Ford Motor Company. It was a separate unit totally, in which he partnered with his young son Edsel to mass-market tractors. Hence the name Fordson. This is the oldest tractor we have and is really a piece of work," Riehlman said.

The Fordson Company could turn out a single four-thousand-part tractor in less than thirty hours. It is kind of cool to see what old Henry Ford did before he made his name with cars. In the year the museum's Fordson tractor was made (1918), Ford produced a half-million automobiles. By 1928, he was done making tractors and went on to sell four million Model A's that year.

The last jewel in the crown of the center is the Brockway Truck Museum. It is obvious this is where Riehlman's passion lies. Inside the giant main showroom of the museum are several large Brockway trucks of different vintages.

"They were not the fanciest truck ever built, but they were the toughest," he said. "And they were made right here in Cortland."

George Brockway founded Brockway Trucks in 1909. They were used for many reasons—overland travel, military Liberty trucks, school buses, delivery trucks, fire trucks, and others. Some of each category is on display.

There is no reason to doubt the company's motto: "The Toughest Truck in America."

"Here is a perfect example of one of our trucks. It is a 1914 Brockway and is the oldest one known to exist. Look how sturdy it still is," he told me as I inspected this ancient yet still impressive relic. "Each truck had its own individual number on an ID plate installed on it. This one is Number 105. The only other one this old is at the Mack Truck Museum in Allentown, Pennsylvania. (Brockway was purchased by Mack Trucks in 1956.)"

Also on display are a 1952 Brockway fire truck, from Truxton, N.Y., a 1973 bright yellow hook and ladder fire truck from Daleville, Pennsylvania, and several other strange looking mechanical creatures.

One unusual item is a 1941 Brockway school bus.

"Everything we get is either given to us or we find it. This was one of our finds," Reithman told me as he scratched his head. "It was out in a muddy field just a total wreck. Peter Grimm purchased the bus, took it home to Troy, and did a complete restoration," he said as he patted the front of the hood.

The bus is now in mint condition. The seats inside are refurbished and comfortable and the bright yellow paint job makes it look like it just rolled off the assembly line.

"Yes sir, this one was a piece of work," he remarked.

Wow Factor

"That's easy," said Bob Mudge, a museum trustee who wandered in during my visit to the center. "Look over here."

"El Viejo" read the painted sign on the back of the 1925 Brockway fire truck.

"It is Spanish for The Old Man," Mudge told me. "A small village in Argentina owned it and they just figured it was about time to trade it in for a newer model. Not having money to ship it, they decided to drive it here. Seventeen thousand miles from La Boca, Argentina, to Cortland. Can you imagine?" he roared.

"Try and picture the look on the faces of the Brockway folks when this old contraption pulled in. Over the fifteen-month trip they went through a dozen tires, three broken axles, two clutches, and God knows how much gasoline. And believe it or not, the Brockway management was so tickled by the story that they gave them a straight, no-cash trade in on the spot. And off they went back to Argentina," he smiled.

"El Viejo" is still used in parades. It is adorned with signs, sayings, and the names of many of the towns it passed through. Needless to say, it is a real head-turner.

The Take-Away

The logo of Brockway trucks is a Husky dog pulling a harness. Because of this, Cortland has been called "Husky Town, U.S.A." It is a fitting sobriquet.

I just cannot say how much I admire Hugh and Chip and Bob and all the others involved in creating and opening this, New York's newest museum. In this day and age of shrinking budgets, a sour economy, disappearing government grants, and a general tightening-of-the-belts, to open a new twenty thousand square foot museum dedicated to life in Central New York is nothing short of miraculous.

The bankers have worked tirelessly to come up with the millions to build this modern venue, and the army of volunteers has worked to exhaustion painting, building, digging, sanding, carpeting, and lighting the expansive space.

What a tribute to the good people of Cortland. And for that I say . . . go and visit and have fun at the Central New York Living History Center.

The Nuts and Bolts

The Central New York Living History Center
4386 County Route 11
Cortland, New York 13077
(607) 299-4185
www.cnylivinghistory.org

• *Travel Suggestion*
Take the Homer Exit (12) from I-81. Make a right at the bottom of the exit ramp. The museum is less than a mile down Route 11 on the left.

- *Center Hours*
  Tuesday through Saturday 10 a.m. to 5 p.m.

- *Admission*
  Adults: $10.00
  Seniors: $9.00
  Children: (6–18) $5.00
  Children under 5: Free
  Active Military Free with I.D.

- *Number of Visitors Annually*
  5,000 (estimated)

Up around the Bend

The nearby Cortland Country Music Park hosts the New York State Country Music Hall of Fame. It is a large room at a campground that is dedicated to the history of country music in the Empire State. There are lots of sequins, guitars, promotional photos, and plaques. The campground has hosted some of country music's greatest names, including Conway Twitty, Tammy Wynette, Kitty Wells, Randy Travis, George Jones, and Loretta Lynn. Visit www.cortlandcountrymusicpark.com to see who is playing when you make your visit to the CNY Living History Center.

Also the city of Cortland hosts thousands of visitors at the Annual Brockway Truck Show the second weekend in August (www.brockway trucks.org). Nearly one hundred fifty vintage Brockway vehicles parade down the street for all to see (and hear . . . I am told it sounds just like the Indianapolis 500 race).

From Here to There

The other museum in this book that is nearest the Central New York Living History Center is the **Museum of the Earth** in Ithaca. It is twenty miles southwest of Cortland.

11

1941 HISTORICAL AIRCRAFT GROUP MUSEUM

Geneseo, Livingston County

*T*here is a wonderful 1941 military aircraft museum in Geneseo, even though there never was a military presence here.

"Mr. Austin Wadsworth started our museum back in 1994," Raublyn Hopkins told me. She is the director of public relations for the museum. "He always had a fascination for the 'big birds' ever since he was a kid, and he just made up his mind that he was going to have a home for them right here in Geneseo."

A "home for them" is a monument to understatement. The 1941 Historic Aircraft Group Museum has big ol' war birds scattered all over its grounds.

"Among our many planes here, we have a Boxcar C-119, a C-47 Dakota, a Russian post-war AN2 Antonov ("Polish built and U.S.A. used"), one of the first T-33s built, and one of the only B-23s left, out of a total of only thirty-three built. Some of our birds are static, some are flyable, and some are undergoing restoration. But all of them are beautiful."

The museum is undergoing a serious case of growing pains. Each year more and more people wander down the flats below the college here, pass through a replica of Checkpoint Charlie, and visit the hangar, the planes, and the nascent visitor's center. Clearly, there is need for more room here at HAG.

"We have a big C-47 Dakota here that dropped paratroopers over the beaches of Normandy on D-Day," Hopkins told me. "It still has its white

'invasion stripes' on it. And we didn't find it, the owner found us," she laughed. "It was a blessing, believe me. He donated it to us."

The budding visitor's center will become a large reception area where guests may view videos on four large television sets, view displays, and shop in the expanded gift shop. There is a large library of World War II books also on site.

One of the largest military air shows in New York is held at HAG every July.

"People come from all over. They love our grass landing strip because it is so evocative of World War II strips in Europe," Ms. Hopkins said with pride.

I had an opportunity to meet Mr. Wadsworth on my visit to HAG. His family goes back a half-dozen generations to the founders of Geneseo.

I asked him if his family sold the land to the sprawling S.U.N.Y. Geneseo campus, which sits high on a bluff and can be seen from the museum.

"No," he smiled. "We gave it to them."

The Wadsworths owned thousands of acres in and around town. He is now the president of the HAG Museum.

"It is just so beautiful what we have been able to do here at the museum," he told me. "We are really keeping history alive here. We have a great staff of volunteers who love what they are doing and believe passionately, as I do, in nurturing the history of our country's World War II military aircraft."

Wow Factor

"Our real wow factor is the heft of the group of large planes we have here," Hopkins said. "Many school groups come here to visit, and the children only know these planes from movies and such. When they stand under the wings of some of our biggest planes, they actually all look up and say 'wow' all at once."

The Take-Away

The ultimate way to see this museum is during the annual air show held on its grounds in July. That is what I did. It was an unforgettable experience. Not only do you get the full involvement of the museum, but also thousands attend to see the aircraft "perform."

The day I was there, more than 60 vintage World War II planes were on display and (constantly) in the air. The star of the show on that day was the original "Memphis Belle," the famous Boeing B17F Flying Fortress that has become legendary through books and movies. She was the first U.S. Army bomber to complete twenty-five missions in combat with her crew intact. Hundreds gathered around her during the show for photographs of the plane and to hear stories from her crew. When she took to the air in a rare "Heritage Flight," the roar of the crowd was deafening.

Having never been to a single air show before, I cannot begin to tell you how impressive this event really is.

The Nuts and Bolts

The 1941 Historic Aircraft Group Museum
3489 Big Tree Lane
Geneseo, New York 14454

(585) 243-2100
www.1941HAG.org

- *Travel Suggestion*
  Leave the New York State Thruway at Exit 46 and travel south thirty miles on I-390 to Geneseo.

- *Museum Hours*
  April through September:
  7 days a week 10 a.m. to 4 p.m.
  October through March:
  Monday, Wednesday, and Friday 10 a.m. to 4 p.m.
  Closed Christmas, New Year's Day, and Thanksgiving

- *Admission*
  Adults: $4.00
  Children (5-12): $1.00
  Under 5: Free

- *Number of Visitors Annually*
  About 1,000, plus school groups

Up around the Bend

A dozen miles west of Geneseo is Letchworth State Park. It is one of New York's greatest natural treasures. One of its waterfalls is actually taller than Niagara. The park's signature gorge, deep and long, is known as the "Grand Canyon of the East."

Be sure and visit the grave of Mary Jemison. She is the legendary "White Woman of the Genesee" who was brought up by Indians in the woods around the park and who now rests there eternally. Her story is remarkable. The gift shop at the entrance to the park sells books on her life. Her grave is marked by one of the most beautiful, realistic life-sized bronze statues you have ever seen.

The park has a full complement of camping options and in 2007 was named several times one of "America's Top 100 Campgrounds."

From Here to There
The other museum in this book that is nearest to the 1941 Historical Aircraft Group Museum is the **Holland Land Office Museum**. It is thirty miles northwest of Geneseo in Batavia.

12

MIKE WEAVER'S DRAIN TILE MUSEUM

Geneva, Seneca County

*A*fter one visit to the Drain Tile Museum, you'd think this item would rank up there with the electric light bulb as far as great inventions go. And to many farmers, that is true.

The concept of field drainage was foreign to most Yankee farmers in the late 1700s. Water seeped into the fields and meadows and created muddy, swamp-like conditions that were a hindrance to farming. That all changed in 1821.

"John Johnston came from Scotland and purchased a large farm here in the early nineteenth century," Alice Askins told me. She is the site manager for the Drain Tile Museum and its sister property, Rose Hill Mansion.

"Johnston's property was plagued with underground springs which kept his land difficult to farm. He was familiar with underground drainage techniques in his homeland and he took a sample tile from Scotland to a potter in nearby Waterloo and asked him to replicate it. He then started using drainage tiles under his fields here to siphon off the damaging water pools. And it worked," Askins exclaimed.

The word of his new technique for "drying the land" went out across the region and farmers and agricultural experts came to little Geneva to see what this new marvel was all about. Soon, tile-manufacturing plants were flourishing in the area, particularly in Waterloo, as more and more landowners clamored for the subterraneous tiles.

In 1838, a crockery maker sent more than 3,000 tiles for Johnston to set underneath his fields. It was only the beginning.

"Imagine what is underneath that magnificent field out there," Askins said to me as she swept her hand over the landscape behind Johnston's home. "Believe it or not, he eventually laid more than 72,000 clay tiles underneath his farm, some fifty-two miles' worth. And this on a three hundred acre farm. His son-in-law, Robert Swan, eventually installed more than sixty miles of underground tiles on his farm. In fact, we are still tripping over pieces of old tiles whenever we walk out there," she laughed. "Of course, his neighbors thought he was crazy for burying perfectly good crockery in the dirt around his house."

Johnston's home is spare, but still shows the glimmer of its early founding. High-ceilinged rooms, wide-open cooking fireplaces, an original 1690 family grandfather clock, and intricate moldings harken back to when he and his family arrived here from Scotland. An intricate Native American basket sits on a high shelf. "Mrs. Johnston bought that from some St. Lawrence Indians," Askins told me. The home is rather spare now, but she told me it wasn't always like that.

"Imagine what this house, really a working farm family house, was like with Mr. and Mrs. Johnston living here with their six daughters," she said.

One fascinating room was son-in-law Swan's office.

"Because of the newness of this drain tile concept, he received hundreds of letters from agricultural experts all over the world. He answered each letter personally. This office got a lot of use," she said.

The office also contains a curious piece of personal memorabilia on the mantel.

The very first clay drainage tile Mr. Johnston ever produced.

The tile museum, officially named the Mike Weaver Drain Tile Museum after the original collector, is behind the house in a stand-alone outbuilding. Inside are nearly five hundred samples of different drainage tiles from around the world. Some are historic.

"Look at this one," Askins pointed. "It is from 500 B.C. and was discovered in Ephesus, an ancient Greek city. We have another one that has an old Native American arrowhead embedded in it. We have many different shapes and sizes for a variety of agricultural uses."

She showed me another unusual one. A German made it in a prisoner-of-war camp during World War II. It was made in 1944 in an American camp, and the German soldier showed his allegiance to his Fatherland by carving a swastika into the actual tile.

The museum also has examples of early trenchers (which laid the tiles in the ground), early drain tile advertisements, and early farm implements.

In March of 1893, in an article in American Gardening magazine, writer and Cornell University professor Liberty Hyde Bailey said, "The Johnston Farm and Rose Hill are together the most important spot in American agriculture."

Wow Factor

"The wow factor here is something you cannot see. And that is the thousands of tiles still underground around the farm. The school kids that come here are simply amazed that we keep finding pieces of tile, some nearly two centuries old. The kids always ask how deep Mr. Johnston 'planted his miles of tiles.' I tell them that he used to say, 'The earth will tell you what to do and where to put the tiles.' They are usually two to three feet under the ground."

Johnston hired dozens of Irish laborers to plant his maze of tiles.

"They were paid twenty-five cents for every thirty-five feet of ceramic tile they laid. And if you notice, this soil is tough and rocky. It was not easy work," Askins said.

The Take-Away

It is kind of weird, I must admit, but when you realize the absolute industry-wide impact of the drainage tile implementation to American farming, well, it is nothing short of remarkable. The museum is very small but with a guide to explain what you are looking at you could easily spend thirty minutes here.

Of course, you must go up the road to Rose Hill to really make this a place worth visiting.

The Nuts and Bolts

Rose Hill Mansion and Drain Tile Museum
3373 N.Y. Route 96A
Geneva, New York 14456
(315) 789-3848
www.genevahistoricalsociety.com/Rose_Hill.htm
Note: Although they are separated by about a mile, one should go to Rose Hill Mansion first to arrange a guide at the Tile Museum. The mansion has a small welcoming center with many items for sale regarding both sites.

• *Travel Suggestion*

Leave the New York State Thruway at Exit 42 and travel south to Geneva. The city sits at the north end of Seneca Lake. The Tile Museum and Rose Hill Mansion are located on the eastern side of the lake, a mile south of N.Y. Route 20.

• *Museum Hours*

May 1 through October 31:

Saturday 10 a.m. to 4 p.m.
Sunday 1 to 5 p.m.
Closed Mondays.
(Again, make all Drain Tile Museum tour arrangements though Rose Hill.)

• *Admission*
Admission to the Johnston House and the Tile Museum is free.
Admission to Rose Hill Mansion:
Adults: $7.00
Seniors: $6.00
Students (10–18): $4.00
Group rates are available.

• *Number of Visitors Annually*
4,000

Up around the Bend
Rose Hill is an impressive, majestic 1839 mansion. It is less than a half mile up the road from the Tile Museum.

The home has been called one of the finest examples of Greek Revival architecture in America. It is built in the "monumental style" and features six classic Ionic columns and a sweeping double veranda. The beige color visible in the kitchen was created by mixing brick dust with white paint. The mansion overlooks Seneca Lake. In 1986 it was listed on the National Register of Historic Landmarks.

The Johnston family tie to Rose Hill is through the marriage of Johnston's daughter, Margaret, to the wealthy owner of the home, Robert Swan. Tours are given of the home, which is massive and filled with antiques.

The dining hall has a huge chandelier; and there are several original pieces of furniture from the Swan family. Many historic photos and oil paintings clutter the walls, including an original landscape by Rembrandt Peale and one by illustrator James Montgomery Flagg. One of the bedrooms even features an 1880s "steam mattress radiator."

"They called it that because it looked like a real mattress. It filled these big rooms with radiant heat. It was very innovative," Askins said. Also on display is a large handmade Victorian bed made in 1850 by prisoners in nearby Auburn prison.

From Here to There
The other museum in this book that is nearest to the Drain Tile Museum is the **National Memorial Day Museum** in Waterloo. It is seven miles east of Geneva.

13

GLENN H. CURTISS AVIATION MUSEUM

Hammondsport, Steuben County

Ask most people to name the most important pioneers in aviation, and they will get as far as the Wright Brothers.

"But what about Glenn Hammond Curtiss?" I ask. Be prepared for the stares.

This museum, tucked away in the stunning Finger Lake wine region of Western New York, pays tribute to the man (and his machines). Glenn Curtiss (1878–1930) is known as "The Father of Naval Aviation" and the "Founder of the American Aircraft Industry."

And yes, he locked horns with the famous Wright Brothers from time to time over the years.

He began his career building bicycles, and then motorcycles, and eventually, airplanes. He was a classic "speed demon," and set and held (for long periods of time) records both on land and in the air. In 1903, he set the U.S. land speed record for a motorcycle, streaking over a mile-long course at 64 m.p.h.

In 1907, he set the unofficial world land speed record at 136 m.p.h. on his self-built V-8 powered motorcycle and was dubbed "The Fastest Man on Earth."

Curtiss went heavily into aircraft production during the World War I years. He was an early contributor to aircraft carrier techniques, pontoon plane sea-to-air aviation, and the "flying boat" concepts (new to the time, these large planes could carry several member crews instead of just the single or double-crew aircraft of the era). He built the sturdy "Jenny"

(JN-4) for the U.S. Army and sold thousands of them. He became an aviation icon and a major Western New York industrialist and employer, and was issued U.S. pilot's license #1. He also made an enormous fortune.

His original aircraft company, Curtiss Aeroplane, is now Curtiss–Wright Corporation. At the end of WWI, his original firm, The Curtiss Aeroplane And Motor Company, was the largest manufacturer of aircraft in America. In 1929, Curtiss merged with the Wright Corporation to form Curtiss–Wright, a company that exists to this day.

Curtiss's career in aviation was relatively short-lived, just 14 years. In 1921, he retired to Florida, which was just beginning to boom. He founded three towns that are still there: Opa-locka, Hialeah, and Miami Springs. He died of complications from an appendectomy in 1930 at the age of 52.

Curtiss is buried in Pleasant Valley Cemetery near Hammondsport, N.Y.

"He was so far ahead of his time it was unbelievable," says Trafford Doherty, Executive Director of the Glenn H. Curtiss Museum. "He was highly innovative and utterly fearless. His legacy continues to this day."

"We really try and tell as much of his story as we can here at the museum. From the early bicycles to the motorcycles and planes, we have over 7,000 square feet of aviation displays, and they really tell a compelling story."

The museum had been located in an old school building in downtown Hammondsport for more than three decades. "We finally found a new, more spacious, location—a former wine storage warehouse—and we moved here in 1992," the director said. "What we have today is a totally unique museum that contains a wonderfully varied collection of fascinating items associated with local history." In addition to our regular visitors, we are seeing increasing visits from local schools and bus tours. The Finger Lakes region is a huge draw for the tourism industry, and the Curtiss Museum in right at the door step."

Doherty is a fountain of minutiae when it comes to the museum and its artifacts. You could say that he has "aviation in his blood."

"I was born and raised right here in Hammondsport," he says. "My Dad, William Doherty Jr., was a World War II aviator and was a director of the Curtiss Museum back in the 1980s. And my grandfather, William E. "Gint" Doherty, Sr., learned how to fly right here in Hammondsport back in 1911."

And who taught ol' "Gint" how to fly?

"You guessed it. None other than Glenn Curtiss himself," Doherty laughed. "So you see, I have been immersed in the Glenn Curtiss story for a long time."

Wow Factor

"The wow factor here is what we call the 'Record Bike.' This is an exact copy of the motorcycle that Curtiss set the world land record on in 1907. It is really so basic you can hardly imagine it going that fast," Doherty says. "It had an air cooled 40 horsepower V8 engine with a shaft drive—no belts, no clutch, and it had to be started by being pulled by a car!" (The original is owned and displayed at the Smithsonian Institution in Washington, D.C.)

The Take-Away

This is an incredible museum that can keep the attention of even those only mildly interested in aviation history. The exhibits are well displayed, and the museum is clean and open (with high ceilings). In the muggy heat of the tourist season, the museum is comfortably climate-controlled. It is fully handicapped accessible and has an interesting gift shop. (Yes, they have a lot of model planes.)

I went to the museum with only a fleeting interest in the history of aviation, but came away totally awed by this small and fascinating place. I was most amazed to see engine parts of the old planes stamped with "Bendix/Scintilla Magneto Company." The Bendix plant was located in my hometown of Sidney, N.Y., and no doubt many old timers that I grew up with had a hand in crafting these intricate machines.

A 75-seat theatre in the center of the museum is used for showing video presentations.

The Nuts and Bolts
   The Glenn H. Curtiss Museum
   8419 State Route 54
   Hammondsport, New York 14840
   (607) 569-2160
   www.glennhcurtissmuseum.org

• *Travel Suggestion*
   Take Exit 42 off New York State Thruway (I-90). Head south on Route 14 through the cities of Geneva and Penn Yan. Veer onto Route 54S to Hammondsport. The trip from the Thruway to Hammondsport is about one hour.

• *Museum Hours*
   The Curtiss Museum is open all year.
   Summer Hours, May 1 through October 31:
      Monday to Saturday 9 a.m. to 5 p.m.
      Sundays 10 a.m. to 5 p.m.
   Winter Hours, November 1 through April 30:
      Monday to Saturday 10 a.m. to 4 p.m.
      Sundays 10 a.m. to 4 p.m.
   Closed: Easter Sunday, Thanksgiving Day, Christmas Eve, Christmas Day, and New Year's Day

- *Admission*
    Adults: $8.50
    Seniors: $7.00
    Students: $5.50
    Children (6 and under): Free

- *Number of Visitors Annually*
    25,000

Up around the Bend

Hammondsport is in the heart of the famous wine region of the Finger Lakes. Wine production and winery tours make up a thriving economic base and tourist engine for the area. Pleasant Valley Wine Company is located just a mile outside of Hammondsport and it is definitely well worth a visit. The "wine campus" consists of many old buildings listed on the National Register of Historic Places. The winery was established in 1860 and is the first U.S. bonded winery in America.

The grounds are gorgeous and the winery tours are totally fascinating. The whole feeling is decidedly European in nature.

The tours last about an hour, and you will not soon forget the magnificent ancient subterranean wine cellars. Just five minutes from the Curtiss Museum, this lovely little spot is a "little bit of Tuscany" right here in the Finger Lakes! This is a great spot! (www.PleasantValleyWine.com)

From Here to There

The other museum in this book that is nearest to the Curtiss Museum is **Mike Weaver's Drain Tile Museum** in Geneva. It is forty miles north of Hammondsport.

14

MUSEUM OF THE EARTH

Ithaca, Tompkins County

*T*he minute you pull off busy Trumansburg Road just north of Ithaca you know that this is not going to be like any other museum you have visited in Upstate New York. Ever.

"We are the largest natural history museum between New York City and Buffalo," Dr. Warren Allmon, director of the Museum of the Earth's parent organization the Paleontological Research Institution (PRI), told me. "PRI shares our campus site and holds over 3,000,000 fossils and an extensive 50,000-book research library."

Despite all of this, what will really catch your eye at first are the dinosaurs running all over the grounds. Well, there's one, and it is in bronze.

"Yes, that is our little logo out there to greet people," Dr. Allmon laughed. "It is a *Coelophysis*. It was a fast-moving edgy kind of dinosaur and that is why we used it for the Museum's logo, that and the fact that it probably lived in New York around 200 million years ago. New York State has no known dinosaur fossil sites except one. That one is in Rockland County and those are just footprints, but they pretty closely match foot bones from this dinosaur that have been found in rocks of the same age elsewhere. And that is why we immortalized him in bronze out front."

The Museum of the Earth is a vast departure from many of the museums featured in this book. Take the physical facility, itself. This is not your sepia-toned Victorian home, or old clapboard Grange Hall or nostalgic one-room schoolhouse. This museum literally rises up to greet you and invite you in. The architecture is majestic and sweeping and the backdrop of the deep-blue waters of Cayuga Lake just down the hill from it make

it one of the most dramatic natural locations of any museum this writer has visited.

Inside the Museum are towering rooms with glass ceilings that hold uncountable display items and exhibits. "PRI has millions of fossils. In fact it holds one of the ten largest fossil collections in the U.S. We made it our policy to have the absolute maximum number of different specimens on display in the Museum at one time as possible. Usually our items number around 650, which is considerably more per square foot than the Smithsonian or other major museums," he told me.

This dazzling kaleidoscope of natural history sparkles at every turn. A mosaic of colors pours in through the large windows, illuminating a fascinating array of displays, exhibits, and hands-on experiences. "Where else in Upstate New York can a kid come to a museum, collect his own fossil, and then take it home?" the director said.

One amazing adornment is the "Rock of Ages, Sands of Time" mural created by local artist Barbara Page. This series of panels wraps the museum in a strand of continuity that really must be seen to be appreciated. Page has created 544 individual contiguous palettes or panels (each representing a million years in time) and colorfully arrayed them down the ramp that connects the upper and lower floors of the Museum.

Each panel highlights the fossils, rocks, and flora and fauna that would have been found along her "river of time." She creatively involved the media she used with her concept. Some of the pigments are interspersed with real pumice to denote the volcanic eras. Shells are prevalent. The colors run from muted pastels to "knock you over" reds and blues. It is more than 500 feet long. It is stunning. (And there is a book version, available in the Museum store.)

There are several full skeletons in the museum. The 13,000-year-old Hyde Park Mastodon brings with it a great story. "We got a call from a man in Hyde Park, N.Y. who was deepening his pond and found some very large bones," Allmon said. "He invited us to come down and explore. We went, three times. By the time we were finished in October of 2000 we had carted out what seemed like everything from the bottom of his pond including muck, mud, trees, leaves, everything. Oh, and we also carted out the makings of a magnificent, complete mastodon skeleton. We have it here, and it is awesome. Experts have called it "the Rosetta Stone of all Mastodon skeletons."

The Museum is heavily invested with its members and visitors. And the mastodon plays a unique role in this. "Over the years, after CNN and others told the story of our Mastodon, we started getting calls and letters from people all over the country asking if they could have a little piece of its history. So we started sending out plastic bags filled with a chunk of mud we found in the pond in Hyde Park to these people all over and told them to 'have at it.' For ten dollars they get a one-gallon zip lock bag filled with stuff. It is called our Mastodon Matrix Project™. We have sent them to individuals, kids, nursing homes, nuns, and just about everybody. We have sent hundreds to teachers who then build a curriculum around the bag and let the kids start going through the stuff with a fine-toothed comb. We encourage them to write back what they have found. More than 3,000 bags have been out to 50,000 people. We call them our citizen scientists."

I asked Dr. Allmon if any of these "lay paleontologists" have ever made a significant find.

"It's all good fun for them and very interesting. People have found bone chips, snails, clams, twigs, seeds, and things like that. Sounds pretty common, doesn't it? Well, just remember, anything they found is at least 15,000 years old. We actually compile all of the data we receive and some of it has been used for actual research on mastodons and their environment"

Wow Factor

"Well, with the skeleton of a 44-foot North Atlantic Right Whale lording over everything, it's hard not to pick her," Dr. Allmon said, "but I think for me the wow factor has to be the building itself. The architects did a great job, and the marriage between building and Earth is marvelous. From the very beginning where you find earthen berms butting up against the parking lots to the gorge garden and to the vast atrium space, this place is conceptually a masterpiece. We hired a husband-and-wife architectural firm, Weiss/Manfredi, who have done some other magnificent work. They are most famous for their grand Women in Service to America Memorial at Arlington National Cemetery. They specialize in blending their projects with the natural environment in which it is to be placed. Everyone comes away from a visit to our museum just in awe of our buildings."

The Take-Away

One of the most impressive things I noticed about this museum is its entrance. After paying your admission, you slowly descend into the earth via a zigzagging downward-sloping ramp. You really do feel like you are becoming one with the Museum of the Earth. It is a nice effect.

And, since the good doctor wouldn't brag on his whale, I will. It seems that from every corner of this 18,000 square foot museum you can catch a glimpse of Right Whale #2030. She comes with an incredible story.

"I always thought this museum should have the skeleton of a giant whale in it," Dr. Allmon told me. "Low and behold, just as the museum was being built, a woman from the National Marine Fisheries Service called me up and said, 'Hey, I've got a beached whale ashore at Cape May,

N.J. Do you want it?' I told her definitely yes, but that we couldn't come and get it for a week or so. She told me it was dead and rotting and it was now or never.

"So our staff drove to Cape May. They found this poor whale at the Coast Guard Station and they spent two days cutting away 16 tons of rotting whale flesh. Afterward, they hoisted what was left onto a flat bed truck and brought her to the museum (which was still under construction at the time). We buried her in horse manure out back for a year to "degrease" her. After that we dug her up, brought her in through an unfinished window, hired some theatre rigging experts from Broadway to hoist her up, and she was here, permanently."

The whale is mesmerizing. Its bones are enormous and her plight, hanging from the ceiling in a museum in far Upstate New York, gives her a massive aura of regalness tinged with sadness. A video is available for you to watch her story unfold. She was registered and tagged (the North Atlantic Right Whale is among the rarest of the large whales, with only 350 known to exist today) when she was ten years old, and died at the age of nineteen after getting tangled in some fishing gear off the coast of New Jersey.

I asked Dr. Allmon why they didn't give the whale a name. "We thought of that once," he told me. "But then we heard from the real whale lovers and they told us that she had been tagged #2030 for the last nine years of her life. That is how they knew her. They suggested we keep that as her name, and we did."

This ocean behemoth is one of the most unusual and remarkable sights you can see in Upstate New York.

"And don't forget to look for those two little bones near her back tail. They are the remnants of the whale's *legs* from 50,000,000 years ago." he remarked.

The Nuts and Bolts
>   The Museum of the Earth
>   1259 Trumansburg Road
>   Ithaca, New York 14850

(607) 273-6623
www.museumoftheearth.org

• *Travel Suggestion*

Trumansburg Road (Route 96) runs up the west side of Cayuga Lake. From downtown Ithaca the trip is less than ten minutes. The Museum is located just south of Cayuga Medical Center.

• *Museum Hours*

Labor Day through Memorial Day
Monday, Wednesday, Thursday, Friday, and Saturday 10 a.m. to 5 p.m.
  Sunday 11 a.m. to 5 p.m.
  Closed Tuesday and Wednesday.
Memorial Day through Labor Day
  Monday to Saturday 10 a.m. to 5 p.m.
  Sunday 11 a.m. to 5 p.m.

• *Admission*

Adults: $8.00
College ID Students: $5.00
Senior with ID: $5.00
Youth (4–17): $3.00
Children: Free
Members: Free

• *Number of Visitors Annually*

30,000

Up around the Bend

Ithaca holds more than a weekend's worth of sightseeing, exploring its natural wonders (as the locals say, "Ithaca is GORGES!"), enjoying some great Finger Lakes wine, and soaking up the international buzz created by the thousands of students who attend Cornell University and Ithaca College from all corners of the world. A walk around the Cornell campus will illustrate why many have called it "the most beautiful college campus in America."

From Here to There

The other museum in this book that is nearest to the Museum of the Earth is the **Sampson Military Museum**. It is in Romulus, which is thirty miles north of Ithaca.

15

SALT MUSEUM

Liverpool, Onondaga County

$\mathcal{P}$eople are returning to Onondaga Lake. And fish are, too.

"There is no validity to the reports that Onondaga Lake is still one of the most polluted lakes in the country," Eric Sopchak told me. He is the Senior Recreational Leader at Onondaga Lake Park, just outside of Syracuse. "It never was. Close, but nowhere near the most polluted."

For years this potential gold mine of a recreational welcome mat to Syracuse was a stinking, fetid, dead lake, due to decades of poisoning by industrial waste and neglect. Now, the lake has started to turn itself around in a big way.

"While the idea of swimming in Onondaga Lake is still several years away, the lake is starting to come to life again," Sopchak told me. "There are more than sixty species of fish now thriving in the lake and it gets cleaner and cleaner by the month."

Onondaga Lake played a long role in the history of the growth and development of Syracuse. It was here, in 1654, that Father Simon LeMoyne, a French-Canadian Jesuit, came to do missionary work in what is now the Syracuse area. He arrived at an Onondaga Nation village along the lake.

"The story goes that the Onondagas were sitting on a vast deposit of underground salt water domes. The springs that this bitter-tasting water bubbled up from were deemed 'evil places' since the Onondagas thought that anything as foul smelling and tasting as this salt water must come from demons or evil spirits. Father LeMoyne knew different.

"The Jesuits showed the Natives how they could boil down giant pots of their salt water brine, leaving only dry salt, which they could use for a multitude of purposes, including medicinal and preservative." Salt soon became one of the most precious minerals in the growing region of Central New York, and its manufacturing and sale eventually made Syracuse "The Salt City," a moniker still used by many today.

When the Civil War erupted, the Union Army was able to take salt-cured meat with them. It was safe and durable. The South had no such item. Thousands of Confederate soldiers died from eating tainted meat and poultry. Not the North, though. In fact, someone once said: "Onondaga salt won the war for the Union Army."

"Almost the entire eastern shore along the lake was dedicated to the production of salt," Sopchak said. "There were hundreds of salt blocks (places where the brine was boiled down into salt), employing thousands of workers. When the glaciers retreated tens of thousands of years ago, they left behind a fortune for Syracuse," he said.

The museum tells the important story of salt in early America and does so with a fascinating yet light touch.

"When the hordes of school kids come through here, they are instantly enlisted to perform in a skit we do illustrating the early days of the salt industry. They love it. There are costumes and props and everything. It really is a surprise how much fun they have when they get here," he told me.

The museum sits in a proud old structure (built in 1933 and actually containing a part of an old salt house) hard on the northern shore of Onondaga Lake. The highlight of any tour is the rare boiler block in the back. Clearly, this is the headliner of the tour. It consists of a dozen large, round pots, each holding many gallons of salt water from the lake. From underneath, each pot is heated and the water boiled down, leaving the precious mineral in the bottom of the pot.

"It was nonstop, around the clock in the block room," Sopchak told me as we walked around the display of pots. "This is where the action was," he said with a smile.

And what action it was. German and Irish immigrants worked around the pots through long shifts, making as little as $3.00 a week. They kept the water levels even, skimmed off the sour brine, and then scooped up the raw salt. (They also invented salt potatoes here in their work camps.) It was hard work under difficult conditions. There were many instances of workers falling into the giant boiling pots or being splashed with skin-searing brine.

"You think that was bad," my guide told me. "Look down here."

Eric took me below, to where the pots were fired. Here, huge, intense infernos kept the pots boiling above. Workers stoked the fires and kept the cauldrons above them just the right temperature for boiling. It was dangerous down here and there are many accounts of workers dying in the salt block house, mostly from fires.

"And that isn't even the worst job," he said. "When the fires died down, the whole pit needed to be cleaned out to prevent creosote from starting a blaze. Someone had to crawl all the way through the boiler duct to clean it out with giant brushes and shovels. It was a tiny place."

"And who got this unfortunate task?" I asked.

"The children. Young boys. They were the only ones small enough to get inside the flues to empty them out. Of course, several died in the act of cleaning out this hell hole," he told me sadly.

There are giant murals on the walls showing the salt manufacturing plants in their heyday, and it is quite remarkable. One enormous wall-sized painting shows the evaporation farms along the lake. Eventually, the salt barons realized that drying the salt water by boiling it was too time-consuming and expensive. They then just laid out hundreds of raised beds along the lakefront, dumped the saltwater into the beds, and then let the sun dry it out and condense it down. It was much slower, but much cheaper. The mural shows this process with gripping detail.

Fifty thousand raised salt beds lining the lakefront.

Incredible.

Wow Factor
"That is easy," Sopchak told me.

Against a back wall stands a barrel. "This is my wow factor," he told me. The salt industry came to a screeching halt in Syracuse on August 26, 1926. Other states, including Michigan and Utah, had discovered great salt sources and were overtaking Syracuse as the leading producers in the nation.

"When Thomas Gale, the last salt baron, decided to shut down his whole operation here, he had the foresight to pack up the last barrel of salt ever produced in the 'The Salt Capital of America.' And here it is," he said.

He then ran his hand over an open-topped barrel that was filled with the last of the Syracuse salt. The barrel has a clear glass top on it to preserve its historical importance.

"That," he told me, "was the end of a huge era in Syracuse's history. Right there in that barrel."

The Take-Away
There is no question that this is a great little museum. It shows, in an interesting manner, the simplicity of this key component in America's development. I mean, when you think of it, it is just a bunch of pots that

boiled up some water. But it is the intricate nature of the process that is so fascinating. The big pots, the hollow log pipes bringing in the water from the lake, the huge fires below, and the sun evaporation concept. It was an intricate and sophisticated process.

One thing that I found really interesting was a giant bell on display. It looks like a large one-room schoolhouse cast-iron bell.

"The raised beds along the lake just sat there all day in the warm weather soaking up the sun and heat, all the while drying the salt," Sopchak described. "But, if you know anything abut Syracuse's weather, well, you know it is unpredictable."

"Whenever a storm approached, as they did regularly off the lake, men would climb up to the top of the many bell towers and ring them for all they were worth. This sent all the able-bodied men and women (and boys and girls) of Liverpool running to the salt beds to join in helping to roll huge wooden pyramids on wheels over the drying salt. Even the nearby schools released the youngsters to run and help. The salt would have been ruined in the rain (or snow)."

He showed me a scale example of the rolling pyramids. They were towering, and weighed several hundred pounds each.

They reminded me of something I once saw in the movie "The Ten Commandments."

The Nuts and Bolts

The Salt Museum
106 Lake Drive
Liverpool, New York 13088
(315) 453-6715
www.onondagecountyparks.com/salt-museum

• *Travel Suggestion*

Exit the New York State Thruway at signs for Onondaga County Park, Route 370. This road runs through the entire park. Liverpool is on the north side of the lake, just five miles from downtown Syracuse. The museum is in the park.

- *Museum Hours*
  May 7 through October 9: 1 to 6 p.m. on weekends.

- *Admission*
  Admission is free but no groups larger than 30 are permitted at a single time. For group tour information, call the museum.

- *Number of Visitors Annually*
  12,000

Up around the Bend
After your museum tour, go for lunch at Heid's of Liverpool. It is the most famous hot dog stand in Upstate New York. They have been serving "Heid's Hots" for more than a century and it is one of the oldest drive-ins in America (www.heidsofliverpool.com). It is located at 305 Oswego Street in Liverpool, a mere two blocks from the Salt Museum.

From Here to There
The other museum in this book that is nearest to the Salt Museum is the **Sims Store Museum**. It is located thirteen miles southwest of Liverpool in Camillus.

16

HOFFMAN CLOCK MUSEUM

Newark, Wayne County

$\mathcal{T}$ime waits for no man at the Hoffman Clock Museum.

As you wander through the several modern showcase rooms in the back of the Newark Public Library, you are accompanied by a constant trilling of little squeaks and squawks, a gentle chorus of small chiming timepieces, the jarring gonging of the big grandfather clocks, and the sharp "wood block claps" of schoolhouse clock hands marking another minute in time.

"Most of our clocks are always working, so it does get a little noisy in there," said Eric Hooker, the curator and conservator of the museum. "We have hundreds of clocks of all kinds and shapes and sizes, from little pocket watches to giant ten-foot-tall grandfather clocks. And grandmother clocks. And granddaughter clocks."

Those are actual names for a category of standing clocks. "They actually call them that, from large to small. Grandfathers run eight feet and up in height. Grandmother clocks are in the six-foot range, and granddaughters run around five feet tall."

While all clock faces generally look the same (to me), the various cases and contraptions they come in can run from the fantastical to the downright beautiful.

"We have some really pretty banjo clocks, and they are really works of art," he said. "It's called a banjo clock because, well, it is shaped like a banjo. But the lengths some people went to to make them attractive is amazing. The ones with the fancy gold leaf and multi-colored artwork on

93

them are known as presentation clocks. These would be custom-made ones to be given as gifts to business partners, brides, etc."

The banjo clocks are mounted on a wall above a beautiful stained glass window which has a "time" theme. I asked the curator why so many of them were made in Massachusetts.

"Simple, really," he began. "Since that was the first part of our new country, the immigrants from Europe came to New England and set up the urban centers there. Soon the craftsman came, and many of them stayed right in Massachusetts after they landed in Boston. The great artisans and watchmakers that came from England and Germany stayed right there. And towns in Connecticut too. Like Winsted, Bristol, Thomaston, Forestville. They are all represented here by fabulous clocks."

One thing that really surprised me here was the sheer beauty of the timepieces. The paintings on the clock cases depicted rural landscapes, houses, birds, farms, etc. The totality of the Hoffman Museum is a unique combination of intricate mechanical expertise married with great beauty and fine art.

Each of the hundreds of clocks has a descriptive card in front of it telling its own unique story. The massive Jennings, a solid mahogany grandfather clock with marquetry that was sold by the Tiffany Company around 1900, is worth more than $15,000. The 1910 International Time Clocks, which got their start in Oneonta, N.Y., and are the earliest beginnings of I.B.M., were a major breakthrough in accurate payroll practices in the beginning of the twentieth century. (And yes, kids can actually take a blank card and insert it into the clock and watch as it stamps the time you were there!)

And there is even a French marble table clock once owned by President Grover Cleveland.

"There were no rules that a president had to give away any gifts they received while in office in the old days, so Cleveland, like many other presidents, simply took the stuff home and sold it," Hooker told me. "Eventually this magnificent clock ended up in somebody's garage sale, where a woman recognized it, bought it, and donated it to our museum," he chuckled.

Wow Factor

"No hesitation here," Hooker said. "The organ clock."

What an unusual piece this is. "This clock spent most of its life right here in Newark," he said. "It ended up in the house right next door to the library. The woman who owned it gave her house to the D.A.R. with the clock still inside it. It wasn't long before it ended up here," he laughed.

The clock is a masterpiece. It came from the Black Forest of Germany and is a handsome piece of furniture. "It was made around 1830, and by the time I got my hands on it, it was a little rough," he said. "It plays eight different German folk tunes at the striking of the hour; each of them is forty seconds long. It hadn't been played in over a hundred years when I found it."

Inside the gleaming mahogany clock case you can see six wooden musicians who move and pantomime playing the folk songs. It is a real crowd pleaser at the museum, obviously.

"Everybody loves this clock. There are only a few working ones like it in the whole country. It took me over two years to get it working again. All of the legs and arms of the little musicians had come loose over time, but luckily I found them all in the clock case. I just puzzled them all together again," he said with pride.

The Take-Away

You don't so much walk into the Hoffman Clock Museum as you are almost magically drawn into it. This museum embraces you. It is colorful, nostalgic, comforting (with the little chimes always going off all around you, much as if you were in your grandmother's front parlor), and extremely interesting. The signage is well done, so no tour guide is needed (except for the playing of the organ clock). The minute detail that goes into each piece is awesome and head-scratching.

"How did they do that?" you'll find yourself saying to yourself over and over as you walk through the display rooms.

One aspect of the museum that really caught my eye was a little, glassed-off corner of the first room. Behind this see-through wall, you will view an old watchmaker's workshop set up as if the jeweler had just left for a cup of coffee. It is neat.

"I got a call from a friend, a gentleman in Philadelphia. He told me that a friend of his, a watchmaker, had died and did I want a watch shop, lock, stock, and barrel? I did and here it is," he said.

The sign reads: "From the shop of Wladyslaw (Walter) Wojnac, 1924– 2009." The tableau tells a story that is quite gripping. "Walter and his family got caught up in World War II when the Nazis came through Poland and killed everybody. Walter was sent to a work concentration camp in Germany, where he survived by working with a camp watchmaker to learn the trade so he could fix the watches of the officers. He knew nothing about this trade, but decided that if they were going to beat him and torture him then he was going to get revenge by becoming an expert watchmaker and learning a trade. He did, and he stayed alive," Hooker told me. "He was a magnificent watchmaker for more than six decades, and this is his entire workshop."

The array in front of you is amazing. The tools, his work desk, personal family photographs, magnifying glasses, etc. "I have been told that a watchmaker could sit right down here today and build a watch just using these old tools of Walter's," Hooker said.

The Nuts and Bolts
    Hoffman Clock Museum
    Newark Public Library
    121 High Street
    Newark, New York 14513
    (315) 331-4370
    www.hoffmanclockmuseum.org (You can actually hear the Organ Clock at this website!)

• *Travel Suggestion*
    Take Exit 42 (Newark) off the New York State Thruway and travel north on Route 14. Make a left on Route 31 and then a left again on Mason Street. The library is on the corner of Mason and High Streets.

• *Museum Hours*
    The clock museum follows the hours of the library.
    Monday through Friday 9:30 a.m. to 9 p.m.
    Saturday 9:30 a.m. to 5:30 p.m.
    Group tours are available by calling in advance.

• *Admission*
    Free

• *Number of Visitors Annually*
    700–800

Up around the Bend
For a whimsical side trip after your visit to the clock museum, travel south on Route 88 about ten miles to the pretty little village of Phelps. This is sauerkraut country, and they throw a huge community festival dedicated to their "money crop" every August. But if you are unable to visit

in August, you really must go to the Phelps Historical Society at 66 Main Street. Walk around back of the grand Victorian home and take a look. Is it? Could it be?

Yes. It is the only two-story brick outhouse in America! It is attached to the main house, which was built by a prominent Phelps physician in 1869. It has connecting doors at each of the two levels of the home and is a classic "six-holer."

Three on the first floor and three on the second!

From Here to There

The other museum in this book that is nearest to the Hoffman Clock Museum is the **Alling Coverlet Museum**. It is located in Palmyra, just ten miles to the west of Newark.

17

TIOGA COUNTY HISTORICAL
SOCIETY MUSEUM

Owego, Tioga County

"*Y*ou are standing under one of the most valuable chandeliers in New York," Tom McEnteer whispered to me.

That sure got my attention.

Tom is a member of the board of the Tioga County Historical Society Museum in Owego. As my eyes lifted to the ceiling of the main showroom of the museum, there it was in all its glitzy splendor.

The "Fireman's Chandelier," as it is known, is a dazzling gold six-foot hanging bauble of exquisite busy-ness. Made by Tiffany, the chandelier hung for years in one of Owego's many firehouses (House #5, "Defiance Hook and Ladder Company"). The several ornate frosted glass globes, which circle the chandelier, are etched with the number 5 on them. The piece itself weighs several hundred pounds and depicts, in reflective gold detail, too many fire department icons to count. Ladders, buckets, helmets, bells, torches, etc. Hundreds of them, in exquisite finite detail. Near the top, nineteenth-century firemen stand on guard in period uniform. The exactitude of the chandelier is positively hypnotic.

"Most people who visit us never look up," Kevin Lentz, director, told me. "We always make it a point to approach them and point it out. They look up and almost fall over at what they witness," he said.

This museum is fantastic. Not only does it tell, in great detail, the history of Tioga County, but tells it in a gripping and personal manner.

The story of Lt. Benjamin Loring is the most amazing.

"Lt. Loring, an Owego native, was in attendance at Ford's Theater the night Lincoln was shot," McEnteer told me. "Being a military man in uniform, he rushed to the presidential box and was one of the first people to attend the mortally wounded president. Lt. Loring cradled Lincoln's head in his arms as they carried him across the street to the rooming house where he later died. We have Loring's bloodstained uniform on display here. Obviously, it is quite a piece of history," he said.

The uniform is on full display in a glass case on the main floor of the museum. The bloodstains are clearly visible.

"The Loring family history doesn't end with Benjamin," McEnteer told me. "His son, known as Todd, was a naturalist who accompanied Teddy Roosevelt on his safaris to Africa. In fact, Roosevelt gave Todd Loring, a non-hunter, a .30 caliber Marlin rifle to use on the safari. One day a lion charged the president's party. Todd took the lion out in mid-air with a single shot between the eyes. The lion dropped within feet of the presidential party. We not only have the rifle that Roosevelt gave Loring, but we have a personal handwritten letter from the president to Loring thanking him for his action."

"There is more," McEnteer said. "Teddy gave the Owego Elks Club (which Todd Loring belonged to at the time) a cigar humidor made out of an actual white rhinoceros foot. And yes, we not only have that rare and unusual item here at the museum, but we also have *another* handwritten letter from Roosevelt presenting this item to him."

As exciting as all of these stories are, they are merely indicative of a veritable treasure chest of historical artifacts stored at this attractive museum. Benjamin Tracy is represented here also. He was a personal friend of President Benjamin Harrison. In fact, Harrison was the best man at Tracy's wedding. Colonel Tracy is one of four Medal of Honor winners from Tioga County and his medal is on display here.

The county was a rich, vibrant manufacturing center once. Industries cranked out everything from bicycles to firearms to cigars to shoes (baby shoes named "O-Wheee-Go").

And motorcycles.

"We have perhaps the only Monarch motorcycle in existence. It was made in Owego in 1913. We have more people call on this one single motorcycle than any other item in our collection," Lentz said as he walked me over to the bike. It was big, compared to newer models, with long three-foot handlebars. It was not hard to imagine yourself flying across the flat-lands of America on the seat of this bad boy back in the day. "Motorcycle fanatics come from all over America just to look at this bike," Lentz said.

Space exploration has been the lynchpin to Owego's success for more than a half-century. The giant Lockheed factory (once IBM) created many items that were key to America's race for space. "Every single manned space mission, from the earliest Gemini to the last space shuttle, had a component on it that was made right here in Owego. In fact, we have the actual computer processor that flew sixteen of those missions on display here," McEnteer showed me.

Exhibit cases scattered around the museum are filled with space memorabilia, from patches to photos to letters from astronauts. And, as if to bolster Owego's sterling reputation as a "Space Town," Doug Hurley, an area native and a 1984 graduate of Owego's high school, was the flight commander on the final space shuttle in July 2011.

This museum is overflowing with tales of Tioga's involvement in everything from the earliest "boneshaker" bicycles to NASA computers.

Come and spend a day here. You will not be disappointed.

Wow Factor

"Our museum has one of the largest private collections of photographs attributed to Matthew Brady in the nation," the director told me.

Andrew Burgess was a longtime friend and neighbor of legendary photography pioneer Matthew Brady. He took many of the photographs attributed to Brady's name and became a partner in his many businesses. Burgess is documented to have taken perhaps the most famous "Brady photograph" of them all. It is the famous photo of Abraham Lincoln and his son Todd. He is also thought to have been the photographer of record of the Lincoln portrait that adorns the five-dollar bill. The Tioga Museum has two hundred Matthew Brady photographs and four original, different studio portraits of Abraham Lincoln.

"Burgess eventually made his way to Owego, where he met and married one of the Owego Tiffanys," the director told me. He and his wife, Eudora, lived the rest of their lives here, but there would be no more photography for Burgess.

"Next to John Browning, Andrew Burgess secured more firearms patents than anybody else (Browning had 952, Burgess 896). He was fascinated with gun making and opened up a firearms manufacturing plant in Owego. He was fabulously successful and made a lot more money from his firearms than he ever did from his photographs," McEnteer said.

The priceless Brady photographs are put on public display periodically. "They are fragile and delicate, so we take great care in them," Director Lentz said. "The museum hopes to publish a book of the photographs in the near future."

The Take-Away

I have been to this museum twice for extended periods of time. During both visits I have marveled at the amount of history reposing here, representing all facets of life. As the director put it so succinctly, "What I love is that our artifacts and memorabilia are not isolated. They are all connected in a grand sense to the development of the nation. From a wooly mammoth's tooth to early transportation to the Brady Civil War-era photographs to the Industrial Revolution to the Space Age, Owego is firmly connected with America's growth and development."

I must put in a special note of appreciation to Lentz, McEnteer, and the hearty group of volunteers that make the Tioga County Historical Society Museum so wonderful. In 2011, massive flooding devastated the village of Owego. The Susquehanna River, which flows at the rear of the museum property, raged out of its banks and swamped the city under several feet of water. "Of the 1,600 structures in the city, 1,200 were severely damaged," McEnteer told me. The museum was one of them.

Recovery efforts were instant and massive. The water, which poured into the museum basement, damaged some articles and the infrastructure, but all of the marquee items (Brady photographs, Civil War items, space items, etc.) were saved.

The last time I visited the museum was the Christmas season in the year after the flood. The museum was festooned with holiday lights and a hundred decorated Christmas Trees for their popular "O Tannenbaum Fundraiser." People were busy with the festivities; volunteers were cheerful, and everyone was grateful at the emergence of their beloved museum from the dark days just a few months before.

More than five hundred of the four thousand residents of the village came through the doors for the opening night of this holiday event to give praise and thanks at the rebirth of the museum. They are a dedicated, involved, passionate, and optimistic group here, for sure!

No wonder that in 2009, Owego, N.Y., was named "America's Coolest Small Town" by Budget Travel magazine!

The Nuts and Bolts

The Tioga County Historical Society Museum
110 Front Street
Owego, New York 13827

(607) 687-2460

www.tiogahistory.org

• *Travel Suggestion*

Take the Owego exit from I-86 (formerly N.Y. Route 17). When entering town, notice the magnificent old courthouse right in the center of town. This majestic landmark, built in 1871, features four three-story towers, one at each corner. Front Street runs directly between the bridge and the courthouse, and the Tioga Museum is just two blocks west.

• *Museum Hours*

Wednesday through Saturday 10 a.m. to 4 p.m. all year.

• *Admission*

Suggested donation: $3.00

• *Number of Visitors Annually*

10,000

Up around the Bend

Owego is in the Southern Tier region of New York. An interesting part of this area's history lies with the Mark Twain connection. Just thirty-five miles west of Owego is Elmira. Twain lived and wrote there for many years. He is buried in the much-visited Woodlawn Cemetery in Elmira. Many famous people are buried there, including Ernie Davis, the first African American Heisman Trophy winner.

Seeking out the Mark Twain connections is fun and easy in Elmira, where he is considered a "favorite son." The trip is short from Owego to Elmira, via the I-86 interstate highway.

From Here to There

The other museum in this book that is nearest to the Tioga County Historical Society Museum is the **Central New York Living History Center** in Cortland. It is forty miles north of Owego.

18

ALLING COVERLET MUSEUM
Palmyra, Wayne County

*W*hat do I know about Palmyra other than Mormons? Nothing.

What do I know about coverlets? Even less.

I had been to Palmyra before to research the birthplace of the Church of Latter-Day Saints. This is where Joseph Smith claimed he was visited by God the Father and Jesus Christ back in 1820. The large, modern Mormon headquarters is located about two miles south of Palmyra. While I admired the visitor's center and the renovated Joseph Smith birthplace and the towering golden statue of the Angel Moroni (who visited Smith four times), I never had the time to venture just up the road to the little Erie Canal town of Palmyra.

I had no idea what I was missing.

"This village has more history to it than any three villages around us put together," exclaimed Bonnie Hays, the executive director of Historic Palmyra. "We have abolition history, Erie Canal history, Winston Churchill history, and immigrant history all right here in this little place."

Palmyra is also home to one of the most unusual museums in this book: the Alling Coverlet Museum.

"We have over sixty full-sized coverlets on display at any given time," Hays said. "Of course we have dozens more, but we have limited space, so we rotate them at intervals so folks who keep coming back here will usually always see a different selection."

The building is a grand, tall red-brick building that was once the home of the Palmyra *Courier Journal* newspaper. It was built in 1901 and is in magnificent condition.

"Mrs. Merle Alling gave us the original collection. Luckily, Mrs. Agnes McLouth Griffith, a long time native of Palmyra, gave us this structure, because it is perfect for displaying something as large as a coverlet. We have over four hundred fifty coverlets in our possession and we keep those not on display in a state-of-the-art vault," Hays said.

"So, what is a coverlet?" I asked sheepishly.

"Don't be embarrassed," she laughed. "Most people haven't got a clue. I always tell them a coverlet differs from a quilt because a coverlet is woven and a quilt is sewn. When we say handmade we mean that someone physically ran the loom. They almost always tell a story in words and iconography. Many of them are a record of sorts with a date, and some are even signed with the name of the weavers. Afterward, a coverlet would simply grace a bed. Coverlets have been called 'American Tapestry.' There were only about two hundred professional weavers in the U.S. in the 1800s, and two of the very best came from Palmyra. They really are works of art."

Are they ever! As I wandered amongst the eighty-inch by seventy-six-inch coverlets hanging from the ceiling (all dramatically lit by track lighting) I could really understand the fascination with this American heirloom. The designs were intricate, the colors were madly bright and decorative, and the history was apparent in the signatures of the weavers.

"One of our oldest jacquard ones is a Mott-made coverlet, from Long Island. It was made for Sarah V. Scudder and is dated 1821," the executive director told me. "It probably took her two days to make in the Motts' weaving factory, and it cost her about $2.00 in materials."

Visitors are shown a short video before going on a tour of the museum, and the presentation shows the importance of the Jacquard loom. Joseph Marie Jacquard invented this revolutionary item in 1804. The process uses a punch card system, which the yarn and material would go through to make the intricate designs on the coverlets. Before Jacquard, the entire setting of the designs was done in a laborious hand- and eye-coordination. With the new loom head, design patterns could be changed as simply as changing a punch card head. This process is actually credited with being the beginning of computer hardware, with the concept of punch card computing being used to control operating machines for the very first time.

I asked Ms. Hays if I could see a Jacquard loom. "Well, yes, if we had one," she laughed. "They are as scarce as hen's teeth to find!"

Wow Factor
To know Bonnie Hays is to know Historic Palmyra. This umbrella organization is the steward group for a series of historic buildings near the Erie Canal. Hays has a wow factor for each one of them.

"In the print shop it is the 1870 Peerless paper cutter (made in Palmyra). Watch this," she told me. She then proceeded to place a giant Rochester city phone book in the jaws of this old black contraption. With a mighty pull of a long iron bar, the diminutive Ms. Hays was able to slice the thick directory in half as if the cutter's blade were a knife going through warm butter.

In the Historical Society Building, she showed me some of the artifacts of several familiar names that were part of Palmyra's history. "This lady is kind of a wow factor to us. Jennie Jerome was her name," Hays said as she held up a portrait of an attractive young woman. "Of course everybody knows her now as Lady Churchill. Yup, her parents set up housekeeping in Palmyra and then moved to New York City by way of Rochester, where they lived for a time. Jennie was born in Brooklyn in 1854. Mrs. Leonard Jerome took the girls to Europe and England, where Jennie eventually married Lord Randolph Churchill."

"So, you mean . . ." I began.

"Correct. She was Winston Churchill's mother!" Hays said. Her mother and father, Leonard and Clarissa Hall Jerome, were married right here in the Western Presbyterian Church on April 5, 1849. Isn't it fun to think that the great Winston Churchill actually has kin here in the Palmyra Village Cemetery?"

In the historic Erie Canal House, you can blow the whistle that called the lockmaster to his post. In the general store you can see some original items that were there when William Phelps first opened the doors in 1868. Ask to see a pair of boots that date back to 1880. As I said, there are wow factors all over this place.

So what exactly is the wow factor at the Alling Coverlet Museum?

"The whole place is just so visually stunning," Hays told me. "People really do stop and say 'wow' when they step into the display room for the first time. With all of the brightly colored coverlets hanging down from the ceiling, gently waving in the breeze, it is just such a gorgeous place of beauty, grace, style, and history."

I couldn't have said it better myself.

The Take-Away

Full disclosure. I am not a fan of coverlets.

That being said, it is quite remarkable what Historic Palmyra has created out of a short two-block area near the canal.

"And we saved it all from urban renewal, don't forget," Hays said proudly.

A good, solid couple of hours could easily be spent wandering in and out of all of the five historic buildings here. In fact, it is set up so that a single price will give you a "trail pass" to all of the museums.

The Phelps General Store has been called one of the most perfect examples of a nineteenth-century mercantile that you will find anywhere in the country. The apartment upstairs, where the Phelps family lived, is a fascinating look back at the 1800s. The furniture, the bathing tubs, the kitchen, everything is perfectly placed as it was when the bustling family business was located just a floor below.

The print shop is made for hands-on experiences for all ages. In fact, kids are invited to print their own stationary using wood blocks and presses that are original to the print shop's beginnings. (Sorry, no kids are allowed to use the paper cutting monstrosity!)

The History Building is packed with twenty-three rooms filled with Palmyra history. Ask about Palmyra's own Increase Lapham, America's first official weatherman. It is a great story!

And when Hays said it all was saved from the dreaded clutches of "urgent removal," she was right.

"We were this close to losing it all," she said while holding up two fingers barely an inch apart. "But we did it, and now we have it for future generations to see."

Congratulations, Palmyra.

The Nuts and Bolts
The Alling Coverlet Museum
122 William Street
Palmyra, New York 14522
The Palmyra Historical Museum
132 Market Street
Palmyra, New York 14522
(315) 597-6981
www.historicpalmyrany.com

• *Travel Suggestion*
Take the New York State Thruway to Exit 43 and travel six miles north. You will pass the Mormon visitor's center on your right on the way into town.

• *Museum Hours*
　　Late Spring to Fall: Tuesday to Saturday 10:30 a.m. to 4:30 p.m.
　　Fall to Spring: Tuesday to Thursday 11 a.m. to 4 p.m.
　　Call for custom appointments.

• *Admission*
　　Adults: $3.00 individual or $7.00 for the trail ticket.
　　Children (12–17) and Seniors: $2.00 individual or $5.00 trail ticket.
　　The trail ticket includes admission to all the museums.

• *Number of Visitors Annually*
　　4,000 (Coverlet Museum only)

Up around the Bend

If you are new to Palmyra, you must visit the Mormon visitor's sites. The Hill Cumorah and Joseph Smith Farm and Family Home and other venues are all located just two miles south of Palmyra on Route 21 (www.hill cumorah.org). Thousands visit here each year. The facility is motor-coach friendly and welcomes all ages for the total "Mormon Experience." Videos, presentations, dioramas, meditation rooms, and of course the beautiful walk up the hill to the giant gold Angel Moroni statue, all contribute to making this an unforgettable, almost surreal, destination.

From Here to There

The other museum in this book that is nearest to the Alling Coverlet Museum is **The Hoffman Clock Museum** in Newark. It is ten miles east of Palmyra.

19

SAMPSON MILITARY MUSEUM

Romulus, Seneca County

*T*his museum may be the only one that is located in a brig.

"Yes, these are the brig quarters for what was the whole military base," Dolores Dinsmore told me. She is the director of the museum at the former Sampson military base. Almost all of the other 498 buildings are gone, and the stark training base has morphed into a bucolic state park. But the brig remains.

"Look how small the cells were," the director said to me as we made our way to the hardcore cellblock. "You'd really have to do something bad to land back in here, like go AWOL or commit a near felony. These were for the baddest of the bad seeds," she said.

The cellblock is divided into a few rooms, which hold two cots each, and a few cells for solitary confinement. The men shared a single communal shower, sink, and toilet. I stepped into the shower stall. I could barely turn around in it. And the amenities were bleak.

"They really did only get bread and water in here," she told me. "Two days of nothing but bread and water, and on the third day they would get a full meal. Then back to bread and water for two more days. You didn't see many repeat offenders in here, that is for sure."

The square building, which houses the museum, surrounds a courtyard. Each room has been transformed to highlight a different phase of camp life. One tells of the construction of Sampson Naval Base.

"They built nearly five hundred buildings over 2,535 acres in just two hundred and seventy days. The camp had its own phone system, fire department, sewage and electric plants, laundry, garage, rail lines, and

hospital. In fact, the 1,500-bed Sampson Naval Hospital was the largest military hospital on the East Coast," Dinsmore told me.

Other rooms highlight camp life, schooling, "off to war," and camp activities. All the major entertainers of the day came by to entertain the troops at Sampson, and a large display shows photos of Bob Hope, Lionel Hampton, Marian Anderson, Joe Louis, and many others entertaining and visiting with the troops here.

"They also had a strong roster of athletics here," the director told me. "In fact, Lt. Commander Jim Crowley, one of Notre Dame's famed 'Four Horsemen,' coached football here."

The displays are very interesting. And every item was donated by either someone who "booted" here or is a descendant of someone who came through the camp.

"I never turn anything down," the director told me with a smile. "We have dozens of uniforms, a hundred different World War II weapons, and armaments, and thousands of photographs. The Navy always took a class photo of the different companies when they graduated. The men received these and usually sent them home to their mothers or sweethearts. The Navy didn't keep any negatives, so the only ones we get are ones brought in to us. Unfortunately, they are not labeled, so it can be quite a trick trying to find a specific person in all these photos," she said.

More than 400,000 Navy personnel booted out of Sampson. It became a school when the war ended. In 1950 it was commissioned again as a boot camp, and 300,000 Air Force troops came here to camp during the Korean War.

Many of the items on display were pilfered by the G.I.s during their overseas duty.

"They were all great scroungers," Dinsmore laughed. "We have Japanese items of every kind as well as lots of Nazi memorabilia."

In front of the museum, as you pass by it to go to the lakefront park, you can see missiles, torpedoes, artillery, and other weapons of war which are part of the museum's collection. Lording over it all is Korean War-era jet.

The tools of the trade are displayed throughout the museum. The men who trained here went on to become butchers, dentists, pharmacist's mates, barbers, radiomen, and gunnery experts.

I asked Dinsmore if she could remember the name of any famous celebrity that actually went to boot camp here.

"Well, I wouldn't call him a celebrity, but everybody knew his name. It was William Patrick Hitler, Adolf Hitler's 32-year-old nephew," she said with a smile. "Really," she said. "He booted out of here during World War II as a pharmacist's mate and they sent him directly to Washington, D.C., where he worked on anti-Nazi propaganda. Creepy, huh?" she said.

Wow Factor

"Without a doubt it's the periscope," the director told me.

We walked over to a corner of a display room and witnessed a long line of kids waiting patiently to peer through an actual submarine periscope. I joined them in line. The experience was, as those around me said, very cool.

"One day some old sailors came in here with that intact periscope. They wanted to give it to us. I didn't ask any questions." It came from the nuclear sub USS *Benjamin Franklin* that was decommissioned in 1993. We had it installed so the eye of the periscope pops out of the roof of the museum. Everyone loves it," she exclaimed.

It was remarkable. In my one 360-degree spin with it I could see bathers almost a mile away on the beach of Seneca Lake.

One forgotten wow factor would have been the base's chapel, long torn down.

"It had a revolving altar," Dinsmore told me. She showed me a photo of it. It was amazing.

"When a Catholic service ended, the whole altar revolved a third of the way, revealing a Protestant altar. When that service ended, a button was pushed and it spun again, revealing a Jewish altar."

It looked like something out of Disney World.

The Take-Away

This museum is very well done. The flow from room to room (camp phase to camp phase) is very efficient and really enables the visitor to capture the whole Sampson story. The displays are well lit and creatively signed. I particularly liked the wall display of the Naval alphabet in signal flags. Of course, the enemy items were interesting to look at also. One in particular.

It was a Japanese "encouragement flag."

"It is the Rising Sun, and the Japanese soldiers and officers have written messages all over it to encourage the soldiers as they went to battle," Dinsmore told me. "We have a Japanese translator working on it now. I can't wait to see what all the messages say," she said.

The Nuts and Bolts

Sampson Military Museum
Sampson State Park
Romulus, New York 14541
www.visitnewyorkstate.org/Sampson
(315) 585-6203

- *Travel Suggestion*

  The museum is on the east side of Seneca Lake. Follow Route 96A 15 miles south of Geneva, N.Y.

- *Museum Hours*

  Wednesday through Sunday 9:00 a.m. to 3:00 p.m. The last tour departs at 2:15 p.m.

  Labor Day to Columbus Day: Weekends only.

  Closed in the winter.

- *Admission*

  Free

- *Number of Visitors Annually*

  8,000

Up around the Bend

This is Upstate's "Wine Country," and there are dozens of fine wineries within an hour's drive of the museum. But for a fun side trip, I would send you up the road just four miles to Ovid. Here you can visit "The Three Bears."

The three public buildings which front the courthouse square are known affectionately as "Mama Bear," "Papa Bear," and "Baby Bear." They have been in continuous public use for more than a century and a half. They descend in size from big to small in exact proportion. The citation for their registry as National Historic Landmarks refers to them as "the only three adjacent Greek Revival public buildings in the United States."

Neat!

From Here to There

The other museum in this book that is nearest to Sampson Military Museum is the **Memorial Day Museum** in Waterloo. It is just ten miles north of Romulus.

20

NATIONAL MEMORIAL DAY MUSEUM
Waterloo, Seneca County

*W*aterloo gets to celebrate Memorial Day. Twice.

"On the weekend of the actual federal holiday we do have some great celebrations," Cyndi Park-Shiels told me. "Our beautiful village park is filled with vendors, live music, food, and performers of all kinds. We have a large parade, and many Civil War reenactors come to Waterloo to exhibit their talents and showmanship. On the Sunday of Memorial Day weekend we have a gigantic car show. Old cars line the main street area for over a mile on both sides of the road. It is a grand time.

"Our second Memorial Day celebration comes on May 30th, which was the actual date of the holiday before Congress moved it to a Monday through the Uniform Monday Holiday Act. On this day we have a second parade, which is usually filled with area veterans. We use this as a day of remembrance and reflection. So you see, we have two Memorial Day celebrations," Park-Sheils told me.

And why do they do this in this beautiful little Finger Lakes community?

Because Waterloo is the nation's official birthplace of Memorial Day.

Directly after the Civil War, a local druggist, Henry Welles, tried (unsuccessfully at first) to get his fellow Waterloo residents to decorate the graves of the many dead from the war. General John Murray later joined Welles in the first organized "Decoration Day," on May 5, 1866. The Waterloo National Memorial Day Museum, of which Park-Shiels is the manager, tells the story of the founding of the holiday and the impact it has had on this little community of 5,000 residents.

"We usually march up to Maple Grove cemetery and lay flowers on the graves of the fallen. After the parade, 'Taps' is played, 21-gun salutes honor the fallen, and we listen to the reading of the Gettysburg Address and General Logan's orders."

General John A. Logan is considered by most to be the "Father of Memorial Day." His famous "1866 Order of the Day" is still read at commemorations all across the nation ("Let us, then, at the time appointed, gather around their sacred remains and garland the passionless mounds above them with the choicest flowers of spring-time. . . .")

The museum on Main Street is housed in the former William Burton mansion. It was built in 1830 and rebuilt in 1860, and is a magnificent Italianate structure that sits tall near the end of the business district. It is listed on the National Register of Historic Places.

Waterloo had to fend off a multitude of other communities around the nation who claimed the title of "Birthplace of Memorial Day." It wasn't until 1966 that it was officially deemed so.

The museum is replete with Memorial Day and Civil War memorabilia. Each room is done in period décor, from furniture to wallpaper.

Display cases hold hundreds of items ranging from small lockets with photos in them to 1860s militariana. Large portraits, wall maps, and archival photos festoon the walls. A docent is usually on hand to walk the visitor down the footpaths of history.

Wow Factor

"Definitely the Memorial Day Centennial Case," the manager told me. "This display covers the events surrounding the one-hundredth celebration in 1966 of Memorial Day, and how Waterloo was nationally recognized as being its birthplace. We are very proud to display the official proclamation signed by President Lyndon B. Johnson, as well as the pen he used to sign it. Just two months prior to that, Governor Nelson Rockefeller offered up his own proclamation. We have his signed declaration in the case also.

"This is the exhibit that gets the single largest reaction from our visitors, because it solidifies in their minds that Waterloo is in fact the official birthplace of Memorial Day."

The Take-Away

I loved this little museum. The Burton House is really a gorgeous early-1800s mansion, and the Museum and historical society here put it to good use. There is hardly an inch to spare! Programs and exhibits change frequently, and even if you are not very interested in the Civil War, there are still a lot of great antiques and local historical artifacts here to paw through.

The Museum is perfectly located near the end of the downtown business district. It is a great starting place to take a self-guided walking tour of this charming little village. There are many nice "mom-and-pop" stores and cafes and restaurants to enjoy and window-shop in.

The front of the red brick museum is usually adorned with red-white-and-blue bunting, giving it a perpetual patriotic flavor.

Ask inside about the whereabouts of the Waterloo residences of a couple of famous folks who once resided here. Dick Clark, of *American Bandstand* fame, once lived here. And Tom Coughlin, head coach of the New York Giants, was born here in 1946.

The Nuts and Bolts

> The National Memorial Day Museum
> 35 East Main Street
> Waterloo, New York 13165
> (315) 539-9611
> www.wlhs-ny.org

• *Travel Suggestion*

> Leave the New York State Thruway at Exit 41. Travel south on N.Y. Route 414 five miles to Waterloo. The village is about 40 miles west of Syracuse.

• *Museum Hours*

> Mid-April to Mid-May: Tuesday through Saturday 1 to 5 p.m.
> Mid-May through Labor Day: Monday through Saturday 10 a.m. to 5 p.m.
> September to Mid-November: Tuesday through Saturday 11 a.m. to 5 p.m.
> Also by appointment

• *Admission*

> Donations gladly accepted.

• *Number of Visitors Annually*

> 1,500

Up around the Bend

This part of the Finger Lakes is loaded with great historical sites. You simply cannot spend a visit at the National Memorial Day Museum in Waterloo without then going to Seneca Falls, "The Birthplace of the Women's Rights Movement." Here are the shrines to the feminist movement, including the amazing Wesleyan Chapel, where the first women's rights goals were written up in 1848, and the National Women's Hall of Fame, among others.

Oh, and if Seneca Falls looks familiar, it is because movie director Frank Capra modeled Bedford Falls in his classic *It's a Wonderful Life* after Seneca Falls. The model for the bridge George Bailey jumped from at the beginning of the picture is here. And you can stay at the Hotel Clarence (named after the "angel" in the movie).

Seneca Falls is just four miles east of Waterloo.

From Here to There
The other museum in this book that is nearest to the National Memorial Day Museum is **Mike Weaver's Drain Tile Museum** in Geneva. It is seven miles west of Waterloo.

21

D.I.R.T. MUSEUM

Weedsport, Cayuga County

$\mathcal{T}$his is a cool spot.

D.I.R.T. stands for Driver's Independent Race Tracks, and this museum and hall of fame pays tribute to the "Kings of Dirt."

"Glenn Donnelly started it all right here back in 1992," Jack Speno, the curator, told me. "Glenn is a legend. He bought the Weedsport Speedway in 1970 and he just never left. The Speedway is behind the museum, and Glenn still lives right up the road from here," Speno said. "It was Glenn's idea to unify dirt racers into a cohesive organization with consistent rules, a coordinated race schedule, and common guidelines. He worked for years at the New York State Fair and created Super Dirt Week there. It really took off and is one of the largest dirt racing events in the country still today."

Dirt motor racing (commonly known as stock car racing in the northern states) took off shortly after World War II. Oval tracks sprang up all over the Upstate New York region.

An even greater surge took place around 1980. "That's when the big sponsorship money really began to draw in the big names," Speno said.

"We have so many of the great, legendary race tracks in our area," Gary Spaid told me. He is the head of selection for the D.I.R.T. Hall of Fame. Great names like Lebanon Valley, Canandaigua, Ransomville, Rolling Wheels, Thunder Mountain, Five Mile Point, Fonda, Afton, and more.

"Man, a lot of great racing has sure gone on around here over the years," he said with a smile.

Dirt track racing is the single most popular form of auto racing in America (despite the glitz and glamour of NASCAR). Nearly 2,000 dirt

tracks can be found throughout every state and Canada. This museum is a treasure trove of D.I.R.T.

When you walk into the museum, the sheer number of extraordinary items on display here immediately dazzles you. Actual racecars are lined up on the showroom floor surrounded by dozens of helmets and racing suits, hundreds of trophies, and thousands of photographs.

"All of these items came from the drivers themselves," Spaid told me. "They are very generous with their personal items and are fully committed to helping to make this museum a success."

The lineup of racers is a virtual Who's Who of dirt racing history. And each car has its own story.

"Johnny Botz was a great racer," Speno told me as we walked through the display floor. "This was his favorite car. It's his famous orange Pinto. He was one of our great champions. As you can tell, he was a big hit in the Syracuse area (the car is orange and white). Poor Johnny died in a garage fire. His Mom called us up and asked us if we wanted his car for the museum," he said in a whisper.

Champion John McArdell's 1962 Chevy five-window coupe is here. Frank Andres's "Mighty Mouse" car with the superhero mouse flying across the trunk is also here.

"I paid $300 for that car. It was found in a field with a tree growing up through the roof," Speno laughed. "We dragged it over here and fixed it up and now it is a big hit with the kids."

Another big car is painted pink and black.

"It's definitely an old one," said Speno. "I forget who drove it, but it was one of the few women drivers. It is a 1936 Ford three-window coupe."

Ron Wallace's 1976 Bicentennial car is here, all decked out in stars and stripes and red-white-and-blue racing colors.

I asked both Speno and Spaid who was the "Dale Earnhardt" of dirt racing. They answered in unison.

"Barefoot Bob McCreadie."

"No doubt about it. He was a great champion. We have a lot of his things here. One of the great similarities between Bob and Dale is the impact they had on the sport," Spaid said. "After Dale died many people stayed away from NASCAR thinking it would never be the same. When Bob McCreadie retired, many said they would never attend a race again, also. He had that kind of an impact.

"Oh, and he got his nickname because he won over five hundred races and once even did it barefoot," Speno added with a laugh.

Wow Factor

The Batmobile.

"I really think I named it," Spaid said as we strolled over to by far the most unusual looking car on the floor.

"I was writing for *Gater Racing News* at the time. Gary 'Hot Shoe' Balough showed up in this old Number 112 at Syracuse for a championship race one year. Boy what a ruckus that caused. The body was a modified Lincoln Continental—it used ram injectors and all kind of unusual and weird modifications. The other drivers complained bitterly about it, but after the judges inspected the car they said he could race it. Gary blew a tire on the first lap and then came from back of the pack to win the race. He had bent the rules but had not broken them and that put him and this car in the history books. No one knew what to call it, so when I wrote about it for the trade paper I just called it the Batmobile and the name stuck."

Balough continued to truck the Batmobile to races all over the east. His luck came to an end when he was pulled over one day and arrested. Convicted of being a part of a multi-million dollar marijuana and cocaine ring, he did nearly four years in prison, thereby ending one of dirt racing's most exciting careers.

The Take-Away

This is the kind of museum where you find guys standing around in front of cars for hours talking and laughing and telling racing stories. They tell of the time they remember seeing this great driver win an incredible race. Or when that famous car made its debut. Or when this old racetrack was first opened out in the middle of nowhere.

It kind of reminded me of when I visited Woodstock. Although I didn't attend the rock festival there in 1969, I like to go there and just listen to the boomers tell of being there and live their stories vicariously. The same happens here.

I do not think I have ever been to a dirt race. But after spending an afternoon here, listening to the great stories of the past, I sure felt as if I had had some dirt kicked up into my face more than once.

By the way, the Hall of Fame part of this museum is also well done. A hundred lighted plaques tell the stories of great drivers from the past, many of them known by colorful nicknames.

Jim "The Pine" Shampine from Clay, N.Y. His plaque calls him "the greatest super modified driver ever." And Jerry "Cookie" Cook from Lockport, "one of the fifty greatest drivers in history." And Elmer "Mad Russian" Musclow, "one of the great pioneers of the sport." And "Gentleman" Harry Peek, "famed for his patented Peek's Charge, proving that nice guys do finish first."

Believe me, Cooperstown has nothing on the D.I.R.T. Hall of Fame.

The Nuts and Bolts

The D.I.R.T. Motorsports Museum and Hall of Fame
1 Speedway Drive

Weedsport, New York 13166
(315) 834-6606
(315) 374-3661
Website: www.dirthalloffame-classiccarmuseum.com

• *Travel Suggestion*
The Weedsport exit of the New York State Thruway is just west of Syracuse, near the New York State Fairgrounds.

• *Museum Hours*
Weekends Noon to 5 p.m.

• *Admission*
There is a very small admission charge, with discounts given to seniors. (Donations are gratefully accepted.)

• *Number of Visitors Annually*
2,000

Up around the Bend
Weedsport is located at the very edge of the Finger Lakes region of New York. A nice side trip from the D.I.R.T. Museum is Skaneateles. This would make a nice introduction to the region for new visitors. The little village is picturesque, quaintly chic, and filled to the brim with charm. It is located on sparkling Skaneateles Lake, and features many nice high-end shops as well as comfortable cafes and restaurants. Known as "The Eastern Gateway to the Finger Lakes," Skaneateles is located just twelve miles southeast of Weedsport.

From Here to There
The other museum in this book that is nearest to the D.I.R.T. Motorsports Museum and Hall of Fame is the **Seward House Museum** in Auburn. It is ten miles south of Weedsport.

OTHER MUSEUMS TO
EXPLORE IN REGION THREE

Corning: Corning Museum of Glass. "One of Upstate's greatest museums. It explores every facet of glass, including art, history, culture, science, technology, craft, and design." (800) 732-6845, www.cmog.org.

Corning: Rockwell Museum of Art. "The finest American Western and Native American art collection east of the Mississippi." (607) 937-5386, www.rockwellmuseum.org.

Cortland: New York State Grange Museum. "The only museum in the state dedicated to the history of the New York State Grange, which was founded in 1873." (607) 753-0337, www.nysgrangemuseum.com.

Cortland: Country Music Hall of Fame and Museum. "Many legendary country music performers have appeared here, from George Jones to Loretta Lynn. The museum contains many artifacts, apparel, and memorabilia of both national and local country music artists." (607) 753-0337, www.cortlandcountrymusicpark.com.

Elmira: National Soaring Museum. "The museum preserves and presents the heritage of motorless flight. There are a multitude of gliders on display." (607) 734-3128, www.soaring museum.org.

Horseheads: National Warplane Museum. "An exciting airplane museum featuring over 70 aircraft. Kids get a thrill out of sitting in the cockpits of such fighting machines as the F14 Tomcat and the TBF Avenger). (607) 739-8200, www.wingsofeagles.com.

Ithaca: Johnson Museum of Art. "The permanent collection here contains more than 25,000 pieces of art, and it is considered to be one of the most important university museums in the country. The building was designed by I.M. Pei." (607) 255-6464, www.museum.cornell.edu.

Penn Yan: Oliver House Museum. "This 18-room mansion was built in 1852. Exhibits reflect this area's rich agricultural heritage. Among the most interesting collection is a large quantity of grape labels. More than 35 million labels were produced in the Penn Yan area up until about 1925. This was a prime grape-growing region and the colorful label art is considered to be the best of its kind." (315) 536-7318, www.yatespast.com/collection.

Rochester: George Eastman House and International Museum of Photography. "The stunning home of the Father of Modern Photography. Eastman shot himself to death in the upstairs bedroom of this mansion on March 14, 1932. The museum houses the largest film archive in the world." (Rochester) (585) 271-3361, www.eastmanhouse.org.

Rochester: National Museum of Play. "The only collections-based museum in the word dedicated to the art of playing. It includes 150,000 square feet of dynamic interactive exhibit area." (585) 263-2700, www.museumofplay .org.

Rochester: Susan B. Anthony Museum and House. "This was the home of the famous civil rights leader for more than forty years. A block away is an amazing bronze double statue of Anthony and abolitionist Frederick Douglass seated in a park having a cup of tea." (585) 235-6124, www.susan banthonyhouse.org.

Seneca Falls: Seneca Museum of Waterways. "This museum celebrates the water industry of the Finger Lakes region. The rear windows of the museum dramatically overlook the Cayuga-Seneca Canal. Seneca Falls's rich heritage was directly tied to the waterways and canals highlighted in this museum." (315) 568-1510, www.senecamuseum.com.

Seneca Falls: National Women's Rights Historic Park and Hall of Fame. "At the National Women's Hall of Fame, our mission all day, every day is showcasing great women . . . inspiring all!" (315) 568-8060, www.great women.org.

Syracuse: Erie Canal Museum. "Located in the only surviving canal weighlock building in America. Out front is the popular statue to the Erie Canal mule named "Sal." (315) 471-0593, www.eriecanalmuseum.org.

Region Four

1,000 Islands/Seaway

Oswego, Jefferson, and St. Lawrence Counties

22

ANTIQUE BOAT MUSEUM

Clayton, Jefferson County

*I*t is very easy to get lulled into the sense that you are actually in an oceanfront community in Clayton. You have to keep pinching yourself to remember that this is a riverfront community.

The St. Lawrence River starts its devolution here, slowly disintegrating into outlets and bays as it exits massive Lake Ontario just a few miles to the west at Cape Vincent. The river flows out of Lake Ontario and downhill in a northeasterly direction past Montreal and Quebec and into the Atlantic Ocean beyond the Gulf of St. Lawrence.

The Thousand Islands form the first fifty miles of the river. There are actually 1,864 islands, ranging in size from rock outcroppings a few square feet in area to 15 mile long expanses with farms and small towns. The international border between the United States and Canada meanders through the islands, never bisecting any single island and dividing the landmass equally between the two nations (although there are more islands in Canada.) Coves and inlets surround the village of Clayton. In fact Carrier Bay, French Creek Bay, and Goose Bay all make for a landscape artist's dream backdrop to this little community of less than 2,000 residents.

"We love our little town, and our museum is the centerpiece to its history," Frederick H. "Fritz" Hager told me. He is the executive director of the Antique Boat Museum.

"We have over 350 boats and tens of thousands of artifacts in our collection, but as you can see we only have room to display half of the collection at one time," he told me. "We're considered the premier freshwater

131

nautical museum in North America. The trouble is, not a lot of people know that. On the other hand, it means we have a tremendous opportunity to grow and reach out and connect people with boats and boating heritage all across the continent."

The museum is awash in boats. Historic boats. Beautiful boats.

"We of course have many classic old wooden boats," Hager said.

And boy, do they ever. The display floor is crammed with gleaming mahogany boats of all eras. Big ones sidle up to small ones. Expensive boats rub bows with boats of a more everyday quality. But all of them shine. The main display floor is a veritable pageant of the history of wooden motorboats in North America.

"We are blessed by our many donors," Lora Nadolski, Director of Programming, said. "We never buy a boat. They're all donated to us. People just know that if they give us a boat, one perhaps that has been in their family for generations, that the museum will care for it like it was our very own."

The museum got its New York State charter in 1981. "It all started with a few prominent residents of our area who got together and held a boat show in the summer of 1965. It was popular and grew every year.

Eventually the idea of a museum was mentioned and it soon became a reality. We bought some riverfront property here in Clayton. Actually all of this was once a shipbuilding yard," Nadolski told me of the museum locale. "Today it is one of the most popular destinations of the Adirondack/ St. Lawrence region."

Today the Antique Boat Museum keeps current to the times by accepting and displaying fiberglass and plastic water pleasure craft examples.

"Still," Hager told me, "no matter what we get in our collection, it is the old wooden masterpieces that people are just in awe of. Among the boats of the 1920s and 1930s that we have are many Gold Cup winners, plus boats that were owned by wealthy and famous residents of the Thousand Islands region. We really want this to be a museum dedicated to boating history so we do have many boats that are very important."

I asked the executive director, "What makes a boat important?"
"Every boat has a story to tell. Its provenance, how it was built, where it was built, who owned it, and what it was used for are all important to boat lovers," he responded.

Wow Factor

It was funny to ask both the executive director and the public programming director of the museum what was their wow factor here. Why? Because they answered in unison.

"*La Duchesse.*"

And I agree. It is a stunner.

"*La Duchesse* was originally built for George Boldt, the proprietor of the Waldorf–Astoria Hotel in New York City and builder of the magnificent Boldt Castle here in the Thousand Islands. The year was 1903 and he created what many consider to be the most luxurious house boat ever built," Hager said.

"And is it ever," Nadolski chimed in. "It has nine staterooms, a full bar, a large dining room, a lavish parlor, a 45-foot-long deck with wicker furniture. It had every amenity imaginable at the time. It was the height of lavishness," she said.

"Yes, it had everything but one item," Hager laughed. "It had no motor! Boldt had his own private tug boat which would pull *La Duchesse* to wherever he wanted to drop anchor, leave it, and then come and pull it back in when he was ready for a new locale," he laughed.

The boat was donated to the museum upon the death of its third owner, Andrew McNally III, heir to the Rand McNally map fortune.

"Mr. McNally was a summer resident of the Thousand Islands and *La Duchesse* was his summer home for more than sixty years. He had always planned on leaving the boat to the museum when he passed away. She's been open for tours here since 2005."

"People are just awestruck when they walk inside," Nadolski told me. "They just can't believe the glamour lavished on a houseboat. From the marble sinks to the brass fireplaces to the gold-stenciled ceilings and the mahogany woodwork, everything is just top-notch on this boat."

The Take-Away

The St. Lawrence Seaway trail (basically New York Routes 12 and 37) is one of the great secret treasures of the upstate region. The route is dotted with many wonderful little towns, some with great history (Cape Vincent), some with venerable recreation opportunities (Alexandria Bay), some with unique small-town charm (Waddington) and some even with urban treats to enjoy (Ogdensburg). But there are very few museums. Perhaps the largest is the Frederic Remington Museum in Ogdensburg. It is wonderful. But another one to cherish is the Antique Boat Museum in Clayton.

When I arrived in the village, I was struck by its character and found it to be quite enchanting. The tiny business district offers many nice little pleasures, including a variety of attractive dining options. The natural setting of Clayton, poised on a peninsula jutting out into the St. Lawrence, affords breathtaking vistas from virtually every corner.

I explored the regal 1903 Clayton Opera House and observed a lively and fairly current lineup of entertainers listed for the coming season. The shops had eye catching window displays and the village seemed to employ a permanent, full-time landscaper. Yes, it was that pretty. And it is *small*.

The Antique Boat Museum is the real cultural anchor in this waterfront community. The architect craftily blended the museum design to evoke the former warehouse/lumberyard location beautifully. It is modern, well lit, and easily accessible to all. The museum is surrounded by water (including the docking area of *La Duchesse*) and attractive perennial gardens. A gift shop offers many unique items, many of a nautical nature.

This museum is a real "find" in the far northern region of Upstate New York.

The Nuts and Bolts

Antique Boat Museum
750 Mary Street
Clayton, New York 13624
(315) 686-4104
www.abm.org

- *Travel Suggestion*

Take I-81 north out of Syracuse about ninety minutes. Make a left on Route 12 to get to Clayton.

- *Museum Hours*

The Museum's galleries and exhibits are open from mid-May to mid-November. The offices and research library are open all year by appointment. Call in advance for actual opening and closing dates.

- *Admission*

Museum Members: Free
Adults: $13
Seniors and AAA Members: $12
Active Military: Free
Children (7–17): $6.50
Family rates are available.
Important: Free tours of *La Duchesse* are included with your admission; however, you must register for the tour when entering the museum. The last tour of *La Duchesse* begins at 4 p.m. The boat is not wheelchair-accessible.

The museum hosts a very popular annual antique boat show during the first weekend in August every year. Call in advance for details, including special entry fees.

• *Number of Visitors Annually*
  35,000

Up around the Bend
You have come this far, why not go just a little bit farther?

Just fifteen minutes west of Clayton (on Route 12) you will find historic Cape Vincent. This is really the end of the road. This town, with roots going back to Napoleon's France, is literally the last stop on the Seaway. The motto for Cape Vincent is "Where the River and the Lake Meet." The view from the head of the St. Lawrence River out over the vast expanse of Lake Ontario is unforgettable. For the best vantage point, head to the 1827 Cape Vincent lighthouse.

Known as Tibbetts Point Lighthouse, it has one of the oldest working lights along the Lake Ontario coast. And it is a great place for a picnic.

From Here to There
The other museum that is nearest to the Antique Boat Museum is the **North American Fiddlers Hall of Fame and Museum** in Osceola. It is sixty-five miles south of Clayton.

23

SAFE HAVEN MUSEUM AND EDUCATION CENTER

Oswego, Oswego County

*I*f you have never viewed the Great Lakes before, it would be difficult to describe them to you. Words like vast, immense, and huge just seem to diminish the incredible proportions of these mammoth bodies of water.

In Oswego, one gets a good sense of the magnitude of the lakes, Lake Ontario in particular. Standing on the shore of the lake here, one, of course, cannot see the other side, some fifty miles over the horizon. Massive cargo ships and oil tankers crawl their way slowly across the panorama. It is about as similar to standing on the shore of a great sea as it gets in the inland continental United States.

It must have seemed like that in 1944 when nearly a thousand refugees, mostly Jewish, were transported from the shores of their war-torn homeland along the Mediterranean Sea in Italy to the frozen climes of Oswego.

"Yes, when many of them first arrived here, they did comment on how similar our great lake was to the Mediterranean," Judy Rapaport told me. Rapaport is current president and a board member of the Safe Haven Museum in Oswego. It is, quite literally, a one-of-a-kind museum showcasing the site of the only refugee shelter located in the United States during World War II.

"In 1944, President Franklin D. Roosevelt issued an order granting temporary residency to nearly a thousand refugees from Europe. Nearly ninety percent were Jewish. The rest were Greek Orthodox, Roman Catholic, and Protestant.

"He invited them to this country for the duration of the war 'as his private guests.' FDR did not want this to be seen as a 'Jewish issue,'" Rapaport told me. "The refuges had fled the Nazi Holocaust and came to Italy. There they heard about Roosevelt's 'invitation.'

"Over three thousand applied and nearly one thousand were chosen, among them the elderly, young children, whole families. Nine hundred and eighty two in all. A young State Department official named Ruth Gruber went and shepherded them on their dangerous journey to America. And they came here to Oswego," she said.

Fort Ontario was a decommissioned Army base in Oswego, located on the shore of Lake Ontario. The refugees were brought from Naples (hence the Mediterranean Sea reference for them) by ship on a harrowing passage to Hoboken, New Jersey, passing the Statue of Liberty. From there they came by train to Oswego.

"They were housed in clean barracks here," Rapaport told me. "Their children went to public schools in Oswego and became boy and girl scouts. Some of the men worked in the local factory. Our little community welcomed these poor, desperate people with open arms." For the first time in years, they could practice their faith without fear.

The Fort Ontario Refugee Shelter was the only shelter for victims of the Nazi Holocaust. They came here from eighteen countries to safety in America.

"It is an unknown story," Rapaport said. "Important, but unknown. The Safe Haven Museum and Education Center in Oswego is dedicated to telling the story of the site of the only refugee center located in the United States during the war. The museum focuses on the 982 refugees and the people of Oswego who welcomed them."

The museum is housed in the last remaining building of what was once a vast complex of barracks, offices, and large gathering halls. The museum looks similar to a little red schoolhouse. It was once the camp's administration building.

"Yes, this is where they were processed into the camp," Rapaport told me.

The walls of the small museum are lined with photographs and informational panels depicting all aspects of camp life. Among the panels are ones titled "Heritage," "Horror," and "Shelter." Other panels educate visitors on the dire situation of the Jews at the time and of the economic and political upheavals in Europe during the war years. One panel, titled "Journey," tells of the treacherous two-week passage from Italy to New York aboard the USS *Henry Gibbons*. Also on display are historical memorabilia from the camp's residents.

"Actually," Rapaport told me, "we have a very large inventory of history from the days of the camp's existence. So much so, that many of the items are located in a special room at the State University of New York at Oswego."

The story of Oswego's refugee camp has been told in books, magazine articles, television plays, and full-length movies. Despite the dark background of the war from which most of the camp's residents came, the refugee shelter was not a place without inspiration.

"They were quite happy here," Rapaport said. "After the war they wanted to stay in the U.S. instead of returning to Europe. Many felt there was nothing to return to. When they came here, there was a stipulation that they had to return. After President Truman signed an executive order, they were allowed to stay in America.

"One refugee, Walter Greenberg, went on to win two Academy Awards for cinema special effects. Another, Alex Margulis, helped to invent the MRI and CAT scan medical procedures. Rolf Manfred, a young refugee here, is called the 'Father of the Minuteman Missile.' They went on to live rich lives in America."

A visit to the unknown, out-of-the-way Safe Haven Museum will move you.

Wow Factor

One of the first things you see when you enter the Safe Haven Museum is a large life-sized cardboard cutout of First Lady Eleanor Roosevelt. She was a big supporter of the camp and worked tirelessly on behalf of the refugees, to make it possible for them to stay in America after the war.

I have been told a story about how indomitable Mrs. Roosevelt could be. A woman told me recently that her grandfather was a sheriff in Madison County (N.Y.) in the 1940s, and one night he pulled over a speeding limousine. When he asked the driver to roll down the window, a woman said to him, "Do you know who I am?"

He replied, "No Madame, I don't. But you sure look like Eleanor Roosevelt."

She answered imperiously, "I *am* Mrs. Roosevelt."

"Well, Mrs. Roosevelt, it is nice to meet you, but I still got to give you a speeding ticket," the sheriff told her.

"Fine. How much is the ticket?" she is reported to have asked.

"Three dollars," the sheriff replied.

"So be it."

She then rummaged in her big black purse as the three men who were in the automobile with her looked on nervously.

She finally thrust her hand out of the window to the sheriff and said, "Here you go, my good man. Here is six dollars."

The sheriff told her the fine was only three dollars.

"I know, Sheriff," Mrs. Roosevelt said. "Keep it. Because I am coming back just as fast!"

Apparently, Mrs. Roosevelt was on her way to Oswego to personally inspect the camp on the eve of the decision to allow the immigrants to stay or make them go home.

Now *that* is a wow factor!

The Take-Away

I have been to Safe Haven twice. You will be surprised by how emotional a visit here can be. "Many tears have been shed in this little museum," Judy Rapaport told me. The displays are excellent and tell the comprehensive story of the setting up of the camp, the selection process for the refugees, the harrowing trip to America on the Liberty ship USS *Henry Gibbons*, and more.

Although small, it is well worth about an hour's visit to this unique slice of history.

The Nuts and Bolts

Safe Haven Museum and Education Center
2 East 7th Street
Oswego, New York 13126
(315) 342-3003
www.oswegohaven.org

• *Travel Suggestion*

Once in the city of Oswego, it is easiest just to follow the many historical signs pointing the way to Fort Ontario, rather than look for the few signs directing you to the museum. Once at the fort, you will see the museum. As mentioned, the fort and the museum share a common space.

• *Museum Hours*

Tuesday through Sunday, 11 a.m. to 4 p.m. Closed Mondays.

• *Admission*

Adults: $5.00
Children: $3.00

Group tours are encouraged to phone in ahead. Check their website in advance because they sometimes have "free days."

• *Number of Visitors Annually*
   Fewer than 2,000

Up around the Bend

The Safe Haven Museum shares a space with the hulking Fort Ontario (www.fortontario.com), built in the 1840s. This towering star-shaped fort sits on the site of a British Revolutionary War fort that was destroyed by the French in 1756. In 1778, the Americans destroyed the rebuilt fort. A "new fort" (circa 1782) sits on high ground, giving it a spectacular vantage point overlooking Lake Ontario. It was here at this fort that the 1944-era refugees were housed.

The fort is awesome. Its earthen works date back to 1759. Many nice historical artifacts can be found within. The powder room is especially interesting, showing how kegs of gunpowder were delicately stored and housed. Tours are given, and are very interesting.

There are several large parking lots around the Safe Haven Museum. You can leave your car at any of these lots and walk to both the museum and the fort.

From Here to There

The other museum in this book that is nearest to the Safe Haven Museum is the **North American Fiddlers Museum and Hall of Fame** in Osceola. It is fifty miles east of Oswego.

OTHER MUSEUMS TO
EXPLORE IN REGION FOUR

Ogdensburg: Frederic Remington Art Museum. "The largest collection of Frederic Remington's paintings and bronze sculptures in America. Of note is his legendary piece *The Charge Up San Juan Hill*, which has been called one of the most famous of all American paintings." (315) 393-2425, www.fredericremington.org.

Oswego: Oswego Railroad Museum. "The Oswego Railroad Museum is dedicated to the historic preservation of railroad history in the Oswego County area. This is depicted in an HO-scale layout along with various static displays. It is sponsored by the Oswego Valley Railroad Association Inc. and is maintained by the members of the club as well as various volunteers." (315) 806-2193, www.oswegocounty.com/oswegocountyrailroadmuseum.

Oswego: H. Lee White Maritime Museum. "Preserving and presenting the maritime history of the Oswego harbor and surrounds, the complex consists of main building exhibits and galleries, outdoor exhibits, the Treasure Chest Gift Shop, and historic vessels arrayed the length of Oswego's West First Street Pier." (315) 342-0480, www.hleewhitemaritimemuseum.com.

Region Five

CENTRAL–LEATHERSTOCKING

Otsego, Broome, Chenango, Madison,
Montgomery, Oneida, and Schoharie Counties

24

BAINBRIDGE MUSEUM

Bainbridge, Chenango County

The museum in this pretty little town of 3,500 on the Susquehanna River is the most spare and one of the least-attended museums you will find in this book. And yet there is something about it that compelled me to include it.

Maybe it is the high-profile names from the past that reach out and grab the casual museum visitor. Borden's Elmer's Glue? Founded in Bainbridge. The first vacuum-canning machine? Invented here. Jedediah Smith, "The Pathfinder to the Sierras?" Born here. The first practical machine which automatically separated milk and cream? Invented here. One of the oldest American pancake mixes? Made here. American Plastics Company, which made everything from hard hats to Fisher Price Pop Beads? Founded here. A politician who introduced and passed a civil rights employment law *two decades before* the Civil Rights Act of 1964? Born here. Condensed milk? Invented here. The longest flat-water canoe race in *the world*? Held here. And on and on it goes.

"You know, when you think of it, we really do have some history here don't we?" Mary Drachler laughed. She is the president of the Bainbridge Historical Society.

Today the village is a sleepy, tranquil spot by the river, with a wide main street dotted with a few small stores and some broad avenues with great Victorian homes. The centerpiece to this slice of rural Americana is a sparkling, monument-studded village green. But in the old days, the factories never stopped.

"Many of these businesses were running concurrently with each other," she said as we toured her one-room museum. "Hundreds were working at the various factories around the clock. Of course the Borden's plant was our main bread-and-butter employer," she said. The name "Elmer" refers to the spouse of Borden's dairy mascot, "Elsie the Cow."

Borden's Elmer's Glue was invented here in 1929, when the company bought a casein (a usually discarded milk by-product) maker and began manufacturing glue out of it. Their first product, Casco Powdered Glue, a predecessor to Elmer's, was introduced in 1932. It was a big hit and was used extensively in industries across the country.

"We are lucky to have some of the last original Casco containers here on display," Drachler told me as she pointed to an exhibit case in the rear of the building. "In fact, we have a sample of almost every product Elmer's used to make."

Indeed, there are dozens on display.

"The Borden's glue factory was the largest employer in Bainbridge for many years," Drachler said. "They had many creative employees who were always looking for new items that would be compatible with the products already being produced, including wood glue and tubes of caulk. They worked around the clock and employed many of the local residents, who were proud to be a part of the company.

"Of course the big boom came when Elmer's School Glue was created. It was non-toxic and safe for children to use and quickly became a best-seller world wide."

The growing economy here had its side benefits too.

"All the youngsters in town found summer employment at Borden's. They would work putting glue bottles into shipping cartons all day and made some pretty good money doing it," Drachler said. "In 1986, the company even arranged for the real cow, Elsie, to come and be in a parade of ours," she laughed.

The sign at the edge of town said it all: "Welcome to Bainbridge. Home of Elmer's Glue. *Stick With Us!*"

The factories in Bainbridge are empty now. But the ghosts of ol' Jed Smith, "Elmer the cow" and his glue, civil rights pioneering legislator Senator Irving Ives, Hansmann's "Just Add Water" Pancake Mix, and much more live on in the dimly lit cases of this repository of memories.

"Sadly, times caught up with the company and with Bainbridge. Canadian and Chinese companies could produce our commodities at a much lower cost and the Borden's slowly began to reduce. The closing of the plant was not unexpected. Long-time employees were offered buyouts and retirement packages, but the doors were soon closed. Many of the workers expected to spend their entire careers at Borden's like their parents or grandparents did, but as in every closing, people and the town moved on," she said wistfully.

The General Clinton Canoe Regatta remains the community's pride and joy. Thousands attend the General Clinton Park each Memorial Day for the finish-line festivities of this 60-mile canoe race of national importance. It began in 1963.

Wow Factor

Ms. Drachler quickly declared that the wow factor was the milk separator display.

The American Separator Company was formed when the Swedish Cream Separator proved too difficult for the average farmer to operate and the original company stopped manufacturing in Bainbridge. Two employees of the Swedish company remained here and developed the practical version of the machine that launched a major industry.

"You just have to realize how long of a process it was to separate the milk from the cream before this machine came along," Drachler told me. "The farmers had to put their dairy product in big pans and let them sit and sit until the cream rose to the top, and then they would use big skimmers to take it off. With these separators, invented right here in Bainbridge, you just dumped the raw milk into a big can and then gave it some mighty spins and out came the milk from one spigot and the cream from the other. It really made a small 10- to 15-head family farm a viable business."

There are several of the earliest models on display here, from the original hand-cranked ones to the later electric models.

"Sometimes I take this old machine down to the park and pour in the milk and let the people watch as I spin it and out comes the cream and milk," she chuckled. "They are still amazed at it."

The Take-Away

The average visitor could blow through this museum in a few minutes easily. However, if you are lucky enough to be here when Mary Drachler is present, you could spend well over an hour without a problem. Many of the static displays are just cases filled with dusty old local memorabilia, but still, the specter of these giant names and inventions and businesses just makes this little museum so wonderful. I mean, who hasn't heard of Borden's or Elmer's Glue? Who hasn't heard of Jedediah Smith the great outdoorsman and explorer (actor Josh Brolin played Smith in a TV miniseries)? Heck, who hasn't heard of Fisher Price Pop Beads?

Oh, and check out my favorite item here. It is an original passenger-room waiting bench from the old Bainbridge railroad station. The neat thing about this item is that the heating pipes went *through* this wooden bench, warming the passengers on and around it. Hard to explain, yes. But you'll know what I mean when you see it.

The Nuts and Bolts
The Bainbridge Historical Society and Museum
38 South Main Street
Bainbridge, New York 13733
Website under construction.
Phone Mary Drachler at (607) 967-8546.

• *Travel Suggestion*
Bainbridge is located one-quarter of the way between Binghamton
and Albany along Interstate 88. Leave I-88 at Exit 8.

• *Museum Hours*
Open Memorial Day through Labor Day, Sunday 2 to 4 p.m. (and by
appointment).

• *Admission*
Free. (Donations are gladly accepted.)

• *Number of Visitors Annually*
500

Up around the Bend
There are many cute little old towns and villages around Bainbridge. The
countryside is beautiful and a drive through this area is quite pleasurable.
I might stop just twenty miles north in Norwich, N.Y. This is the largest
city in the immediate area and besides having a great deal of history on
its own, it is the birthplace of a name very familiar to all the residents of
Bainbridge. Gail Borden, the inventor of condensed milk and the man
most responsible for Bainbridge's glorious past, was born here in 1901.

From Here to There
The other museum in this book that is nearest to the Bainbridge Museum
is the **Northeast Classic Car Museum** in Norwich. It is twenty miles
north of Bainbridge.

25

CANAL TOWN MUSEUM

Canastota, Madison County

*C*anastota is a typical Upstate New York community in many respects. Small downtown business district, a few good restaurants, a wealth of natural beauty, and a storied past. And as in many other communities, most people come seeking the tourist magnet the town is known for. Here, it is the National Boxing Hall of Fame and Museum.

And so, like the many tourists who seek out and find the Hill Cumorah Mormon site in Palmyra, or the Hudson River Maritime Museum in Kingston, for example, they are often surprised that there are other equally interesting (albeit smaller) treasures nearby if they just keep looking. The other treasures that the visitors to Palmyra or Kingston uncovered are featured chapters in this book.

And so it is in Canastota. Thousands come to the Boxing Hall of Fame and Museum each year. Either for vacations, for events, or for the wildly popular Boxing Hall of Fame Induction ceremony. It is a nice place and definitely worth a visit if you are into boxing.

But for those lucky enough to venture into Canastota itself (the boxing venue is outside of the village at the exit from the New York State Thruway), what a reward is waiting for them at the Canastota Canal Town Museum!

This is one jam-packed and totally fascinating little treasure trove.

"Canastota has three nicknames," Joe DiGiorgio, the museum president, told me. "Canal Town, Onion Town, and Title Town. And we try and tell each of these stories right here in our little museum."

The roots of "Title Town" are obvious. "Canastota was ground zero for Upstate New York as far as boxing goes. Many great legends trained here,

some of the earliest boxing movies ever filmed were produced here (using movie machines that were invented in Canastota), and of course today we have the Hall of Fame. Each year we have a terrific Induction Day parade. Thousands come here to cheer on the champions of today and yesteryear as they parade through town sitting in open-air cars waving to the public. It is a grand day," DiGiorgio said.

But it was the Erie Canal that really put Canastota on the map.

"Yes, ours was one of the great little boom towns along the great canal. We are situated midway between the cities of Utica and Syracuse, and we had it all," DiGiorgio said. "Several railroads came through here, many industries sprang up along the canal, and because of our entrepreneurial spirit, many of the great innovators of the day came here to Canastota to make their fortunes and begin their careers."

Don't even get DiGiorgio started on the wealth of Canastota's rich history. His knowledge is encyclopedic and his enthusiasm is unbridled. This was apparent as he took me on a several-hour guided tour of the museum.

"This is our Founder's Room," he said as we gazed over the crowded walls depicting the earliest days of Canastota. I was particularly struck by four extremely handsome original oil paintings.

"These were done by Frederick R. Spencer, a Town of Lenox native who was one of the premier portrait painters of his day (Canastota is in the Town of Lenox). These originals are extremely rare. His works hang in the Metropolitan Museum of Art in New York."

In this room we also meet Nathan Roberts. "This guy was absolutely key to the completion of the Erie Canal. He too lived in Canastota," I was told.

The story of Nathan Roberts is the story of the canal itself. At the time of the construction of the Erie Canal there wasn't a single civil engineer in America. "People, innovators, geniuses stepped forward and made this thing work," DiGiorgio said. "Roberts was a math teacher. He was no engineer. Yet it was his brilliance that came up with the concept of the stair-step locks in Lockport, N.Y. that took the canal up and over the Niagara Escarpment and on to completion. He is one of our greatest stories," the director said with obvious pride.

And on and on it goes. The sum total of what was created in Canastota, all archived here, is overwhelming. In another room, called the Commercial Room, we read about the production of CERTO, once the most popular brand of fruit pectin in the country (now owned by Kraft), here in Canastota. We meet Harry Weed, the inventor of the automobile tire chains. "Yes, it made him one of the richest guys in town," DiGiorgio said. "His company, American Chain Company, is still in existence."

Ideal Cut Glass was a required accoutrement in the salons and estates of the wealthy. The museum has an extensive collection of this exquisite Canastota creation. "Today, these are rare and highly collectible," the director explained as he held up a precious Diamond Poinsettia piece. "Of course, the Great Depression ended this company."

Watson Wagons ("First in the field; Last in the repair shop") were manufactured here, too. These were the first bottom-dumping wagons in the world. "It was quite a business. Fifteen thousand of these dump wagons and military wagons came out of here just for the Allied forces in France during World War I. Tens of thousands of them were sold, but they are now very hard to find," DiGiorgio said. "In fact, we have just come into possession of one of the rarest models, courtesy of the Railroad Museum of Pennsylvania. It is very old but in good shape. We have constructed a glass display kiosk at the entrance to Canastota to hold this wagon for the entire world to see."

For as small a building as this museum is (it was built in 1873 as a bakery), it sure packs a historical wallop!

Wow Factor

Although this museum holds an embarrassment of important riches, DiGiorgio had no problem settling on his wow factor. "I would have to say it is Canastota's connection with the movie industry."

The first successful movie camera was made in Canastota. The American Biograph Company was a major player in the early days of the film industry. Although movies weren't actually made here, the machinery, technology, and creative geniuses behind the new art form were all found right here. Many of the earliest movie inventions were the simple flip-card shows ("peep shows") found in arcades and nickelodeons. Biograph made a fortune on them.

"William Dickson helped start the company. He originally worked for Edison but left, and that caused a great deal of bad blood, including patent lawsuits, between the two. But Dickson's company made a great number of short films, and in fact the company has recently emerged as a player in the twenty-first century in Hollywood," he told me. "In fact, the new American Biograph Company features an old photograph titled 'The Four Fathers of the Biograph.' In it we see Dickson and his partners Herman Casler, Elias Koopman, and Henry Marvin standing right out front on Peterboro Street in Canastota. They bill themselves as 'The Oldest Movie Company in America.' And it all started right here." There are many displays of the early creations at the dawning of the movie industry, including a rare, original "flip card movie," which is a hand-cranked reel holding more than 500 changing cards.

"There is no doubt that Canastota had an important role in the burgeoning movie industry in America," he continued. "In fact, when Walter Edmonds's Canastota-based circus book, *Chad Hanna*, was turned into a movie in 1940, starring Henry Fonda and Dorothy Lamour, they held the premier right here in town at the old Bruce Opera House. The nineteenth-century novel depicts a traveling circus that begins its journey on the Erie Canal here in Canastota. What a night that must have been. The very next day the movie opened in New York. Unlike Edmonds's *Drums Along the Mohawk*, which is a classic, *Chad Hanna* wasn't quite as memorable."

The Take-Away

There are so many little nuggets to be turned up in this museum one hardly knows where to start. Canastota is (was) surprisingly important to the growth and development of many different facets of American life in the last two centuries. Besides the stories and people I have described above, I enjoyed learning about other Canastota wonders like the Sherwood Brothers, who manufactured hundreds of children's sleds, wagons, and roller skates here starting in 1914, or the Canastota Knife Company, which made everything from cigar cutters to knives specially made for removing stones from horses' hooves.

I enjoyed observing the first successful microscope made in the U.S. (1838). And reading of Amelia Earhart's visit to Canastota on August 28, 1928, to christen the town's new airport (25,000 came out to see her). And I chuckled at the sight of the six cars that were in the famous 1908 Great Auto Race Around the World. Believe it or not, they all came to Canastota, to great huzzahs, and spent the night here at the Weaver Hotel on Valentine's Day 1908.

I mean, these are great stories.

But it is the story of the Italian–Americans who came to live in the Mucklands that really grabbed me.

Between 1900 and 1970, Canastota was known as "The Onion Capital of the World." A drained swamp, about five miles across and located just north of Canastota, known as the Mucklands, became the home of dozens of Italian immigrant families who came to work on the railroads and canals and then stayed to onion farm the rich damp black soil (muck) of the area. A whole culture evolved, separate from that of Canastotans who lived in town. The Italians were met with derision at first, but through hard work and perseverance they proved themselves to be as worthy as any entrepreneurs that ever came before them to Canastota.

"People around the world knew of Canastota Onions," DiGiorgio told me. "But the work was dirty, smelly, and very hard. The Italians were looked at as lower-class citizens and they almost never came into town. In fact, we have a newspaper here that has a front page article headlined 'An Italian was spotted walking on Main Street in Canastota!' Can you imagine why on earth that would be big news?" he asked. "Times were so different back then. Carmen Basilio, who was born in Canastota and went on to become a two-weight boxing champion, is reported to have said, 'It was much easier becoming a boxer than working in the (expletive deleted) muck.'"

Even though Basilio, known as "The Onion Picker," went on to become the most famous Italian–American ever to come out of here, my favorite story is that of one Sam Micielli. He lived on Canal Street in the late 1800s, and old Sam would sit on his front porch at night and play Italian folk songs on his ancient concertina for the entertainment of the canal boat passengers drifting by his house. His story is so quaintly romantic and nostalgic that I came away from my visit here thinking this story really paints a picture of what it was like in Canastota back in the boomtown days of the past.

Sam Micielli's 1898 concertina is proudly displayed at the museum in a glass box.

Nice touch.

The Canastota Canal Town Museum is a proud member of the Erie Canalway National Heritage Corridor and part of the National Parks Service Passport Program.

The Nuts and Bolts
The Canastota Canal Town Museum
122 Canal Street
Canastota, New York 13032
(315) 697-5002
www.canastota.com/organization

• *Travel Suggestion*

Canastota is located at Exit 34 of the New York State Thruway. After passing through the toll plaza you will see the Boxing Hall of Fame immediately on your right. Make a left at the stoplight and follow the signs to the Canal Town Museum.

• *Museum Hours*

May and June: 12:00 p.m. to 3:00 p.m.
July and August: 11:00 a.m. to 3:00 p.m.
September and October: 12:00 p.m. to 3:00 p.m.
Closed Sunday and Monday.

• *Admission*

General Admission: $3.00. Call in advance to schedule group or school tours.

• *Number of Visitors Annually*

1,000

Up around the Bend

Since you are in Canastota anyway, a visit to the **International Boxing Hall of Fame** (www.ibhof.com), located just blocks from the Canal Town Museum, might be well worth a visit. It is the "big sister museum" to the much smaller Canal Town Museum. Tens of thousands of boxing enthusiasts visit this sports hall each year.

From Here to There

The other museum in this book that is nearest to the Canal Town Museum is the **National Abolition Hall of Fame and Museum**. It is in Peterboro, about nine miles south of Canastota.

26

MUSEUM OF ODDITIES

Cazenovia, Madison County

*W*here do you go to buy a mummy these days?

Well, I'll be honest. I have no idea. But in the old days you'd just go to a "mummy store" in Cairo and pick one up.

"Mr. Robert Hubbard was one of Cazenovia's wealthiest men and he had a keen interest in exotic things, particularly those with Egyptian heritage," Betsy Kennedy, the director of the Cazenovia Public Library (where the museum is located), told me. "He decided the library museum needed a mummy so he went to Egypt and purchased one," she told me as she swept her hand over a room filled with Egyptian artifacts. "Yes, $2,000 for it all," she exclaimed.

What a bargain he got.

The museum is located in the front part of the village's library, a majestic Greek Revival four-columned masterpiece. Its several rooms (dubbed the "Museum of Oddities") pay archival tribute to a collector of unbridled tastes.

"Mr. Hubbard had an eye for almost everything," Kennedy told me.

And it shows. Case after case of Native American basketry, natural wonders (including some beautiful coral pieces), colorful linens, and "everything Egypt" all crowd the rooms, clamoring for the visitor's attention. One wall has several giant glass cases with stuffed birds and animals in them.

"Yes, the kids really love this stuffed rattlesnake," she said while pointing to a coiled reptile appearing as if in mid-strike.

But it is "Hen" that is the real showstopper at the Museum of Oddities.

"We know the mummy's name is Hen because in the 1940s the library sent the Metropolitan Museum of Art photographs of the objects and they translated the hieroglyphics found on the coffin lid. But what we didn't know was that Hen was a *he* and not a *she*, like we thought for more than a century."

In 1894 Hubbard traveled to Cairo, where he went into a shopping frenzy. He not only purchased Hen for $2,000 (plus another $2,000 to ship the mummy home), but he also purchased a number of other relics including a mummified cat and bird (an ibis).

"It was funny," Kennedy told me. "Our local newspaper, the *Cazenovia Republican*, ran updates about the whereabouts of the mummy on his worldwide sojourn to Upstate New York. When Hen arrived in town, a local art club threw a 'Mummy Tea' and invited all of the townspeople to come and welcome our newest resident. The net profit for the day was a whopping $26.40," she laughed.

And as for the mystery of the sex of the mummy?

"Well, we honestly didn't know the sex of our mummy at the beginning. In 1984 we packed Hen up on a stretcher and slid him into the back of an ambulance and took him to the Oneida City Hospital where they guessed Hen to be a him," the director told me. "Believe me, I got a lot of funny stares when people saw me riding in the back of an ambulance with a 2,110-year-old man next to me!"

This would be the first of several ambulance rides for the mummy. The last one was on May 24, 2007, when the mummy traveled to Crouse Memorial Hospital for a full CAT scan.

"After the CAT scan, there was no mistaking. Dr. Mark Levinsohn showed us the X-ray scans and, well, believe me, it was obvious that our mummy was all man," Kennedy chuckled.

All of this documentation, including a life-sized display of the X-rays of the mummy, is on display. They are nothing short of incredible.

Oh, and the translation of the mummy's coffin lid, done by Egyptologist Ludlow Bull from New York City, showed that Hen was taking some gifts along with him to the hereafter.

It read: "May the Kin of Osiris, Chief of the West, the great God, Lord of Abydos, be pleased to give a mortuary offering of bread, bear, oxen, and fowl for the one beloved of the great God. Hen"

Sounds like he was ready for a picnic when he got there.

Wow Factor

While the main attraction at the Cazenovia Museum of Oddities is the mummy, Betsy Kennedy had a surprising answer for me when I asked her to tell me here favorite wow factor at the museum.

"I'd have to say the stuffed birds," she told me. "They are exquisite. I really like this quetzal," she told me as she pointed to an exotic, long-tailed Dr. Seuss-like character. "It's from Central America and is just so unusual looking and graceful."

She then took me to another display case with dozens of Mr. Hubbard's birds posed in stuffed silence. "But here is my wow factor. This stuffed passenger pigeon."

"Why?" I asked.

"Because it is now extinct and the only place you can ever see a passenger pigeon today is a stuffed one like ours. And it is too bad, really. When the Europeans came to North America, the passenger pigeon numbered in the billions, more than any other bird. Today they are gone. And it is our own fault. I love this little bird. And it is a warning to us all that everything won't be around forever," she said softly.

The Take-Away

I have been through Cazenovia a hundred times over the years. It is a lovely community with a delightful Main Street, many nice shops and restaurants, a lot of history, a respected college, and a gorgeous lake. But a mummy?

The Cazenovia Public Library is a superb small library. Their children's reading room is the cutest one I have ever seen (think a child's garden), and the community has been well served by it ever since Mr. Hubbard gave it to the village in 1890.

The Museum of Oddities is excellent. It is modern and its displays are well documented with unobtrusive signage and dramatic lighting. The mummy room is fun and completely amazing. It is clear that this surprising treat is well taken care of. Betsy Kennedy made a terrific museum guide on my visit to the museum, and it is quite obvious that besides her professionalism and enthusiasm, she really holds the Hubbard collection of oddities in her heart with pride and love.

This is one of the best museums you have never heard of. Give yourself an hour or so to discover its contents.

The Nuts and Bolts

    The Cazenovia Museum of Oddities
    Cazenovia Public Library
    100 Albany Street
    Cazenovia, New York 13035
    www.cazenoviapubliclibrary.org

• *Travel Suggestion*
    Cazenovia is located on N.Y. Route 20, which crosses the state east to west. It is located at the southern end of Cazenovia Lake, about 25 miles southeast of Syracuse.

- *Museum Hours*
  Monday through Friday 9 a.m. to 9 p.m.; Saturday 10 a.m. to 5 p.m.

- *Admission*
  Free

- *Number of Visitors Annually*
  7,000

Up around the Bend

From downtown Cazenovia, go north on County Route 17 nine miles to Chittenango, N.Y. This is the birthplace of L. Frank Baum, author of *The Wizard of Oz*. Every year they hold one of the largest Oz-fests in America (www.oz-stravaganza.com). Usually several of the surviving Munchkins from the original movie come to help celebrate. And yes, the sidewalks are covered with yellow bricks! Plan your trip to Cazenovia during the Oz-fest and you will see two of Upstate New York's great little towns in one afternoon!

From Here to There

The other museum in this book that is nearest the Museum of Oddities is the **Canal Town Museum** in Canastota. It is fifteen miles northeast of Cazenovia.

27

CHERRY VALLEY MUSEUM
Cherry Valley, Otsego County

*T*he Cherry Valley Massacre was one of the most horrific bloodlettings of the American Revolutionary War. It took place on November 11, 1778.

British and Seneca Indian forces converged on the woodland outpost in a reprisal raid for patriot attacks in western New York State. Several hundred combatants, with the British under the command of the infamous Captain Walter Butler and the Indians under the leadership of Little Beard and the Mohawk Chief Joseph Brant, attacked Fort Alden (now Cherry Valley) in the darkness of the early morning. Over a dozen American officers were slain outside their fort (most were living in private quarters outside the fort). The remainder of the Americans were scattered into the wilderness, or hunted down and murdered. Scalpings and terrible mutilations were commonplace. Women and children were among the victims.

"It really was quite awful," Sue Miller told me. Miller is a board member of the Cherry Valley Historical Society and an expert on the history of Cherry Valley. "Stories, books, and even movies have been produced about this event. Our local cemetery has a monument in it which holds many of the remains of the victims."

In the center of a large room at the Cherry Valley Museum sits a remarkable 5-foot-by-4-foot diorama depicting Cherry Valley at the time of the massacre. Sue Miller built it. Enclosed in glass, it features all the natural landscaping of the Mohawk Valley and the rivers and roads leading into Cherry Valley. In the center is the structure that was the target of the massacre, Fort Alden.

"It took me a year to build this, but it was a labor of love," Miller said. As you walk around the perimeter of the giant diorama, there are informational cards describing the timeline of the attack, as well as buttons to push which light up the various locations central to the event. A five-minute audio presentation describes what happened. It is an incredible piece of work.

The Cherry Valley Museum is housed in a handsome 200-year-old mansion located right on Main Street. "This old house is the perfect place for the museum," Miller told me. "We put several thousands of dollars into the structure for renovations and repairs recently, and she is good to go for another hundred years now."

Miller walked me through the warren of rooms in the house. Each one is perfectly decked out in period furniture, old paintings, and an astonishing array of local and regional historical artifacts. There seems to be a little bit of everything here.

"We have theme rooms," Miller told me. She is a frequent presence at the museum (she owns a Celtic merchandise business right next door).

She took me into the "War Room." She pointed to a flag in the corner. "This flag was made by the women of Cherry Valley. Their men carried it into battle with Emory Upton's Regulars at the Battle of Gettysburg," she told me with obvious pride. Other displays in this room highlighted other artifacts relating to Cherry Valley veterans of all other American wars.

"The 'Baby Room' is a special place for 'just kids,'" she said. The room is decorated with a variety of antique dolls, carriages, cribs, and accessories. The "Farm Room" is filled with old farming equipment. The "Fire Room" has many pieces of rare old firefighting apparatus. "This beauty right here," she said while tapping the wooden sides of a large contraption in the middle of the room, "is the second-oldest hand-operated fire pumper in America. It was built in 1800," she told me.

There is an amazing "Music Room" also. In it are several melodeons, the forerunners to the pump organs, as we know them today. These are beautifully crafted pieces of furniture. The sound they make is stunning. "Swan's Melodeons, made right here in Cherry Valley," Miller told me. "Old Mr. Swan was a furniture and cabinet maker by trade, so you can see his beautiful craftsmanship in every organ." The stern-looking visage of Amos Swan looks down on his magnificent creations.

There is plenty to see here, and you will be extremely lucky if Sue Miller is "on duty" the day you visit. If not, go next door to her business, The Plaide Palette, and ask her to show you around the museum.

Ask her about Mr. Swan and his "Frankenstein" experiments. Or about the Cole family Bible, a survivor of the massacre, encased in glass, with its blood-stained wooden shelf covered by a discreet cloth. Ask her about the 1860s treadle-action butter churner that was *powered by a dog*! Ask her about the one-of-a-kind stuffed elephant in the display case (hold on to your hats for that one!). Ask her about the . . . oh, well, you get the idea.

Sue Miller has never met a story she didn't want to tell.

Wow Factor

During my tour of this fascinating little museum, I felt like there was a mini-wow factor around every turn. But to me, the best of them was the smallest of them all.

In a glass case, Sue Miller pointed out a dainty old silver ring. "This is an old Irish Claddagh ring," she whispered to me. "When the Cherry Valley massacre was over, the Indians force-marched many of the civilians on a long, arduous journey through the woods to their camp. One of the villagers, an elderly woman named Mrs. Cannon, was struggling along to keep up with the party. Her Indian captives told her that if she couldn't keep up she would die. Eventually unable to bear any more, Mrs. Cannon fell to the ground. Her daughter, who was accompanying her on the march, Mrs. Jane Cannon Campbell, stooped to aid her.

"Mrs. Cannon whispered to her to carry on and slipped the old Irish ring off her hand and gave it to the younger woman and told her to take it and leave her be," Miller told me in hushed tones.

The Indians then beat the elderly woman to death and left her body by the side of the road.

That ring is here at the Cherry Valley Museum. "It really is an emotional and poignant story, isn't it?" Miller said as we both gazed into the glass case holding the actual ring.

The Take-Away

This museum is for die-hard history lovers. That being said, those die-hard history lovers will be enthralled with the many artifacts here. Cherry Valley really does have quite a story to tell, and I just can't get enough of the tales of the massacre. It appears that the museum operates on a shoestring budget and relies on a cadre of volunteers, but they really pull it off here. I say go and enjoy. The hamlet is lovely, there are a couple of nice places to eat, and the Cherry Valley Cemetery is a wonderful place to stroll and immerse yourself in the history of the area. The impressive tomb holding the remains of the massacre victims is immediately on your right as you enter the cemetery.

Candy Darling, a famous transsexual movie star and muse to Andy Warhol, is buried along the back fence of the cemetery.

The Nuts and Bolts
Cherry Valley Museum
49 Main Street

Cherry Valley, New York 13320
(607) 264-3303
www.cherryvalleymuseum.org

- *Travel Suggestion*

   N.Y. Route 20 goes east and west across the whole of New York State. It was the major thoroughfare until the New York State Thruway opened in the 1950s. I suggest old Route 20 as a much better option for east/west travel. It goes through numerous small towns and villages, highlighting much of the Empire State's history. And the views are wonderful. Cherry Valley has its own exit off Route 20, and is just a mile south of the highway.

- *Museum Hours*

   Open daily Memorial Day through October 15, 10 a.m. to 5 p.m.

- *Admission*

   Adults: $5.00
   AAA Members: $4.00
   Seniors: $3.50
   Groups of 10 or more: $3.00
   11 and under: Free

- *Number of Visitors Annually*

   Attendance has never surpassed 2,000 a year.

Up around the Bend

Cherry Valley is just a twenty-minute drive from historic Cooperstown. The "Village of Museums" is filled with attractions. Don't miss the famous Fenimore Art Museum. It has a wonderful collection of American folk art and representations of the Hudson River School of Art. Cooperstown is a history lover's feast. I suggest you contact *Cooperstown Walks!* for a delightful and fun walking tour (with NO baseball!) of the village (www .cooperstownwalks.com).

Going twenty minutes in the other direction (east) you will come upon historic Sharon Springs, N.Y. This little jewel is undergoing a rejuvenation spearheaded by entertainment celebrities The Fabulous Beekman Boys. They bring their TV film crews here to produce their hit TV programs, have a mercantile business on Main Street, and host several annual festivals that attract thousands to this tiny village each year.

Both Cooperstown and Sharon Springs are fun diversions along the road less traveled.

From Here to There

The other museum in this book that is nearest to the Cherry Valley Museum is the **Iroquois Indian Museum** in Howes Cave. It is thirty miles east of Cherry Valley.

28

IROQUOIS INDIAN MUSEUM
Howes Cave, Schoharie County

*T*housands of cars exit Interstate 88 near Cobleskill every year, drawn by
the muted call of enormous white letters sprawled out over the hillside
identifying the name of this, one of New York's most popular natural destinations. They come by car and van and school bus and motor coach. Are
they heading to the Iroquois Indian Museum?

No.

Just this close to a mecca for generations of year-round tourists, the
Iroquois Museum is like an overlooked cousin to its bright star up on the
hill (and just three minutes away). And that is a real shame.

Dropped in the middle of a lush, green, rolling meadow, surrounded
by thick forests, the Iroquois Museum is positively stunning when you first
come upon it. In fact, you might think you are looking at an alien ship that
just landed for a rest stop here in rural Schoharie County.

The museum is a massive, stylized Iroquois longhouse. As you enter,
there really is a palpable peacefulness that blankets you. The walls inside
this modern (opened in 1992) museum are lined with Native American
art, both paintings and sculptures. The history of the Iroquois Nation is
told in a series of exhibit cases, video montages, and hands-on displays.

"You will notice that you enter the museum and walk counter-clock-
wise here," smiled Erynne Ansel-McCabe, museum director. "That is the
Native American way of doing things. They do it because that is the way a
bean grows around a pole."

Erynne is an articulate, quiet-spoken woman who has a docent's heart.
"Our mission is to be an advocate for the education of the Native American

culture. We use art as the window to the past. We are determined to show that Native Americans, including many with Iroquois ancestry, are alive and well and still producing wonderful and exciting things," she told me.

For most of us, our knowledge of indigenous tribes in Upstate New York comes from our early school days and, of course, from our childhood scavenger hunts through fields and farms for the ubiquitous Indian arrowheads.

"Arrowheads? We got them," the director laughed. She showed me drawer upon drawer of relics, mostly arrowheads, tool pieces, and pottery that have been foraged from the fields and forests of Schoharie County. "People come in here all the time with old arrowheads their father or grandfather left them. Most are put aside for archiving, but some are truly spectacular and merit a display of their own."

She showed me one of these.

"This is one of the oldest pieces we have," she explained as she pointed to a jagged sharp object. "It is one of the earliest known projectile points ever discovered. It is quite rare," she said.

"How rare?"

"Well, this point, known as a Clovis Point, is about 11,000 years old and was used to hunt Mastodons," she exclaimed.

Talk about old.

Some of the most fascinating exhibits highlight Native American lifestyles, lore, legends, and regional history.

"We have a lot of school groups that come here," Ansel-McCabe told me. "Our display case on the subject of Indian stereotypes is always one that gets them thinking."

She showed me a large, well-lit case that highlighted Native Americans in a series of embarrassing advertisements, portrayals, and depictions on tacky souvenirs. "When we get here, the visitors really get engaged. We talk about Native American symbols, like school mascots, for example. Usually the kids think that teams named Warriors, Chiefs, or Braves are an honorary recognition for the Native Americans. Then I show them derogatory Indian caricatures, movie depictions, and even terrible icons from the old souvenir industry (Indian rubber dog toys?), and they start to get the whole picture. They understand what we call the 'slippery slope of stereotyping.' It's fascinating to watch their little minds working," she chuckled.

The director introduced me to Mike Tarbell, a full-time employee who leads demonstrations for the group tours. Mike is a Mohawk. I asked him if he knew his grandparents. "Oh yes," he said. "One side of my family was strict traditionalist in the old ways, and the other side was very progressive."

Mike told me that he could trace his family roots back more than three centuries in North America. I kidded him by saying, "So your people were the ones who were on land pulling the ropes on the Mayflower onto the shore?"

"Um, knowing my family, they were probably on the shore throwing rocks at the Mayflower," he laughed.

Mike summed up the whole theme of the museum this way: "We just want to show the way Native Americans lived and contributed down through the years. As my old Mohawk grandmother used to tell us,

'Everybody is looking at the same thing. They are just seeing it differently. And we must share in all the stories to get the full picture.' That is what we try and do at the Iroquois Indian Museum. Share our story with everyone."

Wow Factor

"That is an easy one," Erynne told me. As we walked together towards an atrium in this tall two-story longhouse, she told me the Native American's image of Creation. "They believe a woman fell from the sky, and as she tumbled to Earth she landed softly on the back of flying geese, which then lowered her to the ground and gently placed her on the back of a giant turtle."

Just about the time she finished telling me that story, we found ourselves standing at the edge of the atrium and, well, there it was! High above us was the glass opening in the roof where the "woman fell to earth." At eye level in front of us is a flock of large, graceful gray geese "slowly spiraling to the ground." When I peered over the edge to the floor below me, I could see a large colorfully painted turtle lazing in a quiet pond. It was all there.

It was an amazing wow factor for sure (although I have to admit, the intricately carved moose antlers are stunning!).

The Take-Away

This museum is very well executed. I knew very little about Native American history in my Upstate New York region when I came into it, but found the whole experience enlightening. I would strongly suggest that you arrange for someone to give you a personal tour of the museum. There is just so much to see, it would be impossible to soak it all up on your own. The museum is bright, colorful, and very comfortably climate-controlled. It is handicapped accessible and has an interesting and eclectic gift shop. Their souvenirs are tasteful and they offer many books on Native Americans and their upstate roots. There is also a large, well-mapped-out nature walk around the 45-acre site.

If you are an enthusiast, you could spend an entire afternoon here. There is a place for children to occupy themselves while the adults tour the museum.

The Nuts and Bolts

The Iroquois Indian Museum
324 Cavern Road
Howes Cave, New York 12092
(518) 296-8949
www.iroquoismuseum.org

• *Travel Suggestion*

Take Thruway Exit I-88 at Cobleskill (Exit 22) and follow the many signs to the museum. The museum is only about four miles from the interstate.

• *Museum Hours*

The museum is open from May through November.
Tuesday through Saturday 10 a.m. to 5 p.m.; Sunday noon to 5.

• *Admission*

Adults: $8.00
Seniors: $6.50
Students (12–17): $6.50
Children 5 to 12: $5.00
Children under 5: Free

• *Number of Visitors Annually*

About 10,000

Up around the Bend

In case you were wondering about the hugely popular tourist attraction with the white letters sprawled across the hillside, well, that would be Howe Caverns. These underground caverns attract tens of thousands of tourists yearly, and in fact are the second-most popular natural destination in the state, behind Niagara Falls. Howe Caverns are located less than a mile up the road from the Iroquois Indian Museum.

For the road less traveled, I would send you to the Cave House Museum of Mining and Geology (www.howecaverns.com/above-ground/cave-house-museum). This museum is operated in conjunction with Howe Caverns and is housed in a magnificent, three-story 1872 limestone hotel that was the inn for early Howe Caverns tourists. The structure is awesome. Exhibits and displays inside tell the story of Lester Howe and his discovery of New York's favorite "hole in the ground," as well as the history of the important cement industry located in the region.

The Cave House Museum of Mining and Geology is located less than five minutes from the Iroquois Museum.

From Here to There

The other museum in this book that is nearest to the Iroquois Indian Museum is the **Old Stone Fort Museum** in Schoharie. It is six miles east of Howes Cave.

29

Northeast Classic Car Museum
Norwich, Chenango County

*T*hey don't make 'em like they used to.

If you want to see style, sophistication, and extravagance in an automobile, go to the Northeast Classic Car Museum in Norwich, N.Y. If it is possible for an automobile to be breathtaking, you will find that right here.

"People are always amazed not only at the beauty of the cars here," said Marty Kuhn, the Museum's Marketing Coordinator, "but also at how beautifully we showcase them."

And she is right. The Museum consists of several large, high-ceilinged buildings that house over 160 cars. Each car (seemingly) gleams under its very own spotlight. As you wander through the facility you cannot help but be awestruck at the craftsmanship that went into these beauties. The cars represent almost every decade of the American auto industry.

"Of course we do feature a lot of Franklins here," Kuhn told me. "They were manufactured in Syracuse from about 1902 to 1934. They were air-cooled and a luxury car of their time. George E. Staley was a large collector of Franklins, and was our greatest benefactor. When we opened our doors on Memorial Day 1997, nearly all of the cars on display were from the private collection of Mr. Staley," Kuhn said.

The Museum's five buildings are packed with cars and trucks of an astounding variety. Some you have heard of. Others, well, I doubt it. Huge, block-long Duesenbergs, sporty post-war compacts, dynamic muscle cars, wood-sided delivery trucks, and much more all jockey for the visitor's attention. Theme rooms add an unexpected element of fun here. The last time I visited here, the theme was "Wild Things/Wild Rides."

It doesn't take long for the concept to come to life as you wander around pristine examples of Jaguars, Mustangs, Cobras, Cougars, Marlins, Pintos, Road Runners, and more.

A classic car museum is a perfect fit in this bucolic city of 7,500. Norwich has many classic familiar nostalgic benchmarks, such as a wide store-lined main street, a village green with a magnificent gold-domed county courthouse, and a century-old movie house (The Colonial) with its original overhanging neon marquee.

Wow Factor

I asked Marc Michaels, Executive Director of the Museum, for his wow factor here. "There are just so many at the museum. But if I really had to make a pick, I'd have to go with the 1908 Mora," he said.

The Mora was only in production for about five years and was manufactured in Newark, N.Y., about two hours west of Norwich. Its early vehicles were powerful and built on "strange looking" chassis, but were quite popular in the region.

"The Mora Motor Car Company (under the anagram Omar) also built a child's automobile, called the Browniekar. It was built on a 66-inch wheelbase and was marketed to boys and girls," Michaels said. "I'd have to give them my vote for the wow factor here simply because they are so rare today. We have both a Mora and a Browniekar on display here. There are only three known Browniekars in existence, and as for the Mora? It is one of only two known to exist, and the only remaining Mora Touring Car. Truly a one-of-a-kind car," he said proudly.

On a personal note, my wow factor would have to be a car with direct local ties to the town I live in. It is a rare seven-passenger 1928 Cunningham Berline. Mrs. Esther Wilber, the doyenne of the respected Wilber banking family of Oneonta, N.Y., owned it. This custom limousine is an eye-popper. Mrs. Wilber had it tricked out with all the latest amenities of the era. She had a coal box on the floor to warm her feet (it was used with ice to cool her in the summer), linen window shades, a microphone to talk to her driver, electric cigarette lighters, and perhaps one of the first automobile burglary alarms ever made. It is the only known original Cunningham to be found anywhere.

Oh, and this nearly one-hundred-year-old car has just five thousand miles on it!

The Take-Away

I took our thirteen-year-old son with me when I visited the Northeast Classic Car Museum. I figured if there were nothing here to interest me (I am not a car buff), there would surely be something here to interest Joey. To my surprise, we both enjoyed our ninety minutes here thoroughly. The cars truly are dazzling . . . and huge! The Museum looks like a warehouse of giant Lifesaver cars: bright reds, brilliant yellows, cool-to-the-eye greens, and even cars painted purple! And of course enough small-windowed black sedans to fill the parking lot behind the movie set of *The Untouchables*.

There are instructive signs at each vehicle, but if you can hook up with a guided tour your visit will be greatly enhanced. The building is air-conditioned, handicapped-accessible and very comfortable. The gift shop carries a wide variety of "old car themed" toys, gifts, books, and T-shirts.

The Nuts and Bolts
The Northeast Classic Car Museum
24 Rexford Street (N.Y. Route 23)
Norwich, New York 13815
(607) 334-AUTO (2886)
www.classiccarmuseum.org

• *Travel Suggestion*
   Norwich is located on Route 12. It is equidistant from Binghamton
   and Utica, both of which are about an hour away.

• *Museum Hours*
   The Museum is closed only three days of the year: Christmas, New
   Year's, and Thanksgiving Day. It is open 9 a.m. to 5 p.m. daily.

• *Admission*
   Adults: $9.00
   Children 6 to 18: $4.00
   Children 5 and under: Free

• *Number of Visitors Annually*
   10,000

Up around the Bend
Just about a block down and across the street (45 Rexford) is another great
little museum.
   The Chenango County Museum (www.chenangohistorical.org) is
housed in an old red brick public school building and is jam-packed with
artifacts telling the story of the Chenango County area and its people.
The back room has giant stuffed animals peering down from the ceiling
at you, and the display cases carry everything from photos to local Civil
War items to Victorian hair wreaths(!).
   The museum has recently expanded to include the historical contents of the old Norwich Pharmaceutical Museum, which also will be
housed here. Norwich Pharmaceutical manufactured the first pain tablet

to garner widespread use, Norwich Aspirin. They also invented Unguentine, the first anti-bacterial antiseptic dressing. Oh, and Pepto-Bismol. Yup, invented right here in 1901!

The building was originally a neighborhood school, the 1892 Ward School Number 2.

Located nearly across the road from the Northeast Classic Car Museum is the small yet interesting Bullthistle Model Train Museum. It is run with an entirely volunteer staff. You might venture over and see if it is open.

From Here to There
The other museum in this book that is nearest to the Northeast Classic Car Museum is the **Bainbridge Museum**. It is located twenty miles south of Norwich.

30

NATIONAL ABOLITION HALL
OF FAME AND MUSEUM

Peterboro, Madison County

*T*his museum is unique in that the story is literate and textual rather than archive-laden.

"The story of the underground railroad is basically a story that was relayed orally between people and organizations. "Almost nothing was written down for obvious security reasons," Norm Dann told me. He is on the Board of Directors (they call it the "Cabinet of Freedom") at the National Abolition Hall of Fame and Museum.

"Our buildings and historic sites around Peterboro tell the story. Our museum is more of a learning experience. Our displays are designed for someone to spend twenty minutes *looking at* the panels, or two hours *reading* the panels. We believe we are suited perfectly for both types of visitors."

The museum is located in the Smithfield Community Center just off the village green in Peterboro, a hamlet of under three hundred people. Built as a Presbyterian church in 1820, this majestic old structure reaches high into the sky, with a pointed roof topped with a three-sided clock face (yes the clocks work) crowned with a cupola that holds the original one-ton bell. Oh, and an antique weathervane oversees it all.

This site is considered by many to be the birthplace of the abolition movement in New York State.

"On October 21, 1835, a large anti-slavery convention was to meet in Utica. Wealthy Peterboro resident Gerrit Smith attended as an observer. Utica businessmen and politicians threatened attendees if they didn't leave the city," Dann told me. "Smith was outraged at this affront, and

stood up and invited the four hundred or so delegates to 'come to my home in Peterboro' where he would host them."

Smith was as surprised as anybody when so many of them made the thirty mile trek from Utica to Peterboro. Many of them rode their horses, secured wagons and carriages, or even walked the distance. One large group of one hundred men hailed a canal boat on the Erie Canal and rode it (all standing up for lack of seats) to Canastota. There they disembarked and walked the final nine miles to Peterboro. By this time Smith had directed the employees at his estate to go door to door asking for help, a room for people to stay, and even food to comfort the masses heading their way.

"This little community rallied and responded in a beautiful way to Smith's entreaties," Dann said. "And they came right here," he whispered as he tapped his foot on the old wooden floor of the Community Center. "Yes, it all started right here in this building."

Dann, who is a Professor Emeritus at the State University of New York at Morrisville, is also the author of several books on the abolition movement as well as a biography of Smith.

"Smith was fully engaged in the movement. There is a difference between being anti-slavery and being an abolitionist. Anti-slavery advocates simply agreed with the notion of ending slavery. Abolitionists, like Gerrit Smith, were activists who pledged their fortunes, homes, energies, and even their lives to seeing slavery banned from the country. Smith was a strident abolitionist who dedicated his life and his money to the cause."

I asked Dann how wealthy Smith really was.

"Well, his father made the family fortune in the fur trading business in association with his young friend, businessman John Jacob Astor. Smith's son Gerrit later used the family money to buy hundreds of thousands of acres of Upstate New York property. In his lifetime he was certainly worth millions. Today that would translate into *billions* of dollars."

Hence, the role Smith took on as the unofficial "banker of the abolition movement."

Wow Factor

As mentioned earlier, the museum and hall of fame contains many informative panels, diagrams, plaques, and biographies. There is a lot of reading in this large one-room museum. But the story of the Underground Railroad, one of America's most intriguing, romantic, and daring chapters, is impossible not to get drawn into.

"I would have to say the wow factor right here at the museum is these colorful and informative panels," Dann explained. "There are eight of them, each highlighting a different stage of the abolitionist movement.

They carry such titles as 'Colonial and Revolutionary Period,' 'Freedom Now,' 'North Star Shining,' and 'The Terrible Swift Sword.' They are wonderful, and people love them. And they are portable," he laughed. "Even though they are about six feet tall, they fold right down, we pack them into cases, and we can carry them wherever we are invited to make a presentation.

"But I would really like to suggest a different wow factor than these panels. But it isn't here. Yet," he continued.

"We actually own a large wrought-iron slave collar from the early 1800s. It is heavy and was literally locked around a slave's neck. Then an iron chain was attached to it and the other end of the chain was attached to the iron collar of a slave behind the first one. And so on. This is how they transported slaves: in trains [chained-together lines] called coffles. The inhumanity involved is amazing. This is a very valuable item, and one that I take with me to show people at our presentations. They are shocked, to say the least.

Unfortunately, we have yet to derive a security system at the museum where we feel comfortable leaving such a rare and valuable piece here for long periods. But soon, I hope, that will be different."

"Why?" I asked him.

A smile crossed his face. "Well, you want to know my dream?" he asked. "I want us to reconstruct Gerrit Smith's mansion right across the street on the village green where it once stood (it burned down in 1936). We have photographs of the building, and if we ever get that built it will house our museum and we can bring our artifacts, such as the slave collar, there for permanent display.

It'll cost probably a half-million dollars to do, so it is still just a dream of mine. All we need is a very big donor," he said with a chuckle.

The Take-Away

This tiny hamlet is loaded with history. The Gerrit Smith Estate is a National Historic Landmark and is just a block away from the Community Center which houses the hall of fame and museum. The two venues make for a very interesting afternoon in this community with only two retail businesses. The estate grounds are dotted with many informative plaques describing the history of the Smith home as well as informing the visitor about the several existing buildings.

One of the buildings is the original family estate laundry.

Dann told me a fascinating story about this building.

"Gerrit Smith's first wife died shortly after they were married. He then married Ann Carroll Fitzhugh. She had been raised in Maryland by a wealthy slave owner. His new wife begged Smith to go into the South, find the black nanny who raised her, buy her her freedom, and bring her to Peterboro to live. Smith did this.

"He contracted a fellow abolitionist in Skaneateles to go and find 'Harriet,' the nanny. He gave this man a blank check and basically told him not to come back without her. This man went to Maryland, but the trail led further when he discovered she had moved to Kentucky. He went there and finally found his wife's beloved nanny. But there was a problem," Dann said.

"The nanny had married and now had five children. So the man contacted Smith and asked what he wanted him to do."

"What did Smith reply?" I asked.

"The word came back to "buy them all." So he did. And when no stage coach would transport the black family to the north, Smith told his man to 'buy the stage coach and bring her up yourself.' And he did!"

The woman and her family moved to the Smith estate at Peterboro, where she became the family laundress. Her laundry building still stands in restored condition.

"The amazing thing is that this nanny, Harriet, still has descendents that live in the Peterboro area," Dann told me.

The Hall of Fame induction ceremonies are held every two years. "We hold them at Colgate University, which is just fifteen miles away."

I asked Norm Dann if any single induction presentation stuck out more than the others.

"Well, they are all moving and well-attended. Often times, family members of the inductees come to the ceremony to witness the event. The year that John Brown was inducted, 2007, was an especially exciting year. Alice Keesey Mecoy, his great-great-great-granddaughter, came for the ceremony. She spoke eloquently of her famous relative and was overcome with emotion that he was finally being recognized for the hero to the movement that he really was. There wasn't a dry eye in the house that night," he said.

The history centered in Peterboro is kind of amazing. Like the Underground Railroad was. When you find it, the place tells its story with exciting detail and interest and you will be rewarded by having been to the actual starting place of one of the most important movements in American history.

The Nuts and Bolts

National Abolition Hall of Fame and Museum
5255 Pleasant Valley Road
Peterboro, New York 13025
www.abolitionhof.org
(315) 366-8101

- *Travel Suggestion*

Leave the New York State Thruway at Exit 34. Travel south on Oxbow Road (County Route 25) nine miles to Peterboro.

- *Museum Hours*

Open weekends mid-May through September, 1 to 5 p.m. (or by appointment).

- *Admission*

$3.00

- *Number of Visitors Annually*

500

Up around the Bend

Other than the Gerrit Smith sites there is very little to see in Peterboro. You might, however, take a little stroll around the hamlet's original public green. Fronting it is a gorgeous 1820 Georgian mansion impeccably restored to its early splendor. It is now the Charlotte Amalie Inn and Bed and Breakfast and it is really quite extraordinary ([315] 684-3555).

Just one-quarter mile north of Peterboro on the road to Canastota (County Highway 54) you will find a curious historical marker on the right hand side of the road. It was here in 1880 that the first Holstein-Friesian Cattle Association began.

The man who founded this organization was Gerrit S. Miller, Gerrit Smith's grandson.

From Here to There

The nearest museum to the Abolition Hall of Fame and Museum is the **Canal Town Museum**. It is located in Canastota, about nine miles north of Peterboro.

31

New York State Museum of Cheese

Rome, Oneida County

*A*fter leaving the gift shop/admission office at the Erie Canal Village, you walk over an arched wooden bridge built in 1844 that crosses one of the earliest modifications of the Erie Canal. "The birth of the *new* New York began right here," said Melody Milewski, the museum's director. "From this spot, near this bridge, the Erie Canal began transforming New York into the Empire State."

That is a pretty impressive statement.

As we wandered over the bridge we could look down at a life-sized Erie Canal packet boat, moored under the bridge. "We give rides on that in the summer. The kids love it. We pull it along by mules and horses, just like they did nearly two hundred years ago," she told me. We next crossed over a set of railroad tracks and headed into the main park.

Why the train?

"Well, you can't say Erie Canal without saying railroads, so we built one right here," she laughed. "Of course, the railroads and the canals were great friends at the beginning but soon became rivals. Rome was really a transportation hub," she told me. "We have an original narrow-gauge train which takes the kids on a rail trip around our large park."

Ok, so we have canal boats and trains, but where is the cheese museum?

"Right over there," she said, dramatically pointing to one of the largest, most majestic old barns I have ever seen.

188

The barn was built in 1862 in a nearby village (Verona), and dismantled and reconstructed here in 1987. "The first cheese factory was in Rome, N.Y., but there is nothing left of that structure. Our barn was constructed to withstand time. And it sure has," she said.

"My husband, Michael, was here at the time it was moved, and helped in the construction," she told me. "In fact, my whole family has been here for many years. I started out when I was a teenager, my husband has been here for more than thirty years, and my kids and even my grandchildren come to the village and help out. Some days there are four generations of my family working in some capacity here. We can't get enough of this old place," she said softly.

The cheese museum is wonderful. The amount of space inside the old barn (90 feet by 34 feet) is really surprising. Wide-open floor spaces give way to cheese vats and bins and worktable displays in the summer. The vast "make-room," where the cheese was actually made, is faced with large wagon doors that the farmers would drive up to and unload their milk. "You could say we were the first drive-in," the director said.

Extensive signage and display panels clearly and interestingly describe what was once one of the biggest industries in New York.

A large old wall map near one of the dioramas particularly fascinated me. It was an 1899 map of the state with a little circle denoting each cheese factory in New York.

"Remember, cheese making was a family business. Every farm did it. It was hard work and the women did a lot of it, while the men were tending the animals and the farm chores. Eventually a wealthy farmer named Jesse Williams decided it was the right time to act as a clearinghouse for all of the little cheese factories around the state, so he built the first manufacturing plant right here in this barn. It revolutionized the industry. Now quality, consistency, and control could be regulated. It really was huge," Milewski said.

As we pored over the large 1899 map, I asked her how many little circles were on it. "We tried to count them all one time, but gave up at around seven hundred individual cheese making farms in the state. So you can really see, it was a big deal," she laughed.

One corner of the upper floor holds a curious item. An old-fashioned stand-up bar.

"Sure, we have this antique bar in here (from an old Rome hotel) to remind everybody that cheese was the first snack at a happy hour. Our cheese and crackers . . . we started it all," she said.

The authentic nature of the cheese barn and the village has not gone overlooked. "The Discovery Channel and The History Channel have both come here to film. They like to feature my husband in their shows because his old, long beard makes him look like he belongs to another era," she chuckled. "The packet boat was featured in the 'I Love New York' tourism commercials, too. Also, the local grade schools were so impressed with our story out here that in 1983 they formally lobbied the New York State Department of Education to institute an Erie Canal curriculum in the fourth grade."

Wow Factor

"That would be the Big Cheese," the director fairly shouted.

She guided me to an exhibit that displayed all sorts of cheese making records set in the past by those in the area. One stood out.

"'The Big Cheese,' it was called," she said as she pointed to an old photograph. "It was the largest wheel of cheese ever produced up to that time. It weighed 12 tons and represented the single day's output of 10,200 cows. It was encased in an enormous wheel and sent to Washington," she told me.

And sure enough, there it was. In an old sepia-toned depiction you can see President Andrew Jackson in front of the White House cutting a slice of cheese from the gargantuan wheel. The date was February 22, 1837. Stamped in large letters across the cheese wheel are the words, "Martinsburgh, N.Y. Cheese Factory."

The famous chunk of cheese is long gone but a historic part of this grand event still remains! The original 1837 wheel case, which carried the upstate cheese to the White House, towers more than seven feet in the air next to the exhibit. "Visitors love to stand inside it and get their pictures taken," the director laughed.

The Take-Away

I must admit I experienced a roller coaster of emotions when I first visited the Erie Canal Village. As I pulled into the empty parking lot (in all fairness, the park was closed this day) I couldn't help but be chagrined at the sight of weeds growing up through the pavement. The tall, old-fashioned lampposts were forlorn and gave the place a look of a forgotten souvenir.

I remember the old Adirondack theme parks of my youth. Fantasyland, Storytown, Gaslight Village, Land of Makebelieve, Frontierland, etc. There were lots of them. They all (for the most part) eventually suffered a fate of neglect, disinterest, and loss. I couldn't escape that feeling at the Erie Canal Village. Several of the buildings appeared to need paint and minor repairs. It had a patina of woefulness about it.

Having said that, I was delighted to discover that this place really does have a lot of spunk. Melody Milewski, the director, is an enthusiastic interpreter of the past, and was one of the most engaging tour guides I have experienced on my long and fascinating journey in writing this book. As we strolled through the fairly desolate grounds (remember, the park was closed the day I was there) I was holding my breath as we neared the Cheese Museum.

What a relief! The New York State Cheese Museum is a very well done and absorbing look at the cheese industry of Central New York. I was ushered into the first level of a truly massive, impressive three-story barn that was an original nineteenth-century cheese factory, which had been moved here many years ago. The cheese-making exhibits are quite interesting and attractive. The various steps along the cheese making process are told with photos and static exhibits, all including original, historic tools and implements. I loved it all.

The barn itself is one of Central New York's great treasures. The director showed me portions of the wall and ceilings that are exposed and glass-covered so as to show the exquisite and complicated construction methods. Through a glass portion in the ceiling, you can see way up to the cupola on the roof. It was not just an adornment, I was told, but rather acted as a cooling duct to keep the cheese products "refrigerated." Through another glass panel you can look up and see the behemoth winches that hauled the cheese tonnage from one floor to another. The Shakers had nothing on the clever and practical cheese makers of Central New York.

The effort to rekindle Central New York history here is not insignificant. All of the many buildings on site were donated, dismantled, and reconstructed here at the "village." The church came from Maynard, N.Y. (1974), a schoolhouse came from Wood Creek (1975), the tavern came from McConnellsville (1978), the settler's house from Ridge Mills (1979), and so on from the livery stables to the Victorian playhouse to the print shop and other showpieces.

The first waterway you cross over when entering the park is the "Enlarged Canal," built between 1836 and 1862. This was the first change in the original canal. The amazing thing about the Erie Canal Village is that if you walk way into the rear of the park, you can still see some original remnants of the one and only *first* Erie Canal (1825). It is as if you are witnessing a holy revelation. Now, this is history.

I have lived near the famous Farmers Museum in Cooperstown most of my life, and I have visited it many times. If that place, flush with cash and with a deep-pocket angel to keep it vibrant (the Stephen Clark Foundation [Singer sewing machines]), can continue to thrive, one can only imagine what this historic canal village would be like with a sprinkling of cash from the State or another source. I know that this is a private enterprise now, but still it is an almost reverential place. This village is really a shrine to New York's history, with the first shovel of dirt for the Erie Canal being turned here on July 4, 1817.

I encourage the powers that be to come, visit, and support this unique place. If the public is still willing to come and experience nineteenth-century life among the canal village's boats, trains, and buildings, then at least, even in these incredibly difficult budget times, outside money should come forward to bring this nostalgic living history primer back to a vibrancy fitting for the new century to enjoy.

And if the village survives and perseveres, no small credit should be given to Melody and her four generations of family who continue to pour their hearts and souls into the Erie Canal Village every day.

They are heroes.

The Nuts and Bolts
The Erie Canal Village
Route 49
5789 Rome/New London Road
Rome, New York 13440
www.eriecanalvillage.net
(315) 337-3999

• *Travel Suggestion*
From the west: Take the New York State Thruway to Exit 33, and follow the signs to Rome. From the east: Take Exit 32 from the Thruway and follow the signs to Rome.

There are many signs to the Erie Canal Village, or just make your way to Route 49, which leads you to it.

• *Museum Hours*
Open Memorial Day Weekend through Labor Day
Wednesday to Saturday 10 a.m. to 5 p.m.; Sunday noon to 5 p.m.
Closed Monday and Tuesday.

• *Admission*

You are advised to contact the website for the many variations of admission prices (admission plus boat ride, admission plus train ride, family admission, etc.).

Note: The website also will contain the many events which continuously change at the park. These include holiday events, free days, Pirate Days, Halloween Fright Nights, etc.

• *Number of Visitors Annually*

5,000

The Road Less Traveled

Rome, N.Y. is steeped in history. The Revere Copper Company here, founded by Paul Revere in 1801, is the oldest manufacturing company in the U.S. Francis Bellamy wrote the *Pledge of Allegiance* here in 1892 (his grave in Rome Cemetery is etched with the words of his paean to America). The thirty-year anniversary of the original Woodstock ("Three Days of Peace and Music") concert was held here, disastrously, in 1999 at the mammoth Cold War-era Griffiss Air Force Base.

But for one of the true historic icons in Upstate New York, just travel a mile back into the city of Rome from the Erie Canal Village to Fort Stanwix. This fort, "The Fort That Never Surrendered," is a national monument and one of the most accurately reconstructed Revolutionary War forts in the state. It is said that this was the site of the "first flying of the American flag in wartime," on August 3, 1777. A new multi-million-dollar visitor's center has greatly enhanced the experience of visiting this historic place, which is located right smack dab in the middle of downtown Rome.

From Here to There

The other museum in this book that is nearest to the Museum of Cheese is the **Canal Town Museum** in Canastota. It is twenty miles southwest of Rome.

32

OLD STONE FORT MUSEUM

Schoharie, Schoharie County

A visit to this historic little corner of Schoharie County is like visiting a miniature version of Williamsburg, Virginia. A *much smaller version.*

The Old Stone Fort "campus" includes a 1700s home, a 1780s Dutch barn, a 1830s law office, and a 1890s one-room schoolhouse, as well as one of the most beautiful and picturesque old churchyard cemeteries you'll ever find.

And a fort.

"Our Old Stone Fort was built in 1772 as a church and later fortified into a fort during the heat of the Revolutionary War," Daniel Beams, the museum curator, told me. "It really was just a rural church until after the Tory Uprising during the Burgoyne campaign of 1777. Then it became a fort and the Johnson/Brant Raid of 1780 etched its glory in our local history." That would be Col. John Johnson and the Mohawk Indian Chief Joseph Brant.

The raid's purpose was to decimate the frontier towns known to some historians as "Breadbasket of the Revolution." It succeeded.

"The enemy came sweeping through the valley, some eight hundred loyalists and Native Americans, and torched everything," Beams told me. "In fact General Washington was so devastated about the loss of the 80,000 bushels of wheat here that he wrote a letter to Congress asking for help to feed his troops. The raiders also burned the entire nearby farms and villages and forced the residents to flee into our church, which was then known as Lower Fort. Two other forts were nearby. The Upper Fort was bypassed and the Middle Fort was besieged for about six hours, but not reduced."

The British fired upon the fort several times, but to no avail, and moved on and out of the valley. A cannon ball hole still can be seen along the roofline of the fort.

"Kids love the old cannon ball hole," Beams told me. "Most other Revolutionary War forts are 'cleaned up' for visitors so the students can hardly believe that a war took place right here in their own back yard. Seeing the hole (which has a sign near it telling of the event) really brings home the importance of this building as a historic fort."

The Old Stone Fort is a stunningly beautiful structure that sits on a high promontory in a shady glen of trees. The gleaming white stones give the church an air of pastoral beauty. An oddity is the decoration you can see covering the front of the church/fort.

"Yes, the folks who were instrumental in the building of this church had their names inscribed on the stones," Beams told me.

It is an amazing sight. From afar, it just looks like some fancy handi-work in the stone. But up close, the names of the ancient Dutch and German families of Schoharie who took part in forming the church are clearly visible. Each is done in sturdy yet graceful script. It is a very unusual thing to see.

Tim Murphy is the legendary figure around here. The "Savior of Schoharie" was a marksman and outdoorsman of mythic proportions.

"Many people who come here already know about Tim," Beams said. "He was our own Paul Bunyan. Except that he was a real person. Many stories and 'tall tales' about Tim Murphy have been passed down through the generations. Of course his actions at the Battle of Saratoga are the stuff that legends are made of.

"It is fairly well-documented that on October 7, 1777, Tim, then a member of the famed Morgan's Rifle Corps, climbed a tree on the battle-field and with a single crack felled the British leader, Brigadier-General Simon Fraser. Now, there are some contradictions to this historical event, but Tim Murphy settled here, so we certainly discuss that version of the story," Beams told me. Although originally from New Jersey, Murphy is buried nearby in the Middleburgh Cemetery.

The museum itself has more than 50,000 historical artifacts on display and archived within. Its contents tell the story of the early settlers of the Schoharie Valley and their involvement in the Revolutionary War. And yes, there are even a few of Tim Murphy's personal belongings here as well.

"We have his pocket watch, his will, and an IOU with his personal mark on it, plus other items of Tim's, here at the Old Stone Fort," the curator told me. "One of the oddest items is a chunk of Tim Murphy's coffin. Apparently, when his body was moved from his farm to the Middleburgh Cemetery somebody was thoughtful enough to save us a piece of his coffin," he smiled.

The Old Stone Fort was listed on the National Registry of Historic Places in 2002.

Wow Factor

"Well, it really doesn't have anything to do with the Revolutionary War, but I think one of our wow factors here is the Old Deluge #1," Beam said. He walked me over and showed me the oddest thing. Basically just a "water bladder" on wheels, Old Deluge is one of the oldest fire engines in the U.S.

"We really can't find many that are older in the country. It was built in 1731, the year before George Washington was even born. It was just a water pumping mechanism, but it did yeoman's service in New York City before heading to Schenectady, Esperance, and then finally here. It was one of two fire engines ordered from a company in England. They came over by ship together. The other one is still around also. It is in the Fire-fighting Museum in Hudson, N.Y."

The Take-Away

I must admit I am a little biased about the Old Stone Fort. I have had the great pleasure of being the featured speaker there on more than one occasion. The folks are wonderful and warm and inviting. And they know their stuff! Just ask any of them about a certain historical factoid about the fort and, well, stand back, because off they go. The grounds are almost park-like. The whole campus is set on a beautiful dead-end road. The buildings and the cemetery are a perfect place to wander and explore on a warm summer evening.

As I mentioned before, the churchyard cemetery is a treasure trove of local history. Notice the tall white obelisk to the right of the main entrance. This is the grave of David Williams. His story is told on the base of his grave marker. It was Williams and two friends who stopped British Major John Andre as he was en route to give the plans for the capitulation of West Point to the British in the Revolutionary War. After being stymied by the clever officer, it was Williams who asked the key question.

"Will you please take off your boots, sir?"

Inside Andre's boots were Benedict Arnold's plans for the taking of West Point. Because of the actions of David Williams and his two fellow soldiers, West Point was saved. Williams later moved to Schoharie County after the war.

Major John Andre was hanged on October 2, 1780.

The whole story is told on Williams's grave here at the Old Stone Fort.

The Nuts and Bolts

The Old Stone Fort Museum
145 Fort Road

Schoharie, New York 12157
(518) 295-7192
www.theoldstonefort.org

• *Travel Suggestion*
From I-88 (which goes between Schenectady and Binghamton), take
Exit 23 and travel three miles south on Route 30 to the museum.

• *Museum Hours*
Open May 1 through October 31
Monday through Saturday 10:00 a.m. to 5:00 p.m.
Sunday noon to 5:00 p.m.

• *Admission*
Adults: $5.00
Seniors: $4.50
Children aged 5 to 17: $1.50
Children under 5: Free.

• *Number of Visitors Annually*
7,000

Up around the Bend
Just twenty miles south of Schoharie once stood the Blenheim Covered
Bridge. It was the longest single-span wooden covered bridge *in the world.*
Just looking at it made you wonder: "How did they do that?"

It was built over the Schoharie Creek in 1855 and was one of only a
handful of two-lane covered bridges in the country. Sadly, it was destroyed
during the Great Flood of 2011 caused by Hurricane Irene. The storm
did what no other element could do for over a hundred and fifty years.
Destroyed the historic bridge.

A Herculean effort is now under way to locate and secure pieces of the
old bridge. Groups of volunteers have been scouring the riverbanks looking for any and all sizes of bridge parts. Among the structural components
already located downstream is one that is forty feet long. It is the hope of

these history lovers that FEMA will ultimately provide funding to rebuild the Blenheim Covered Bridge.

The whole area around Schoharie is dotted with farm stands and craft stores, and the months of September and October are certainly the busiest times. Like harvest times in the past, the autumnal wonders of this "Breadbasket of the Revolution" region once again burst with pumpkin patches, cider mills, fruit stands, and quilt displays for the thousands who visit here annually.

From Here to There

The other museum in this book that is nearest to the Old Stone Fort is the **Iroquois Indian Museum** in Howes Cave. It is ten miles west of Schoharie.

OTHER MUSEUMS TO
EXPLORE IN REGION FIVE

Amsterdam: The Noteworthy Indian Museum. "Developed from over 60,000 artifacts, this museum displays and interprets much of the Mohawk Indian history." (518) 843-4671, www.greatturtle.net.

Binghamton: Roberson Museum and Science Center. "The Roberson engages people of all ages and backgrounds by providing community-relevant exhibitions and programs in art, science, and history." (607) 772-0660, www.roberson.org.

Canajoharie: The Arkell Museum. "Features an extensive collection of American art including Winslow Homer, Childe Hassam, and Andrew Wyeth. Inside the museum is a second museum dedicated to the story of Beechnut baby foods. The company was founded by Bartlett Arkell." (518) 673-2314, www.arkellmuseum.org.

Cooperstown: The Farmers Museum and Fenimore Art Museum. They are across the road from each other. "Once the farm owned by James Fenimore Cooper. It now houses everything from the Empire Carousel to the Cardiff Giant." The Fenimore Art Museum sits on beautiful Otsego Lake and houses everything from Hudson River School masters to an extensive collection of Native American masks." (607) 547-1450, www.farmers museum.org.; www.fenimoreartmuseum.org.

Cooperstown: The National Baseball Hall of Fame and Museum. "The shrine to America's pastime." (888) 425-5633, baseballhall.org.

Greene: The Greene Museum is operated by the village's historical society. It is a real eye-opener! Much of Greene's history is represented here. Be sure and check out the local success story of the Page Seed Company as well as viewing the "parachute wedding dress." Oh, and wait till you read the story of the famous "Shooting Elliotts." Their guns are even on display here! (607) 656-4981. www.greenenylibrary.org.

Oneida: Oneida Community Mansion and Museum. "This massive 95,000-square-foot mansion was the longtime home of three hundred members of John Humphrey Noyes's Utopian movement. Oneida Silverware got its start here." (315) 363-0745, www.oneidacommunity.org.

Oneonta: Yager Museum at Hartwick College. This museum of culture and art is an actual teaching museum. It occupies a small but attractive first floor area of Hartwick's Yager Hall. The exhibits change frequently and they are always top-notch. Paintings, sculptures, fabrics, and oddities make this a fascinating stop in the "City of the Hills." Willard Yager was a noted archeologist and anthropologist who left many of his relics and artifacts to the museum which now bears his name. http://www.hartwick.edu/academics/museum.

Rome: Sports Hall of Fame and Museum. "The only municipal sports Hall of Fame with its own museum in New York State." (315) 339-9038, www.when-in-rome.com.

Utica: Munson-Williams-Proctor Institute and Museum of Art. "The striking building was designed by famed architect Philip Johnson and was so innovative that a model of it was exhibited at the U.S. Pavilion at the Brussels World's Fair of 1958." (315) 797-0000, www.mwpi.org.

Region Six

ADIRONDACKS/NORTH COUNTRY

*Franklin, Clinton, Essex, Herkimer, Hamilton,
Warren, Fulton, and Lewis Counties*

33

REMINGTON ARMS MUSEUM

Ilion, Herkimer County

"*W*e still have over a thousand employees working around the clock at Remington," Fred Supry told me. If he isn't the longest working employee here, I don't know who is. Fred recently retired after almost 46 years here.

"But who's counting," he laughed.

"I started here as a teenager, and it was always a great place to work," he told me as we strolled the aisles of this modern, well-lit museum. Each giant case held another chapter of the storied Remington name here in Ilion.

I mentioned to Fred that the sign at the edge of town read "Welcome to Ilion. Birthplace of the typewriter."

"Yes, there was almost nothing the Remingtons couldn't make. We made some of the first typewriters, sewing machines, bicycles, cutlery, and more. But it was the guns that put us on the map."

Eliphalet Remington began manufacturing weapons and ammunition near Ilion in 1816.

"The Erie Canal came right through town, so this was a perfect place for the plant," Supry told me. "Remington had a whole fleet of barges carrying his product out to the masses. It was a very busy place."

The museum starts with displays of old man Remington's first rifles and progresses through the decades. There are long-barrel guns, 1816 flintlocks, pistol rifles, side-by-side shot guns, the first "on top" shotguns, and of course the "rolling block carbines," which really changed the face of armaments forever.

"The rolling block made here really was groundbreaking. It was the most successful single-shot rifle ever made, and it really made us the premier gun maker in America," Supry said.

In the early days, just the barrels were made here in Ilion. The other two parts of the rifle were contracted out.

"That's where you get the phrase 'lock, stock, and barrel,'" Supry smiled.

As we walked through the museum, I couldn't help but notice the almost boyish exuberance Supry showed towards his former employer's products and history.

"Look here," he said excitedly as he pointed to one particularly crowded display case. "Annie Oakley."

Inside the case I saw photos and placards telling of Oakley's great talents as a sharpshooter. Also inside was one of her guns (a Remington, of course). It was a 1925 pump-action repeater. This would have been made the year before she died.

"It was her favorite shooting rifle," Supry told me.

The many marquee names on display at the museum really bespeak the popularity of the Remington firearms down through the years.

"General Norman Schwarzkopf is a major Remington collector and has visited our factory. So has NASCAR driver Dale Earnhardt. Wrestler Stone Cold Steve Austin also collects, and has been here. Irlene Mandrell, one of country music's Mandrell Sisters, even went to our shooting school here in Ilion. Of course she then bought several guns from us," he smiled.

"Here is something special," he said. It was a copy of a letter from General George Armstrong Custer dated 1873. The letter (the original is in the corporate headquarters) tells how pleased he is with his new Remington rifle. It reads in part: *"The number of animals I have killed with the Remington is not so remarkable as the distance at which the shots were executed. 250 yards or more was not uncommon."*

Another large display case shows the commemorative rifles signifying benchmark issues of Remington arms. In it you can see beautifully hand-tooled artwork adorning rifles with plaques on them reading "1,000,000 made," or "10,000,000 made." It is very impressive.

The museum ends at a well-stocked, attractive gift shop. The Remington logo is everywhere, from shirts and ball caps to gun cases and coffee mugs. You can get almost everything here, except a gun.

Wow Factor

"Well, one of the most unusual stories is told in this display over here," Supry told me as we walked to a large case in the back. In it, the story of Tom Frye was told. It was great.

"Tom was a Remington salesman who was also one of the country's greatest competition shooters. To advertise our new Nylon 66 repeating cartridge, they sent Tom out for public exhibitions using it. Once, he shot (over a period of fourteen straight days) at more than 100,010 thrown wood blocks. Can you believe he hit every one of them but *six*? And look," he pointed, "it's all right in here."

In the case are photos of Frye accomplishing his feat and the actual Nylon 66 firearm he used, as well as two of the actual wood blocks from the demonstration. In pencil, one of them bears the inscription #1 and the other reads "#100,010." Of course there is a bullet hole in each wood block.

The Take-Away

So many elements of the Remington story are told here that you find your head constantly twisting and turning just to see it all. In one wall case are a series of huge ornamental guns given to Mr. Remington by the Chinese government. Another displays fancy rifle engravings (some of the intricate handiwork on a custom rifle can take a year or more to create). All along the top walls, near the ceiling, is a collection of original paintings from which the famous Remington calendars were created. Among the artists represented are J. C. Leyendecker and N. C. Wyeth. The paintings are worth a fortune.

One curiosity that drew my attention was a Remington bicycle, one of their first. It had strings holding up the fenders, and each bike came with an attached leather holster.

To put a Remington pistol in?

The history of the Remington Arms Company is literally the history of America.

This is an excellent museum.

The Nuts and Bolts

The Remington Arms Museum
14 Hoefler Drive at NY. Route 5S West
Ilion, New York 13357
(315) 895-3200 (Call in advance for current hours and times.)
www.remington.com

• *Travel Suggestion*
Take Exit 30 of the New York State Thruway, then follow Route 5S West three miles to Ilion. The factory and museum will be on your left.

• *Museum Hours*
Monday through Friday: 8 a.m. to 5 p.m.

• *Admission*
   Free

• *Number of Visitors Annually*
   7,000

Up around the Bend
Gems Along the Mohawk is a wonderful place to visit, just six miles east of Ilion in Herkimer. Not only do they have a great waterfront restaurant here, they also have the best gift shop in Upstate New York! The big shop is packed with items from around the state, all segmented out by region (Niagara, Adirondacks, Capital District, Hudson Valley, etc.). They also have one of the largest selections of local history books on sale anywhere. Out in front of the gift shop is the Mohawk River and what else . . . canal boats! This is the best place in Central New York to take a ride on the Erie Canal. The *Li'l Diamond II* is a comfortable 60-passenger tour boat that takes you up the river and through the locks. The narration along the way by the captain of the boat is interesting and fun. (www.gemsalongthemo hawk.com).

From Here to There
The other museum in this book that is nearest to the Remington Arms Museum is the **New York State Museum of Cheese** in Rome. It is thirty miles west of Ilion.

34

NORTH AMERICAN FIDDLERS
HALL OF FAME AND MUSEUM

Osceola, Lewis County

*T*iny Osceola, population just over two hundred, is the most remote locale of any museum I researched for this book. Located just outside the Adirondack Park, the hamlet lies deep in the north woods, along a small rural road. As you make the journey to this museum you will find yourself muttering, "Boy, this is out in the sticks."

And it is.

Lewis County sprawls over 1,300 square miles, yet contains only 27,000 souls, ranking it as one of the most sparsely populated counties in the country. Osceola feels more like an outpost than a town. It consists of a small four-corner crossroads with a hotel on one corner ("The World Famous Osceola Hotel"), a house on another, a hunter's rental property on the third, and a general store/gas station on the last corner (actually called the "Osceola Outpost," sorry no credit cards here!).

This is outdoor sports country, and most of it revolves around winter. Snowmobiles are as common as four-wheelers here and the area, smack dab in the middle of the Tug Hill Plateau, annually racks up some serious snowfall totals (in January 1997 the area around Osceola saw a six-and-a-half-foot snowfall in *twenty-four hours*, a world record).

Yet they are a hearty bunch up here along the Salmon River. As the snow melts and life returns to normal (usually around May), the joyous sounds of fiddle music can be heard emanating from a 150-year-old farmhouse up on Comins Road.

"Our fiddler's group has been together since 1976," Leona Chereshnoski, the museum's co-curator (with her daughter), told me. "We bought this old house in 1981 and put the museum up front and our Hall of Fame out back."

Ms. Chereshnoski has fiddle music in her blood. "My Mom, Alice Clemens, was a co-founder of it all. She was one of the best fiddlers in the region, and always wanted to put up a museum and facility right here in God's country. Mom fiddled for 70 years. In fact she gave a performance a month before she passed," she told me.

The back room is apt to warm any fiddler's heart, even in Osceola's notoriously cold, snowy winters. Portraits of legendary fiddlers line the long walls of the hall. "There are two sets of nominees every year, one from New York State and one representing North America. As you can see," she pointed out, "there are quite a few Canadians honored here."

The plaques under each portrait tell an interesting story of this centuries-old art form. Being a novice, I asked the curator a simple question. "What is the difference between a fiddle and a violin?"

"There is no difference whatsoever. It's all in the way the instrument is played," was the emphatic reply.

Some of the names leap off the wall. Others are obscure. All are fascinating.

Bob Wills, the "King of Country Swing," was in the initial class of inductees. Johnny Gimble (Class of 1987), Mark O'Connor (1991), Roy Acuff (1998), and Jay Ungar (2004) are all legendary American fiddlers who have notched every honor imaginable, from the Kennedy Center Honors to Grammy Awards to induction into the Grand Ole Opry.

"But here, look at some of our New Yorkers," Chereshnoski said. "This is Ms. Telletta Bourne Atwell (1983). She was a music teacher. Her high school bands played at the 1939 World's Fair as well as the 1965 World's Fair, both in New York City.

"Don Messer—why, everybody along the St. Lawrence River with a radio of any size could listen in to his fiddle show from Ontario, Canada. Here's Hilt Kelly from down around Delaware County. They say he taught almost every Catskill fiddler how to play. And Old "Jack" Daniels here was chosen to play his fiddle at the one-hundredth anniversary rededication of the Statue of Liberty," she said as we slowly walked along the rows. Below many of the inductees' portraits are cases holding their fiddles, bows, performing outfits, and more.

The front section of the building is the museum. It consists of several rooms filled with fiddles, instruments, and personal memorabilia from the great musicians highlighted in the Hall.

"This is the luthier's room. A luthier is someone who makes or repairs fiddles," she informed me. There are dozens of old violins on display here. Some defy description. One strange one in a display case drew my attention.

"Lord only knows how old that fiddle is," she chuckled as we stared at the most unusual musical instrument I have ever seen. It was a cigar box with a couple of strings hanging off it and a piece of leather keeping it all together. "Yes, it sure is ancient," she whispered.

I could only imagine the heavenly sounds that old fiddle must have made a century or more ago.

Wow Factor

"I love this old luthier's cabinet," she said. The tall wooden cabinet with three glass doors in the front held a dozen fiddles of varying sizes, all hanging upside down.

"The craftsmen had to hang them this way so air could circulate all the way around the fiddle. Each shelf would hold an instrument in various stages of repair. One shelf was taller than the other to hold the larger violins and such. It really is a special piece, isn't it?" she said softly.

Chereshnoski opened up the middle glass door and gingerly took out one of the smaller fiddles. Its burnt-orange wood glistened under the spotlight. She caressed it gently.

"This was my mother's fiddle. She taught twenty-seven children how to play using this instrument."

Alice Clemens thought the fiddle was "God's Blessing on Four Strings."

The Take-Away

This small museum has a lot of soul to it.

Maybe it's because since it began it has been a place where strangers with the common denominator of a fiddle become like family. Maybe because it evokes the happy sounds of laughter and dancing in this spare, remote region of the state. Maybe it is because of the very nature of a fiddle itself. I have always associated a fiddle with the music of America's past, of a simpler time, a happier time. All of that is present within these old walls.

The museum grounds cover about twenty acres. An outside pavilion is used for fiddle concerts and gatherings. "We do about sixteen concerts a year out in the back," the curator told me. "Hundreds of people come from far and wide and make a day of it."

One thing I did find rather amusing was a case in the front of the display room. Inside it was an honor the museum received. It was the prestigious New York State Governor's Arts Council Award. "We were thrilled to receive that award," she told me. "What an honor for a fiddler's museum. Several of our members went down to the city and accepted the award from the folks who sat on the Board of the Council of the Arts. It was quite a time."

As I looked at the list of luminaries who made up the Board, I could only imagine what a hoot it must have been to see a few of those North Country fiddlers all dressed up and receiving their awards from newsman Dan Rather, Academy Award nominee Rosie Perez, and opera diva Beverly Sills!

The Nuts and Bolts

North American Fiddlers Hall of Fame and Museum
1121 Comins Road
Osceola, New York 13316
(315) 599-7009
www.nysotfa.com

• *Travel Suggestion*

As I said, this place is remote! Any directions to the museum can be confusing, but if you are coming from the north it can make a little sense. Travel on I-81 and get off at Exit 37. Head east. This will take you to the larger community of Redfield, where you can follow the blue fiddle signs to the museum five miles away.

• *Museum Hours*

The museum is open when there are events (concerts, picnics, shows, etc.) on the grounds. Traditionally this is from Memorial Day to the end of October. Events are frequent. You are welcome to call in advance to arrange to visit the museum at your convenience.

• *Admission*

Free

• *Number of Visitors Annually*

3,000

Up around the Bend

Twenty-five miles west of Osceola is the village of Pulaski. The entire center of the community is listed on the National Register of Historic

Places. The salmon is king here, and a great festival is held every year when the fish are running on the Salmon River. The Selkirk Lighthouse is a landmark (just west of the village on the shore of Lake Ontario). Its architecture is stunning and it is a much-visited tourist destination. Plus . . . it is reputed to be haunted. As a bonus, this 1838 working lighthouse is one of only a handful in the country where you can actually reserve to spend the night inside . . . just you and the ghosts. (www.salmonriverlight housemarina.com).

From Here to There
The other museum in this book that is nearest to the Fiddler's Museum is the **Safe Haven Museum** in Oswego. It is fifty miles west of Osceola.

35

ROBERT LOUIS STEVENSON
MEMORIAL COTTAGE AND MUSEUM
Saranac Lake, Franklin County

*T*his museum is a most unspectacular place. And yet there is something so important about it that it produces goose bumps on your arm the minute you step onto the property.

The ordinary-looking little cottage lies at the end of a dead end street, overlooking the Saranac River. It is white with green trim, and boasts a wide veranda and a split rail fence around a small yard. I stepped up onto the porch and first noticed a small bronze plaque. It was a historical marker adorned with a curious image of a bed on it. This would be the famous "cure beds" that hundreds would lie on as they recuperated here in the cold, crisp Adirondack air. Tuberculosis was the scourge.

Saranac Lake resident Dr. Edward Trudeau was the savior.

I walked around the front of the house and noticed a much larger bronze bas-relief plaque next to the front door. It shows the image of a tall, gaunt man in heavy woolen clothing and a hunter's cap. The legend reads: "Here dwelt Robert Louis Stevenson during the winter of 1887–1888." The sculptor's name is Gutzon Borglum, of Mount Rushmore fame.

I knew this was going to be interesting and I hadn't even stepped inside yet.

"Welcome, friend," said Mike Delahant, curator. "Come in and let me tell you the story of Robert Louis Stevenson."

For two hours, Mike regaled me with incredible stories of the great author's time spent here, in a place Stevenson called "The Little Switzerland of the Adirondacks."

"He came from Scotland to New York City and was extremely ill and was coughing up blood by the time he got here," Delahant began. "In fact, Stevenson personalized his coughing fits as 'Bloody Jack.' They suspected tuberculosis and he was looking for options for a remedy. Many of the experts told him to go to a 'dry, clean climate' to battle the disease. Colorado Springs was one option. The Adirondacks was another one."

As his ship, the steamer "Ludgate Hill," neared New York City his conditioned worsened, precluding a journey to faraway Colorado. His traveling party, consisting of American-born wife Fanny, his mother, and a stepson, chose Saranac Lake as the destination for the writer's recuperation.

Dr. Edward Trudeau had been producing remarkable results here with his studies on the immune system and his radical yet commonsense cure tactics to battle TB. Many famous people came here for the cure, and Stevenson was one of them.

Stevenson was in rough shape by the time he arrived, after an arduous journey from New York. He traveled from New York City by riverboat up the Hudson, then by rail to Plattsburgh, then by train aboard the still-under-construction Chateaugay Railroad to Loon Lake. The last twenty-five miles was by stagecoach.

"Trudeau never even knew the writer was in town until Stevenson got settled in and summoned the doctor to the Baker residence (his rental home and now the museum)."

Saranac Lake went star-crazy once the word got out about the dashing young author from Scotland living up at the Baker's farm and hunting lodge.

"Andrew Baker was a prominent guide and we even have the tent poles from the numerous tents he set up on their property for decades to lodge the so-called 'sports' that came from the cities for hunting and fishing excursions," Delahunt said. "The Bakers had never rented out an actual portion of their home until they made the arrangement with Stevenson during the winter of 1887–1888. In fact, the museum is four of the six rooms occupied by the author.

"The folks in town flipped when they found out that he was the author of *The Strange Case of Dr. Jekyll and Mr. Hyde.* The book was less than a year in print, and yet by the time Stevenson came to America there were already plays being performed of it."

Stevenson's arrival in New York City was unwittingly well-timed. In 1887, British authors had no copyright protection in the United States and he was totally unaware of the degree to which his books were being pirated over here. That is, until the *Ludgate Hill* docked.

"The public's Jekyll and Hyde fever was at full throttle when he arrived," Delahunt said. "In fact, he was actually accosted by American publishers upon his arrival."

While Stevenson convalesced in Saranac Lake, many of the major publishing firms in the country made the pilgrimage to the Baker residence to present him with astounding offers of royalty deals for future works.

"Charles Scribner, one of the great publishing giants of the era, actually tried to woo Stevenson into signing with his company by sending him up a favored pair of ice skates. We have them here in the museum," the curator told me.

"Scribner offered him a king's ransom in royalties. Stevenson was to be paid $3,500 for twelve essays and $8,500 for a full-length piece.

Stevenson's great *The Master of Ballantrae* got its start right here in this old house. He came to Saranac a poor, sickly man and left a millionaire (in today's money)," Delahant told me.

In one room are the writer's actual desk, chair, and day bed. Stevenson's dashing dark-purple smoking jacket and velvet hat are hanging on a rack as if waiting for the writer to return from an afternoon of ice-skating on Moody Pond (his ice skates are in this room, too). The writer's bedroom looks much as it did when he was writing during the long winter nights.

Dr. Trudeau visited him in this bedroom often. "Stevenson spent a lot of time in that bed," Delahant said as he pointed to the original bed still in the center of the room. "In fact, Trudeau once was quoted in the newspaper as saying: 'He was propped up on pillows with a pad of paper on his knees, cigarette in one hand, pen in the other. The room was filled with blue smoke and pages of manuscript tossed carelessly about the bed and the floor.'"

Stevenson was a chain smoker, which no doubt exacerbated his ill health. ("In fact, when asked his advice, Dr. Trudeau told the writer to 'stay in the Adirondacks and quit smoking!'") Mrs. Baker was no fan of his smoking, and it was a constant source of great friction between the landlord and her guest.

"Look over here, Chuck," Delahant said as we crossed the living room floor to the fireplace. "These are the most famous cigarette burns in the world," he laughed.

And sure enough, there they were. A series of deep dark burns etched into the massive mantelpiece above the fireplace, where the writer would leave errant cigarettes. You can almost hear the sounds of feisty old Mrs. Baker shouting and cursing at the famous writer echoing through the house today.

Mary Baker was once asked why she didn't repair the mantelpiece after her now-famous guest vacated the cottage. "Yes. See that! He 'bout ruined my mantelpiece," she said to a reporter. "I wanted my husband to build me a new one, but no one will let me do it. So there they are. It is all a lot of nonsense to me," she muttered.

The various rooms on the ground floor, where the writer and his family lived that winter, are crowded with amazing memorabilia. "Yes, we have the finest collection of Stevenson lore in the *world*," Delahant told me. In one case is a lock of the writer's hair from when he was an infant, in a corner sits an actual washtub he would have used. Letters from famous people, like President Herbert Hoover, and a signed photograph of actress Sarah Bernhardt line the shelves.

There is one note in particular that I found fascinating. The great sculptor Gutzon Borglum, a friend of the writer (although they never met), became a charter member of the Stevenson Society after his death. He returned year after year to the annual Board of Directors meetings. One year he couldn't attend. He sent a telegram, dated August 28, 1926, announcing he would not be there.

> Greetings to you and the speaker of the day, Mr. Bigelow. Sorry I cannot be with you. I am working on a big national monument on Mount Rushmore, Black Hills. Sincerely, Gutzon. Borglum, Mount Rushmore, S.DAK

Wow Factor

"For an author as prolific as Stevenson you would think there would be signed copies of his books all over the place," the curator told me as we walked over to a small display case in the back writer's room. "Not so."

Inside the case is the jewel of the collection. A signed first edition copy of *Treasure Island*. "He gave it to the young son of Mary Baker when he departed the residence. 'To Ralph Baker from the author. Christmas, 1887.' You will never see another one like that," Delahant told me.

I was amazed at how many wow factors there are spread throughout the five rooms of this museum. The signed book is definitely one of them, and is perhaps the rarest, most valuable item here.

But you have to admit; the cigarette-burned mantelpiece is pretty awesome!

The Take-Away

This museum and Grant's Cottage (also in this book) are completely different from almost any other museum you will find. It is not hyperbole to say that you can really feel the writer here (much as you can feel President Grant in his cottage).

This cottage is stuffed with Victorian era frou-frou. The fact that the cottage is so much as it was the day Stevenson left is really amazing, and adds tremendously to the impact of a visit here. There is a solemnity to it, an air of importance that is undeniable. Stevenson was a handsome devil, perhaps the Johnny Depp of his day. He was a charmer and a ladies' man, and was loved by all who met him. He was a world traveler. He was a supernova in the world of writers. He is one of the most translated authors in history. He was a boy genius (he had just turned 44 years old when he died on the South Pacific island of Samoa).

You can actually feel all of that as you wander from room to room in this rooming house where he spent that cold winter of 1888.

The world needs more people like Mike Delahant. His grandfather was the caretaker here, as was his father. And now Mike. He has fought a lonely fight against those who cannot see the importance of this little white house with the green trim. Those who see only a valuable piece of real estate here. Mike has poured a life's worth of sweat equity and money into keeping this flame alive for future aspiring writers who want to come and experience this hallowed upstate literary shrine.

And money is tight. Very tight.

"Yes, we need much, that is for sure," he told me. "We try and keep it open to the public every day. My wife and I live in the back of the building, so if somebody wanders up on the porch, I am right here to welcome them in."

And you never know who that "wanderer" might be.

"A couple of years ago I looked out and saw this elderly gentleman being escorted by two younger men approaching the house. I went out to greet them. The old guy ended up being the chairman of one of the most famous Wall Street financial firms of all times. I gave him a tour of the cottage. He was a big fan of Stevenson. Afterwards, he sat himself down in Robert Louis Stevenson's very own chair and said, "What do you need, Mike?" He was 103 years old and remembered that his mother read to him the author's work *A Child's Garden of Verses* when he was small.

"I thought for a minute, realizing this was the real deal. The cottage had been built directly on the ground and was in danger of shifting. So I went for it," the curator said. "I told him what I needed was a basement. He asked me to send him the paperwork"

Within three weeks this Wall Street tycoon sent Mike Delahant checks totaling $184,000. Hence the brand new basement.

"The man was a saint. He ultimately lived to be 107. I wish somebody like that would walk up here today. I could really use a public restroom and a parking lot," he laughed.

Like I said, you never know who that wanderer might be!

The Nuts and Bolts

The Robert Louis Stevenson Cottage and Museum
Stevenson Lane
Saranac Lake, New York 12983
(518) 891-1462
www.robertlouisstevensonmemorialcottage.org

• *Travel Suggestion*

Leave the Northway (I-87) at Lake Placid/Keene (Exit 30). Follow Route 9N to Keene and then pick up Route 73 to Lake Placid, and then Route 86 to Saranac Lake.

The drive to the Stevenson Cottage from the Northway is about a half hour.

Note: Saranac Lake straddles two New York counties: Essex and Franklin.

• *Museum Hours*

9:30 a.m. to 4:30 p.m. daily. Closed for lunch noon to 1 p.m. Closed Mondays.

• *Admission*

Adults: $5.00
Under 12: Free

• *Number of Visitors Annually*
   500

Up around the Bend

The Olympic Village of Lake Placid is a mere ten miles east of Saranac Lake. One of the prettiest villages in Upstate, Lake Placid pays tribute to its Olympic bloodline at every corner (it hosted the 1932 and 1980 Winter Olympics). Some of the original venues and training grounds are right in the village and a plethora of shops sell winter sports clothing and equipment. The giant ski slope, the Olympic cauldron, the bobsled runs, and more are all nearby. The Olympic Center is open for tours. Here, Jack Brooks's American ice hockey team stunned the Russians with a 4–3 victory in the 1980 Olympics.

Sports Illustrated called "The Miracle on Ice" the greatest sports moment of the twentieth century.

Famed abolitionist John Brown's farm and gravesite are located next to the giant ski jump. Singer Kate Smith, of "God Bless America" fame, was a forty-year summer resident of Lake Placid and her large pink mausoleum in St. Agnes Cemetery is one of the most visited sites in the village.

From Here to There

The other museum in this book that is nearest to the Stevenson Cottage is the **Slate Valley Museum** in Granville. It is 120 miles southeast of Saranac Lake.

36

WILDLIFE SPORTS AND
EDUCATIONAL MUSEUM

Vail Mills, Fulton County

I can't think of a spookier job to have in Upstate New York than to be the night watchman at the Wildlife Sports and Educational Museum.

You enter the cavernous fourteen thousand square foot facility and are greeted by more than one hundred stuffed deer heads all mounted and crowding several long walls. Their eyes stare out ghostlike as you pass by in review, reading the plaques which trumpet each dead deer's legacy. "Largest rack ever in North America," "Most points ever scored by a bow hunter," "World Record Gun Kill," and so on. Like I said, it is spooky.

"These here are the best of the best," Bob Kazmierski told me as he guided me around the wildlife mausoleum. He is the owner, president, and director of the museum and, clearly, its driving force. "That over there is the world record rack," he said as he pointed to a definitely sad-looking deer head high up on a wall. "1914, out of Wisconsin," he told me as I stared at the impossibly tangled horns intertwined over the deer's head. "It's been on magazine covers and had books written about it," he said proudly.

Sixty-five of the greatest taxidermy artists in North America are responsible for this unique entrance into this truly unique museum. The building seems as large as an airplane hangar. "It is our mission to tell the story of the evolution of outdoor sport in America," Bob told me. "We have skins, horseshoes, pelts, guns, bows and arrows, rods and reels, and of course one of the largest taxidermy displays anywhere."

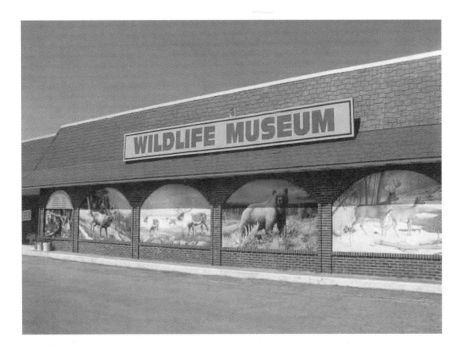

This is not just your deer head hanging over the fireplace mantle display, either. You'll see stuffed rattlesnakes that appear coiled and ready to strike, huge bears standing on their hind feet, a huge Southern New York Woodland Buffalo (the largest stuffed animal here), an albino deer, a two-headed calf, an eighty-pound salmon, a polar bear, and the biggest pike ever pulled from the Great Sacandaga Lake (which is nearby), a forty-six pound Northern Pike.

And a lion.

"This is the most expensive item in the place," Bob told me with pride as he pointed to a nearly indescribable display. A huge African lion is seen in full power fighting a duel to the death with a large spiked sable antelope. The word "visceral" hardly describes the tableau. "I paid $19,000 for that lion," Bob told me. "Worth every penny."

This place really is a treasure trove of "outdoors America." They have a bow and arrow that dates to the early 1600s. Some of their Kentucky rifles are the only ones left in existence. And then there is the stuffed passenger pigeon.

"That's the rarest item in the whole place," Bob told me.

Imagine, a place where stuffed regal lions storm the savannah, huge trout dance above painted waters, and the largest deer ever caught (a 400-pound Saskatchewan white-tailed deer caught in 1989) poses silently for all the world to see, and the rarest item in the museum is a little bird.

"Yup," said Bob. "Ain't none of them left anymore."

Wow Factor

"You're gonna love this item," Bob told me as we wove in and out of aisles crammed with every imaginable sporting item. We stopped in front of a large glass case exhibiting hunting traps of all kinds and sizes. Bob pointed to one in the lower left corner. It was a large old flat trap that looked like it could kill a human being.

"I'd have to say that is the wow factor in the museum," Bob said.

"Why?" I asked.

"Can you imagine that we found that trap up in the Adirondacks a few years ago? We brought it in for our museum. It was set up in the mountains to catch a bear. And the trap was set more than one hundred twenty years ago. When we found it, the trap had never been tripped. Think of it," he grinned. "That thing sat up there in the mountains for over a century just waiting to catch something, anything. And it never did. With all the wild animals, and hikers, and storms and falling branches, that thing just sat there waiting to take a chunk out of somebody or something. And look," he said as he pointed.

"The darn thing is still set."

The Take-Away

If you are not a hunter or fisherman or outdoors sportsman, you will be lost at this museum. It is attractive and fascinating, what with the hundreds of stuffed animals and birds. The real stories though are the ones about each of the individual species and the chase to bag, shoot, trap, or kill these beasts.

If you are lucky enough to meet Bob or any of the other volunteers here and have them take you around, you will be fascinated by the eye-opening stories of the great outdoors. Bob is a walking encyclopedia of nature facts,

Upstate New York history, and everything hunting and fishing. He is also a wildlife taxidermist, artist, and sculptor. Many of his works are on display.

I must say there is a certain beauty to all of the huge, violent, muscular "eat or be eaten" taxidermy on display. But the faint of heart, beware. It is quite graphic. (You'll know what I mean when you see the lion chomping down on the antelope.)

Kids, however, cannot get enough of this stuff and in fact make up more than half of the total of visitors each year.

The museum also houses the New York State Outdoorsman Hall of Fame. Bob Kazmierski is, of course, an inductee.

The Nuts and Bolts

The Wildlife Sports and Educational Museum
Corner of Route 29 and 30
Vail Mills, New York 12010
(518) 762-7925
www.wildlifesportsmuseum.com

• *Travel Suggestion*

Leave the New York State Thruway at Exit 27. Follow Route 30 north through Amsterdam. Keep going about eight miles to Vail Mills. The museum is right at the busy four corners intersection with Route 29.

• *Museum Hours*

Memorial Day to Labor Day, seven days a week, 10:30 a.m. to 5 p.m.

• *Admission*

There is a nominal admission price. Call for details.

A large number of bus coaches stop at the museum. For up to thirty guests, the fee is $8.00 per person.

For school groups of thirty or more, the cost is $4.00 per student.

• **Number of Visitors Annually**

3,000

Up around the Bend

If you have never been in this part of Upstate New York, I would suggest that for the "road less traveled" you do simply that. Take a drive! The Great Sacandaga Lake is right at your doorstep and many little villages adorn the shoreline. Mayfield would be a good place to start. Just north of Vail Mills, Mayfield has about eight hundred citizens and really reflects the small-town life in the foothills of the Adirondacks.

Oh, and don't forget to stop and see the liquor store that was built to look like a giant whiskey barrel! The Adirondack Whiskey Barrel and Spirits Store is located at 2474 Route 30, Mayfield. (To see a video, visit http://adirondackwhiskeybarrel.com/Location.html.)

From Here to There

The other museum in this book that is nearest to the Wildlife Sports and Education Museum is the **National Bottle Museum in Ballston Spa, N.Y.** It is twenty-five miles east of Vail Mills.

OTHER MUSEUMS TO
EXPLORE IN REGION SIX

Blue Mountain Lake: The Adirondack Museum. "It has been called one of the nation's most beautiful museums. With a backdrop of the glorious Adirondack Mountains, the campus consists of nearly two dozen buildings. The rustic furniture collection here is the largest in the U.S." (518) 352-7311, www.adkmuseum.org.

Croghan: American Maple Museum. "Founded in 1977 to preserve the history and evolution of the North American maple syrup industry." (315) 346-1107, www.americanmaplemuseum.org.

Gloversville: Glove Theatre Museum. "In the 1930s the historic Glove Theatre was one of the first movie houses in the U.S. to have sound equipment. The museum also has vintage candy machines and original, 1930s usher uniforms." (518) 773-8255, www.glovetheatre.org.

North Creek: North Creek Depot Museum. "Where Teddy Roosevelt first learned that William McKinley had died and that he, Roosevelt, was now President of the United States." (518) 251-5842, www.northcreekdepot museum.com.

Plattsburgh: Battle of Plattsburgh Museum. "Dedicated to developing and operating the Battle of Plattsburgh Interpretive Center and the War of 1812 Museum. The battle here was the last major engagement of the War of 1812." (518) 562-3534, www.battleofplattsburgh.org.

Tupper Lake: The Wild Center. You can explore the 31-acre campus on marked trails. There are theaters with high-definition films, plenty of hands-on activities, and hundreds of live animals from rare native trout to porcupines, hawks, and many other often hard-to-see residents of the woods and waters. (518) 359-7800, www.wildcenter.org.

Region Seven

THE CATSKILLS

Delaware, Greene, Ulster, and Sullivan Counties

37

HANFORD MILLS MUSEUM
East Meredith, Delaware County

I learned a brand new phrase on my most recent visit to Hanford Mills Museum. The phrase is "in situ."

"There you go, you learned something new today," laughed Liz Callahan, the energetic and amiable director of the museum. "It basically means you are where you were. A place that has not moved or been transferred. That's us!" she exclaimed.

Hanford Mills Museum is one of the top five mill museums in America. There are only about fifty, and this little Delaware County gem is among the best of the best. The facility sprawls over lawns and fields and forests and ponds. There are seventeen buildings in the complex, from small ice-block storage sheds to massive woodworking barns. The place positively oozes history.

"The Hanfords started this place well over a hundred years ago," Callahan told me. "Their buildings are still here, their workshops are still here, and in fact their homes are still here. All the buildings are preserved and open to the public. We are very proud that this historic place is fully authentic and fully operational."

The large clearwater pond is a dramatic centerpiece and bucolic backdrop to an image right out of a Grandma Moses sampler. The barns are bright red, the old horse wagons are waiting to be loaded, the Kortright Creek bubbles along providing the water that brings this place to life, and the sound of the 1890s steam boiler whistle harkens back to days of old. The staff is articulate and very knowledgeable about the history of the mill and the area.

I talked with Bob Adair, also known around these parts as "Woodworker Bob." Bob is an interpreter at the mill and also operates the woodworking shop. He knows this place like the back of his hand. He ought to. He was born here.

"My grandmother was Anna Hanford. Her uncle, John Hanford, and cousins Will and Horace Hanford, were the founders of Hanford Mills. I was born here at the mill, right over there," Bob told me as he pointed to the second floor of the old post office which is at the entrance to the property. (It now also houses the museum's shop, admissions, and office.)

"Yes, this place was always buzzing with excitement. I started out at a sawmill, worked for many years at one, my father's first job was at a sawmill, and now that I am retired I still come to the sawmill every day."

Woodworker Bob just can't get the sawdust out of his blood. "I love it here," he told me. "The romance of working with tools that are more than a century old just cannot be described. People like to see me make butter tub covers, which is a specialty item we make. The barrel head machine used in the Mill was actually invented just down the road in Oneonta by William Mickel. I still use the very first machine that Will and Horace used to make thousands of tub covers. It was purchased by the Hanford's in 1876. Works just like new," Woodworker Bob laughed.

Hanford Mills is a living trust in many ways. The place is generally quiet, with an up-tick in the summer tourist months. If you do visit, you should plan to come during one of their many annual festivals. An active lineup of lumberjack shows, steam engine jamborees, miller's harvests, cooking events, junior woodsman's camps, and more really bring this place to life.

"The ice harvest festival in February is one of the most unique events in the area," Callahan told me. "Our pond freezes over and the public is invited to join us in harvesting (cutting) the ice blocks and putting them on the sleds. They are then taken to the ice shed where, packed expertly in sawdust (no electricity!), the ice will still be usable in the summer months. Just like they used to do it in the old days. We always get a large crowd, and it is great fun."

Hanford Mills Museum is a little gem of a place tucked away in the beautiful hills of northern Delaware County. In the autumn, it is unforgettable here.

Wow Factor

I have been to the mill several times, and without a doubt the wow factor here is the giant water wheel. You walk into the bowels of a hulking old barn that sits astride Kortright Creek. There, in front of you, is a gigantic wooden water wheel, sitting silent and ominous. At the shout of "let her go!" the water from the creek is shunted into the barn and the monster wheel slowly creaks to life.

Soon more than 6,000 gallons per minute of clear cold creek water is cascading over the 13-foot-tall wheel as it starts whirring and spinning faster and faster. As it does, dozens of giant pulleys and belts, powered by the wheel, become activated and the place comes alive. To witness this display of waterpower is an awesome experience, one that is unmatched in Upstate New York.

"The Hanfords bought this Fitz Water Wheel in 1928," the director told me. "It is one of the only ones like it in the country."

I asked her what the reaction to this dramatic event is like when she brings the many school groups that visit Hanford Mills down to watch the wheel in action.

"I don't want to say they are scared, but it gets awfully quiet all at once. The kids stare at this huge towering wheel spinning and the water splashing and the belts whirring and the whole building just shuddering, all just a few feet in front of them. Their eyes are as big as saucers," she laughed.

The Take-Away
Be sure and schedule your visit here during an event or festival. In the autumn, the mill is gorgeous and is a perfectly lovely place to spend the afternoon. There is not a lot to *do* here, but there is a lot to *see*. For a guided tour of the complex, I would suggest you set aside at least an hour to really see and enjoy it all. The staff and volunteers at the Hanford Mills Museum are dedicated to preserving not only one of the last working mills of its type in the state, but also of preserving a way of life now long gone.

A century ago, the four corners out in front of the mill would have been as busy a place as any in this rural county. Wagons lined up to deliver or pick up products at the mill. General stores selling wares to the folks who trekked in to East Meredith from afar. A couple of churches. A classic old one-room schoolhouse (still here), and more. This is the kind of snapshot of life a hundred years ago that was played out all across the country in small mill towns just like this one.

It is not hard to imagine the ghosts of the Hanford family scurrying around to mind their stores and mills. This place is a great, living reminder of those simpler days of old.

You will enjoy your visit to the Hanford Mills Museum. And don't forget to ask them to turn on the water wheel!

The Nuts and Bolts
Hanford Mills Museum
73 County Highway 12
East Meredith, New York 13757
(607) 278-5744
www.hanfordmills.org

- *Travel Suggestion*

   From Oneonta, go east seven miles on Route 23 to Davenport Center. Here, at the junction of Route 23 and County Route 10, you will see the sign for the museum, which is just another three miles down the road.

- *Museum Hours*

   May 15 through October 15: Wednesday to Sunday 10 a.m. to 5 p.m.

- *Admission*

   Adults and children over 13: $8.50
   Seniors and AAA: $6.50
   Active and retired military: $4.25
   Members and children under 13: Free
   About 20 percent of all visitors are school groups. Contact the museum to make special arrangements for your group.

- *Number of Visitors Annually*

   About 7,000

Up around the Bend

A perfect companion to any visit to the Hanford Mills Museum is the West Kortright Centre (www.westkc.org).

   This beautiful arts and entertainment venue is located just two miles up the road from the mill. The venue is a stunning classic 160-year-old Greek Revival church situated in a hollow along a dirt road. Now a National Historic Landmark, the center has a full schedule of live entertainment, focusing mostly on world music and international arts. If you nail a perfect summer evening at the centre (after an afternoon at the mill), you will forever remember the experience of hearing and seeing top-notch international stars performing in a tiny, pristine, acoustically perfect old church. The pews are original, as is the stained glass. The entertainment runs from Shakespeare to jazz to Zydeco to folk singers to dance troupes to live theatre.

   It is in the middle of nowhere, but seems in the middle of everywhere.

From Here to There
The other museum in this book that is nearest to the Hanford Mills Museum is the **Maywood Depot Museum** in Sidney Center. It is located twenty-five miles west of East Meredith.

38

GREATER FLEISCHMANNS MUSEUM OF MEMORIES

Fleischmanns, Delaware County

From the late 1800s up to today, the fortunes of the village of Fleischmanns have risen and fallen like a bad batch of yeast. Only don't say it was Fleischmann's Yeast. That was the gold standard of yeasts!

Charles Fleischmann brought the secret of his "miracle yeast" with him to America in 1865. He turned his product into the first commercially produced yeast (sold in cakes) and helped usher in the era of mass-produced bakery products. Over the next several years, he continued to grow his company and create other inventions that were successful. By 1870, when he created the first commercially made gin in the country, he was one of the richest men in America.

And he started looking for a summer place.

"Mr. Fleischmann first came to Griffin Corners (the village's first name) around 1881," John Duda, one of four trustees of the Fleischmanns Museum of Memories, told me. "Of course he was fabulously wealthy so money was no object to him. He built a nineteenth-century version of the Kennedy compound right here in the hills overlooking the village. Five gigantic mansions in all, for various family members. One of them is still standing," he told me.

Years later when the Fleischmann family decided to pack it all in and leave for the Midwest, they donated a large baseball field to the community for general use.

"To show their appreciation, the village decided to rename itself after their benefactor," Duda said. "In fact, baseball was an important part of

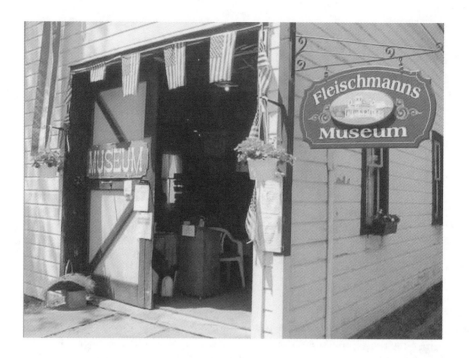

our town's growth. We had this big beautiful field, we fielded a team of stellar ballplayers (including two of Fleischmann's sons) and soon a regional league sprang up. There was some great baseball played in those days. Even major league players came up to play pick-up games. Of course, they had to play under assumed names for contractual reasons. We know that Miller Huggins and Honus Wagner, both Baseball Hall of Famers, played here in Fleischmanns," Duda said.

The Museum of Memories is chock full of local history, railroadiana, sports memorabilia, and thousands of photos of the community's heyday as a major Catskill resort.

"The hotels up here were mammoth," Peggy Kearney, another museum trustee, told me. "We had dozens of these huge hotels all over the hills around town. There is only one left," she said.

The last survivor is a hulking four-story place called the St. Regis (now Oppenheimer's St. Regis). I drove the half-mile out of town to see it. The blue cement pool, the dozens and dozens of colorful chairs dotting the landscape, and the huge dining facility all reminded me of an era when this area was the most popular destination out of New York City for many resorters, during the early part of the twentieth century.

"Yes, we were hopping here in Fleischmanns, long before things started to get busy down in Sullivan County," Duda told me. "The families would stay all week, but the men would come up on the trains Friday and go back to New York City on Sunday. They called them 'Husband Trains' or 'Crying Trains' because so many woman wept when the men left the depot to go back to the city."

Sullivan County would follow soon after to become the home of the famed Borscht Belt.

One of the most interesting sections of the Museum of Memories is what is known as "School Corner." The documentation of the past hundred years or so of the community's school history is exhaustive and very interesting.

"We have many graduates who come back here after decades, and they can still find their faces looking back at them from any of these dozens of school class photos. In fact, the earliest class photo we have, taken on a school class trip to Washington, D.C., in 1936, was just brought in to us two weeks ago," Kearney laughed.

A surprising section of "School Corner" is one dedicated to old "excuse notes." These were actual notes taken to the school nurse or principal that were donated to the museum years ago. The notes, in their simplicity, bespeak the rural nature of life in Fleischmanns over the last century or so.

"Please excuse my daughter from school as she has to help her father birth a calf this morning," read one. "My son won't be in school today because he has extra chores to do," is another. Of all of them, however, my favorite was this cryptic one, dated December 14, 1952: "Georgiana was out of school on November 30 for an illegal reason."

Makes you wonder, doesn't it?

Wow Factor

"Our two stars," Duda told me.

He walked me to a case containing historical material regarding Amelita Galli-Curci. "Of course people don't know her today, but she was a great opera star during a period of between 1910 and 1920. She was hailed as "the world's greatest coloratura," he told me.

She was extremely wealthy, having been one of the most successful of the early operatic recording stars. She had worldwide fame and yet decided to live for many years in the lush green mountains along the Delaware and Ulster County border in Fleischmanns.

"Her mansion, Sul Monte, was built here in 1922. It is still occupied today," he said.

The other shining star in Fleischmanns's past is legendary entertainer Gertrude Berg.

"Berg's father, Jacob Edelstein, bought the sprawling Fleischmanns compound when that family moved out. Edelstein's daughter used to entertain the guests at the compound by singing, dancing, and putting on theatrical productions. That young girl was Gertrude Berg," he said with a smile.

Berg, known to millions of her fans as Molly Goldberg, was a true pioneer in radio and television, and in women's issues. She was the first actress to ever win a comedy Emmy Award, and she won many other show business awards over her long career. She won a Tony Award for her role in the 1959 Broadway production of A *Majority of One*.

"We all love our dear Molly here in Fleischmanns," Ms. Kearney told me. "We have family photos of her, signed scripts, her books, some of her personal letters, and many other artifacts from her career. And of course we have her forever right here, too," she whispered.

Gertrude "Molly Goldberg" Berg is buried in the Clovesville Cemetery in Fleischmanns.

The Take-Away

This little museum is right up my alley. Lots of local history, an enormous photographic archive, some curious pieces (including lots of old telephone memorabilia from the town's historic central phone station), and much more. And . . . some vintage Opera and Hollywood material to boot!

The museum is located inside an old carriage house right behind the Skene Memorial Library. Andrew Carnegie donated some of the money to build the ornate library in 1901.

An unusual side to Fleischmanns is its incredible multicultural diversity.

"We have a large segment of Hasidim who live here in the summer, as well as a large segment of Mexicans and Mexican-Americans who have found us over the years. We have Mexican stores and cantinas as well as Orthodox households and Yeshiva summer camps. We also have many residents whose families go as far back as the American Revolution. It makes for a great mix. If nothing else, Fleischmanns is one of the warmest and most welcoming communities you will ever find," said Duda.

The Nuts and Bolts

The Greater Fleischmanns Museum of Memories
Main Street (behind the Skene Memorial Library)
Fleischmanns, New York 12430
Trustee Peggy Kearney: (845) 254-5311
Trustee John Duda: (845) 254-4104
There is no specific museum website. For area information: www
.margaretville.org (click on Fleischmanns)

• *Travel Suggestion*
N.Y. Route 28 goes the whole length of the western Catskills, from Oneonta to Delhi to Andes to Margaretville to Fleischmanns to Big Indian to Phoenicia and on south to Kingston. It is one of Upstate's loveliest mountain roads. It passes several beautiful bodies of water that are reservoirs that serve as water suppliers to New York City. Fleischmanns sits on the border between Delaware and Ulster counties. New York State–owned ski resort Belleayre Mountain is five miles away.

• *Museum Hours*
Open Memorial Day through Columbus Day, Saturdays 11 a.m. to 3 p.m.
The museum will also be open random days in the summer and by special appointment. You are advised to call first before going on a day other than Saturday.

• *Admission*
  Free (Donations are gratefully accepted.)

• *Number of Visitors Annually*
  1,000

Up around the Bend

Just six miles up Route 28 from the museum is Arkville, N.Y. This little community has a rich railroad history and is the home of one of the best small train excursions in Upstate. The main business district has some small shops and eating options, but the real draw is the Delaware and Ulster Rail Ride. The train ride (www.durr.org) stays busy all summer long, and is extremely active when the leaves turn this region into a crazy quilt of autumnal colors. The Arkville train depot has a nice, small gift shop with railroad souvenirs.

From Here to There

The other museum in this book that is nearest to the Fleischmanns Museum of Memories is the **Old Stone Fort Museum**. It is fifty miles northeast, in Schoharie.

39

Trolley Museum of New York

Kingston, Ulster County

From Brooklyn to Kingston, these trolley tracks have wandered through the years until they reached here, their final destination.

The Trolley Museum was founded in Brooklyn, N.Y., in 1955, but for many years it had no tracks or building of its own. The Brooklyn group had done a good job of collecting and preserving trolley cars and subway cars that would otherwise have been scrapped and lost to history. The collection was scattered far and wide, from Philadelphia to Coney Island, but they had no way to run the cars.

Kingston, meanwhile, had some interesting railroad trackage that was no longer being used. In 1983, arrangements were made to bring the cars to Kingston and put the trackage to use. It was a marriage made in heaven. The trackage begins in the historic Rondout area of Old Kingston and runs out along the Hudson River.

The Rondout area itself is abuzz with trendy shops, pubs, cafes, and restaurants. The physical setting is wonderful, with boats gliding by on the Rondout Creek, old-fashioned-looking gas lamps, and brick and stone paved walkways.

The Trolley Museum is a working museum, with rows of actual train tracks stitching across an industrial area at the end of the shimmering business district. When you arrive, you look over a faux wrought iron fence and into an old train yard where several trolley cars in varying states of renovation sit idly. Up and above it all is a large building with a small sign denoting it as the "Trolley Museum of New York."

The building is a re-creation of the one that the railroad used for the same purpose one hundred years earlier: housing and working on the rail equipment. In fact, this building is built on the same foundation as the original railroad building.

This museum is great.

As I walked into the yards for my pre-arranged visit (the Trolley Museum was officially closed the day I got there), I was met by a small army of museum greeters. I was introduced to volunteers, conductors in period clothing, motormen, tour guides, and Jon McGrew, the museum's president.

"All aboard," the motorman hollered as a bright orange-and-cream-colored trolley car inched closer to me. I got on, and off we went. The sign over the motorman read "Johnstown #358."

"We got this one, which was originally from Johnstown, Pennsylvania," McGrew told me. "Its life began in 1925, and it was an electrified trolley. It later ended up in Stone Mountain, Georgia, which is where we got it."

It was a beauty. After a nine-year restoration, the results are spectacular. The paint job was immaculate. The genuine rattan seats were comfortable and reversible, so you were always facing forward, both coming and going on your trip. The gleaming brass work and the wood sides and ceiling shone like new. The windows were wide open to catch the river breeze. I asked Jim Steipp, our motorman for my private trolley ride, how he liked his job.

"Who wouldn't like it," he said. "I get to dress in these cool clothes every day and take folks on this wonderful trip. And I don't even have to steer," he smiled.

And what a ride it is. The trolley ride takes you a mile out of the Rondout, clinging to the Hudson River on the last half of the trip. It rolls right along the water's edge, and the view is one of the best along the whole river. The Hudson is wide here, making a stunning palette for everything you see. The mountains across the river, the sweeping homes and mansions hugging the far side, the old Rhinecliff train station directly across from you and as the centerpiece for this magical canvas, the ancient Kingston Lighthouse right smack dab in the middle of everything. The bluestone lighthouse marks the confluence of the Hudson River and Rondout Creek.

When the Hudson River School painters described awe-inspiring vistas of the river, this must have been what they were talking about.

The trolley ride ends at a park.

"We let visitors off the trolley here for about fifteen minutes before we return," McGrew told me. "They love to wander through the park or walk down to the water to just sit and admire the view." Kingston Point Park marked the area where the largest port on the river between New York and Albany once stood.

"It was the busiest of places back then," McGrew explained. "Dayliners, which plied the Hudson with large steam-powered excursion passenger ships, would bring tourists up from New York City as far as here, and another whole group would sail down from Albany. They all met right here at this park. There once was a large amusement park right here for the entertainment of the tourists."

After a far-too-short stop at the park we flipped our seats over and headed back to the museum. When we approached, a large metal door slowly opened and we slipped right in. It then closed behind us. (I remember a similar scene like this in a James Bond movie once, only I think it involved space ships.)

Inside the "shop" you will find an astonishing array of vintage trolleys from around the country and around the world. Some of the destination signs on the front of the cars sound wistfully familiar: The Bronx, Coney Island, and Vanderbilt Avenue.

"And over here are our cars from around the world," McGrew told me. "We have a 1910 car from Brussels, Belgium." He showed me the lemon-yellow car. It was gorgeous. "And yes, they still have trolley cars over there today," he smiled.

Also on display are a 1912 Gothenburg tram, a Swedish trolley car, plus a 1952 car from Hamburg, Germany. All of them, including trolley cars from Brooklyn, have informational signs in front of them.

Wow Factor

"Which one is the oldest in the museum's collection?" I asked.

The museum president walked me over to a relic from the past that still exuded great charm and class. "This one right here," he said as he patted the side of a colorfully painted car. "This is an 1897 electric street car from Oslo, Norway."

"I love this car. And not just because of its age. The craftsmanship of it all makes it so unique. It is made of wood, not metal, and it is just in such beautiful condition. It is reported to have been used by the King of Norway." And then the museum president thought for a minute.

"But, still, I think the wow factor for the visitors has to be the trolley ride. They stare out over the Hudson with wide eyes as it unfolds in front of them. The trolley car puts them into an aura of nostalgia and then the view along the ride just knocks them out. Because of our tracks running right along the water, we believe that the Trolley Museum here in Kingston really offers a unique and wonderful experience for our museum guests."

The Take-Away

This museum does not disappoint. It is a thrill for all ages to take the trolley ride out along the river, for sure. Once back inside the shop, the old cars stand at attention as you walk by in review, reading of their history and lineage. The shop is a bit dusty and cramped, but despite the grit, this museum has heart.

The whole Rondout area is alive with renewal. On the day I was there, as dusk descended, the street lamps came on and whole clutches of walkers filled the sidewalks. The restaurants and cafes lit up with an amber glow emanating from within. Laughter and chatter filled the riverfront.

And there, at the end of the line (literally) stood the Trolley Museum ready for the future yet proud of its past. I think the museum is perfectly situated in this historic area, and I would encourage any and all who visit the Rondout to stop in and answer the clarion call from Motorman Jim, "All aboard!"

The Nuts and Bolts
The Trolley Museum of New York
89 East Strand Street
Kingston, New York 12401
(845) 331-3399
www.TMNY.org (also on Twitter and Facebook)

- *Travel Suggestion*
  The museum is located about two hours north of New York City and an hour south of Albany. Leave the Thruway at Exit 19. Follow the signs to "Historic Kingston Rondout Waterfront."

- *Museum Hours*
  Open Memorial Day to Columbus Day
  Saturdays, Sundays, and holidays noon to 5 p.m.
  Charter bus tour groups by appointment.

- *Admission*
  Adults: $6.00
  Children and seniors: $4.00
  Children under 5 ride for free.
  Note: There are no set times for the trolley rides down to the Park. The museum staff simply waits for a small group to gather and then takes them on the trip down the old Ulster and Delaware Railroad

causeway to the riverfront. The rail ride is about a mile each way, with a short stop at the park at the end. It takes a total of about fifty minutes.

- *Number of Visitors Annually*
  Unknown

Up around the Bend

That's an easy one. Just cross the street!

The Hudson River Maritime Museum is a gleaming, modern show-case of the history of commerce and trade along the Hudson River. It is housed in an old warehouse with graceful red bricks. It is the only museum solely dedicated to the preservation of the history of the Hudson River. Many ships dock along its three hundred and fifty feet of river front-age, and boat rides out to the Rondout lighthouse begin here.

You can't miss this museum. The giant 1898 steam tugboat *Mathilda* sits in its backyard.

This is a first-class museum well worth the five hundred paces from the Trolley Museum. In fact, the Trolley passes the Hudson River Mari-time Museum and can stop there on request. More than 20,000 tourists a year visit the Maritime Museum (www.hrmm.org).

From Here to There

The other museum in this book that is nearest to the Trolley Museum is the **Gomez Mill House Museum** in Marlboro. It is twenty-five miles south of Kingston.

40

CATSKILL FLY FISHING MUSEUM
Livingston Manor, Sullivan County

*T*he permanent sign hanging from the front door of this museum should read: "Fish Tales Told Here"

"We are the largest fly fishing center of its kind in the world," said Jim Krul, Executive Director of the Catskill Fly Fishing Center and Museum. "People come from all over the world to immerse themselves in our history and lore. And being situated on one of the great trout fishing rivers in the East (Willowemoc Creek) doesn't hurt either," he said.

We started our tour on the outside. All along the attractive log building that is the museum are a series of bronze-cast plaques. This is the museum's version of their Hall of Fame. Other than writer Zane Grey, I hardly recognized any of the names. But then, I am not a fly fisherman.

"All of these people are key to the growth and development of fly fishing in America. Among the names are champion fishermen, sports writers, creators of innovative fishing equipment, and more. And there are several important women honored on the wall also," Krul told me.

"Julia Freeman Fairchild, for example. In 1931, she organized the very first fishing organization for women. It was called The Women Flyfishers Club and she was president of it for more than forty years. She was quite a gal."

The stories of all of the Hall of Famers are interesting, and eventually, as we slowly walked around the entire building looking at the dozens of plaques, I did recognize a name on the wall.

"What is he doing here?" I said incredulously.

Krul smiled. "I knew you'd say something when we reached him. Who doesn't know Robert Redford! He was inducted into our Hall of Fame in the Class of 2007. He is such an amazing person, a conservationist, a naturalist, and a benefactor to so many of the great causes our museum stands for. And of course there was that little movie he once made."

A River Runs Through It, I offered.

"Yup. More people became interested in fly-fishing after that film than from anything else we have ever done for a century. It really gave us, and the sport, such a tremendous boost."

Among the many supporters of the museum are Supreme Court Justice Sandra Day O'Connor, former Federal Reserve chairman Paul Volcker, talk show host Sally Jesse Raphael, and actors Rip Torn and Mark Ruffalo, as well as Donald Trump, Jr., who sits on the Board of Directors.

Krul's enthusiasm grew tenfold once we opened the front door to the museum. And for good reason.

"Just look at this!" he fairly shouted, spreading his arms out wide. "It takes my breath away every time I come in here."

It *is* wonderful.

The gigantic room features hundreds of artifacts from the fly-fishing timeline. From the very first reed rods to the latest, most sophisticated lures. Everything is very intricate, all items are displayed professionally, and they all have a unique story to tell. It is curious how such a tiny little thing as a handmade fishing tie can have such a long and interesting story. Be sure and ask about the "pink" tie that was colored using (ahem) something natural from a stuffed red vixen fox found at a bar in downtown Roscoe.

Artwork lines the high walls, photos by the hundreds tell the story of the sport and its people, and long lines of display cases show off the mementos of lives spent standing in the river. One item that will definitely catch your eye is sculptor Paul Theising's nine-foot-tall carving of a brown trout, nicknamed "Big Mo." Don't worry, you won't overlook that!

Many international visitors come to the museum each year. "We have a revolving display which changes every year. It features a different country each year, and they send items for us to display." Italy was the nation featured during my visit.

"My favorite," Krul told me, "was the year we featured Japan. They sent a delegation over to present the items to us. We had a big ceremony, and then the Japanese gentlemen asked to go down to the creek and fish. We watched them from afar. The relationship between the Japanese fishermen, the outdoors, the river, the fish, the whole thing, was just amazing to watch. It was so reverential to see the respect they showed for nature. They caressed each fish they caught, said a prayer over them and then released them back into the Willowemoc. Many of us had tears in our eyes," Krul reflected.

In his own version of a "lightning round," the executive director has a flashy bon mot for all of the revered names honored at the museum. Lee Wulff? "Died in a plane crash at 86. He was the 'Father of Catch and Release.' A towering man." His wife, Joan Wulff? "Quite simply, the greatest fly caster in the world." Lefty Kreh? "One of the greatest pioneers of the sport." Rube Cross? "A hustler. First one to turn this sport into a business. A genius." Ed Hewitt? "He did it all. He was featured in *LIFE* magazine in 1946." Herman Christian? "He could smell the best fishing spot on the river. He was the #1 fishing guide." Art Flick? "He was the first to match the fly to an actual insect through photography, and to document the actual insect hatching cycles. He owned the West Kill Tavern over in Schoharie. He'd catch bugs and put them in his beer cooler to 'slow them down.' This would keep them for a couple of days to be professionally photographed. Poul Jorgenson, the greatest fly tyer of all time, would photograph them."

And on and on it goes.

Wow Factor

"We try and feature some of the famous people who were known to love fly fishing," Krul told me as he pointed to an odd mixture of ordinary items. "These all belonged to Clark Gable. He was one of Hollywood's most recognized fishermen and was photographed fly fishing many times."

Among the movie star's memorabilia in the possession of the museum are his writing desk, a chair, some monogrammed tableware, some small personal items, and his fishing rods and reels. His wicker creel hangs in the display, also. Next to his fishing items are those of his wife, actress Carole Lombard.

The Take-Away

Not being a fly fisherman, I would say that for those like me, an hour might be enough time spent here. If you *are* a fly fisherman, or want to be one, you'll never want to leave.

Clearly this is a spot as near to heaven as any fisherman can get. The Willowemoc runs about twenty-five miles long, intersecting with the Beaver Kill. Nearby Roscoe is known as "Trout Town U.S.A." This small region of the western Catskills is among the richest trout fishing centers in the U.S. Even President Jimmy Carter has been known to show up and put on a pair of rubber pants and wade into the water to try his luck.

Livingston Manor is located in the heart of the Catskill Mountains and is known as "The Birthplace of American Dry Fly Fishing," and this medium-sized museum does it great honor.

A word to the wise, though. To enter the fifty-three acre museum grounds, you have to drive over a seemingly small, arched bridge over the Willowemoc. I slammed on the brakes when I made the turn at the museum sign. I really didn't think my small car would fit over the rattling boards to the other side. I slowly crept over and into the museum parking lot.

When I mentioned this to Mr. Krul, he chuckled. "Oh, don't worry about that old bridge. The UPS guy barrels over it every day to bring us packages."

I felt a little sheepish.

It would be very hard for me to pick a more peaceful, beautiful, natural setting for any other museum I visited for this book. Or for any other museum, anywhere. Period.

The Nuts and Bolts

The Catskill Fly Fishing Museum
1031 Old Route 17
Livingston Manor, New York 12758
(845) 439-4810
www.catskillflyfishing.org; www.facebook.com/cffcm

• *Travel Suggestion*
Obviously, the best way to reach the museum is to access it off Route 17. There are not a lot of signs along the highway, so I would suggest you exit at Roscoe. From the exit you will see signs pointing you to the museum on Old Route 17 (which runs parallel to the main highway). Also, by going this way you will have to pass the Roscoe Diner on your way to the museum, making the route back to those garlicky pickles familiar to you when you return.

• *Museum Hours*
April through October: 10 a.m. to 4 p.m. daily
November through March: Tuesday to Friday 10 a.m. to 3 p.m.; Saturday 10 a.m. to 4 p.m.
Note: Call in advance, as the museum has 35 event days during the summer.

- *Admission*
  Adults: $4.00
  Students 14 and under: $2.00

- *Number Of Visitors Annually*
  8,000

Up around the Bend
After a visit to the museum, make the short five-mile trip to the Roscoe Diner. It was built on busy Route 17 in 1967 and is considered to be one of the most popular eating establishments in Upstate New York. Located approximately halfway between New York City and Binghamton, the diner, known for their huge sandwiches, free table-side bowls of garlicky dill pickles, and towering desserts, has been known to serve as many as two thousand meals a day!

From Here to There
The other museum in this book that is nearest to the Catskill Fly Fishing Museum is the **Greater Fleischmanns Museum of Memories**. It is located about twenty-five miles northeast of Livingston Manor.

41

Maywood Depot Museum

Sidney Center, Delaware County

"All aboard for Maywood!"

Perhaps one of the most popular places to house a museum or historical society in Upstate New York is in an old railroad building. There are many. Small country depots. Large train stations. Historic railroad buildings. Yes, Upstate New York was "railroad country" many decades ago, and these old buildings, all of them, played a part in it.

Few of them tell it with more charm and nostalgia than here at the Maywood Historical Museum in the old Sidney Center train depot.

The building is small, but its importance was large. The little depot sits on a high bluff overlooking the tiny pastoral village below it. The view from the Maywood Depot is lovely. Sidney Center sits in a natural swale in a landscape consisting mostly of hills and mountains. Because of the geographic depression the village sat in, it was difficult (if not impossible) for the old freight trains running through here to crawl down into Sidney Center and then claw their way up and out of it. So, ingenuity stepped in and gave the village its unique footnote in history.

The "largest floating trestle in the East."

The trestle was constructed over the community so the trains could keep their speeds at an even pace coming through here carrying milk, freight, mail, passengers, and livestock.

"By the 1870s our giant horseshoe trestle was nearly 3,000 feet long, in two sections," Bob Pomeroy told me. Bob is an officer at the historical society located at the depot. "It was over 100 feet in the air. It was quite a sight to see."

Bob told me one of his favorite childhood memories of the old floating trestle.

"I remember when I was a kid in the 1950s, we had a real bad snowstorm. We had a couple of feet of snow on the ground in town. And because the trains still needed to get through, the O&W sent one of their big snow trains with a big 'V' plow on the front of it to clear the trestle. Well, remember, the trestle was up there," he said while pointing to the sky. "So when the plow came through clearing the tracks, all the snow up there had to go someplace, didn't it?

"You guessed it. It all came down on the houses and streets below and dumped another foot on top of us," he laughed. "Oh, people were a might mad at that."

The Maywood Depot was the hub of activity in Sidney Center's heyday (the trestle was torn down in 1959). Today it is a restored marvel. Though very small, it is not difficult to conjure the images, sights, and sounds of the once-bustling depot of the past. The floors are in excellent shape, the wooden wainscoting gleams, the gilded ticket cage shines like new, and the large baggage room in the rear of the building is now used for a variety of community events.

The front of the building houses an amazing array of historical artifacts related to the village and the railroad that came through here, the Ontario and Western (or the "O&W," or the even more familiarly heard "Old and Weary").

The old railroad photos papering the walls are a truly amazing look at the history of the O&W, and some of the items housed here are especially historic.

"We have the only complete collection of O&W railroad lanterns in existence. Each color was swung by a trackside attendant to signal a particular condition. Yellow meant caution, red meant stop, white meant a flag stop, etc.

"We are very proud of our collection of lanterns," Pomeroy told me as he pointed them out in a large display case. "They are rare. No reproductions here," he laughed.

Other sources of pride are the 125-year-old blueprints for the depot and the floating trestle. They are all displayed in the small, crowded museum.

"Sidney Center doesn't have a lot any more," he said. "Especially since our big, main church burned down recently. But we do have Maywood, and we are extremely proud of its history and its future. We have a sturdy bunch of volunteers who work very hard to keep it up so nice here, and we get railroad buffs who come here and tell us this depot is as nice as they have seen anywhere in the country."

The small gift shop sells many items with the Maywood Depot logo on them, as well as many books on railroad history.

Wow Factor
When I asked Bob to tell me the "wow factor" item here at Maywood he got real quiet.

"You know, despite all of the great railroad history we have here, the real story is right over there on that wall," he said, as he pointed to a display on the wall leading from the front of the building to the baggage room. "Now that is a story."

On the wall is a tribute to the "Seven Sons of Sidney Center."

These were seven native sons of the little community who went off to serve in the Vietnam War and never came back. All seven died within 51 days of each other. On the wall are photographs of the young men smiling back at you from now-40-year-old picture frames, the newspapers telling of their deaths, the letters of condolence from the White House, the cemetery flags, the Vietnam Wall name rubbings.

The national press, newspapers, and magazines came searching through the back roads of Delaware County looking to tell this sad story oh those many years ago. Many reported it as "the largest loss of life in the war proportionate to the size of the community from whence the boys came." It would take years for Sidney Center to recover from this tremendous blow.

"Yes," Pomeroy said as he scratched his head, "those boys are the real story to be told here at Maywood."

The Take-Away

What is not to like about this little treasure? It has something for everyone, and the people really love to show you around. It is very small, and a half hour should be more than enough time spent here.

The inside of the depot is packed with interesting local and railroad history, and the view outside is gorgeous. Even though the giant floating trestle is gone, it is not hard to imagine it winding its way above the little town below. I strongly suggest that you make your visit on a Sunday night in the summer. That is when they hold their community ice cream socials, and the feeling of small town U.S.A. really presents itself on those evenings.

The Nuts and Bolts

The Maywood Historical Society and Museum
Depot Street
Sidney Center, New York 13839
(607) 369-7592
www.mhgonline.org

- *Travel Suggestion*
  Sidney Center is located off I-88 (Exit 10), between Sidney and Unadilla. Travel down the Back River Road (not N.Y. Route 7) about a mile, and turn left at County Route 23. Go eight miles to Sidney Center and turn right on Depot Street.

- *Museum Hours*
  May through December: every Saturday 10 a.m. to noon
  May through September: every Tuesday 10 a.m. to 2 p.m.
  Special appointments are welcome.

- *Admission*
  Free (but donations are more than welcome).

- *Number of Visitors Annually*
  1,500

Up around the Bend
For a fun side trip, make your visit to the Maywood Depot on a Sunday summer night to enjoy the ice cream social, and then head over to the Unadilla Drive-In (just ten miles away) for an old-fashioned outdoor movie. It has been here for as long as anyone can remember, has a great snack bar, and shows double-bills of first-run movies. There once was a drive-in theater around every corner in Upstate New York. Now there are fewer than two dozen. For more than six decades (and under only three owners), the Unadilla Drive-In (www.drive-in.ws) has been a summertime tradition for grown-ups and kids alike.

From Here to There
The other museum that is nearest to the Maywood Depot Museum is the **Bainbridge Museum**. Bainbridge is fifteen miles west of Sidney Center.

OTHER MUSEUMS TO EXPLORE IN REGION SEVEN

Catskill: Thomas Cole Home and Museum. "Cedar Grove is the home of the Father of the Hudson River School of Art." (518) 943-7465, www.thomascole.org.

Coxsackie: Bronck Museum. "Built in 1663 by Dutchman Peter Bronck, this is the oldest home in the Hudson Valley." (518) 731-6490, www.gchistory.org.

Kingston: Hudson River Maritime Museum. "Its collections are devoted to the history of the shipping, fishing, and boating industry on the Hudson River. Kingston was once the busiest city on the river between New York City and Albany." (845) 338-0071, www.hrmm.org.

Ossining: Sing Sing Prison Museum. "Artifacts from the most famous prison in the Eastern U.S. In the old days when they sent you "up the river to the big house," it meant up the Hudson River to Sing Sing Prison!" (914) 941-3189, www.ossininghistorical.org.

Phoenicia: Empire State Railway Museum. "Housed in an 1899 train depot, this museum tells the story of railroading in the Catskills. Includes three antique rail cars. At one time, the Ulster and Delaware Railroad came through here non-stop, 24 hours a day, carrying the rich and famous to the grand hotels of the Catskill Mountains." (845) 688-7501, www.esrm.com.

Prattsville: Zadock Pratt Museum. "Zadock Pratt's home highlights the life and times of the man who once built the largest tannery in the world here." (518) 299-3395, www.prattmuseum.com.

Rhinebeck: Old Rhinebeck Aerodrome Museum. "America's original living museum of antique Airplanes. Take a ride over the Hudson River in a 2-seat 1929 New Standard biplane." (845) 752-3200, www.oldrhinebeck .org.

Region Eight

HUDSON VALLEY

*Columbia, Dutchess, Putnam, Westchester,
Orange, and Rockland Counties*

42

GOMEZ MILL HOUSE MUSEUM
Marlboro, Orange County

*T*he roots of Judaism in America run deep and strong through the centuries. If you were to diagram the ascendancy of Jews in America, this house would stand alone at the very apex of the chart. Gomez Mill House is the oldest continuously occupied Jewish dwelling in the country, and is one of the oldest of all homes in the nation. Over forty owners have resided here, including five great historic families who crossed the doorsill of this elegant stone structure that straddles the Ulster and Orange County borderline.

Luis Moses Gomez was the first.

Gomez was a pioneer in many ways. He was a Sephardic Jew whose family was persecuted during the Spanish Inquisition and fled to France the year he was born, 1654, and then settled in England as merchants. By the time he arrived in New York City in 1703, there were fewer than 100 Jews in the city's population of 4,500. Gomez, a respected and successful merchant, soon became a leader of the tiny Jewish community. He served as *Parnas* (president) of Congregation Shearith Israel, America's first Jewish congregation. In 1728, he led the drive to build the first synagogue, the Mill Street Synagogue, which opened its doors in 1730.

Richie Rosencrans, program coordinator at the site, told me that because Gomez could not become a citizen of the colonies under oath to the British Crown and in the name of the Church of England, he purchased an Act of Denization in 1705. The decree allowed Gomez the right to conduct business, purchase land, and engage in commerce in New York without any interference or threat. It gave Gomez the right to

expand his entrepreneurial practices, but came at a heavy cost. The price of fifty-eight pounds sterling was costly, the equivalent of about $25,000 in today's money.

Gomez eyed the Hudson Valley for its lush forests and natural resources, and for the trading opportunities both on the River and on the settler trails north.

In 1714, he bought the first lot of what would be about 6,000 acres here in Marlboro. He set up lumber mills and lime kilns, and built a stone blockhouse for a trading post. The milled wood and processed lime were sent downriver to New York, where they were used by the growing population to build the city.

The house is magnificent in a quiet, solemn way. During my private visit to Gomez Mill House Museum, I walked from room to room and from floor to floor in awed silence. The setting is almost religious in its power and simplicity. The rooms are spare, and appointed with many original family artifacts and antiques.

"People are really amazed at what we have here," said Rosencrans. "The paintings, rare antiques, and personal family heirlooms convey the long history of the house. And we have many items from all the five families."

Well, when I hear the phrase "five families," I think of the movie *The Godfather*. But here, the phrase refers to the famous inhabitants of Gomez House through the centuries.

Wolfert Acker was the second owner. A Revolutionary patriot, he expanded both the house and his business." In the Acker bedroom we find the Acker family handmade (circa 1760) Bible box, and nineteenth-century personal items. "Here is an odd piece," my guide said. "We all thought it was just a bedside table until one day the top came off and we realized what it actually was." He showed me. It was a custom-made "hidden" commode!

The wealthy aristocrat Edward Armstrong was owner number three. His family fought for the British during the Revolutionary War and decided to stay when the war ended. His wife, a southern belle, did not like the rustic Mill House and insisted that Edward build a plantation mansion, which he did on the famed Danskammer point. They then gave the Mill House to his eldest son William Henry and his bride as a wedding present. William spent most of his time here as a "gentleman farmer" and was an animal breeder and patron of the arts.

Another owner, probably the most famous, was Dard Hunter. "He was a legendary papermaker and paper historian, and was an active member of the Arts and Crafts Movement." On display is a copy of a hand-made book: every aspect of the book was made entirely by hand. Rosencrans pointed out that Hunter produced 210 copies, of which one is in the Smithsonian Institution. "And of course, we have a copy here," he smiled.

The copy (#124 of 210) is in the library of the house in a glass case. The minute detail in the making of this ornate book is incredible. Many of Dard Hunter's other works are in this room, including some hand-printed books, glass watermark plates, and some "Half Moon"-themed stained glass.

Martha Gruening bought the house next, in 1919. "She was a founding member of the NAACP, an author, a lecturer, and an educator. She used an inheritance to purchase the Mill House to open up a Libertarian School for children 'of all color and backgrounds.' We have a number of items from the Gruening era. Plus this little extra," Rosencrans said with a wry smile as we walked over to the mantel of a nearby fireplace in the "Gruening Room." He showed me a photo of the Depression-era retreat,

Camp Moodna, run by social worker Rose Gruening, Martha's sister. He also showed me a book.

"This book was written by Ernest Gruening, Martha's brother. Does the name ring a bell with you?" he asked me.

It did. Ernest Gruening was a governor of the Alaska territory before it was a state, and was later one of the first pair of U.S. senators from Alaska. He was one of only two senators to vote against the Gulf of Tonkin resolution authorizing U.S. force against North Vietnam. As a U.S. senator, Gruening was also responsible for introducing a Congressional resolution to establish the nationwide 911 number!

Wow Factor

The Gomez Mill House Museum is really a secret treasure. And inside it are many exquisite individual secret treasures. Priceless books in the library, an original Jenny Lind bed in the bedroom, an antique two-man "slaw board" for making coleslaw in the kitchen, two deep brick fireplaces bookending the expansive living room, secret compartments (to stash illegal booze during Prohibition?), an original ten foot tall Gomez family grandfather clock, and more all make this a living, breathing repository of Americana along the Hudson.

But still I am drawn back to a single piece of paper hanging on a wall.

"The wow factor has to be the wonderful decree of freedom on display," Dr. Ruth Abrahams, executive director of the museum, told me. She was talking about the Act of Denization. It is a large piece of parchment, busily decorated with scrolls and flourishes. In the upper left-hand corner is the image of Queen Anne. It is hand written in Latin, the official language of the European courts. There are signatures, seals, a cloth tax stamp, and extravagant lettering, all bestowing the right to become a legal denizen of New York to Luis Moses Gomez. It is dated 1705.

"This document is so remarkable it has a generic appeal to all freedom-loving people. The language is extraordinary for the time, giving Gomez unimpeded freedom to pursue commerce and trade, secular activities, ownership of land, etcetera. He acquired this document because he would not take an oath to the Crown in the name of the Church of England. So he received this official 'release' that allowed him to adhere to his personal religious beliefs and morals and yet still have the rights of other citizens living here at the time. I like to think of it as part green card, part letter of credit and part passport," she said with a smile in her voice.

Another incredible piece of paper that fascinated me, also displayed on a wall, was the Gomez "family tree." Researched in the 1930s by famed New York architect Lafayette Goldstone, it features hundreds of names of descendants who made their mark in the family's history.

And what names they are.

If you look closely at the tiny print on the document, you will see names that came alive in our history books, and all of them related by birth or marriage to Luis Gomez. Names like Benjamin Cardozo, who sat in the U.S. Supreme Court from 1932 to 1938. Also both Ephraim Hart and Benjamin Seixas, original signers of the 1792 Buttonwood Agreement which created the New York Stock Exchange.

Another familiar name found here is Emma Lazarus. We, of course, know Emma as the poet whose immortal words are inscribed on the Statue of Liberty. The document also carries the names of dozens of church leaders, philanthropists, politicians, and others, touching virtually every facet of life in the early decades of America. One can spend a great deal of time just studying this single document.

The Take-Away

The Hudson River Valley is noted for its extravagant estates, from FDR's birthplace in Hyde Park to Washington Irving's castellated mansion "Sunnyside," to painter Frederic Church's Moorish mountaintop aerie "Olana," and others. Still, this old stone dwelling located on the west side of the Hudson carries with it a disproportionate amount of historic heft on its own. The property's ancient stone walls snake their way between the counties of Ulster and Orange, and the small English gardens (created by Andrew Jackson Downing, "The Father of American Landscaping") dazzle in the bright summer sunshine. The site positively exudes importance and awe. The tours are especially interesting, and are conducted by professional and passionate docents. They are fun and fact-filled and document each of the "five families" who resided here with respect and historical prospective.

Next time you are in the Hudson Valley I would strongly suggest you put the Gomez Mill House Museum, "The Hudson Valley's Secret Treasure," on your "must see" list of things to do! Any visitor will enjoy the juxtaposition of such a small, beautiful site containing such a colossal amount of U.S. history.

The Nuts and Bolts

Gomez Mill House Museum
Mill House Road
Marlboro, New York 12542
(845) 236-3126
www.gomez.org

• *Travel Suggestion*

From Kingston take Route 9W south through the small towns along the Hudson (you will pass the Walkway Over the Hudson). It is a little longer this way (the trip will take you about a half hour), but the little communities you pass through are worth the extra time. Curiously, several of the signs in town refer to Marlboro as "Marlborough," instead. As my guide Richie Rosencrans told me, "They took the 'ugh' out of Marlboro a few years back."

• *Museum Hours*

Wednesday through Sunday 10 a.m. to 4 p.m.
Guided tours are required for entry.
Tours are given at 10:30 a.m., 1:15 p.m., and 2:45 p.m.

• *Admission*

Adults: $8.00
Seniors: $6.00
Ages 6–16: $3.00
Under age 6: Free
Discounts are offered for groups of 10 or more.

• *Number of Visitors Annually*
4,000

Up around the Bend
Just ten miles north of the Gomez Mill House Museum is the magical Walkway Over the Hudson. This new state park is the world's longest and highest pedestrian walkway. It straddles the Hudson River between Highland (on the west) and Poughkeepsie (on the east). It is an easy, flat stroll offering some of the most magnificent river views in the world. It is totally unusual and totally awesome (www.walkway.org). The walk is a little over a mile long, following a renovated elevated railroad line.

Since its debut in 2009, nearly a million walkers have "walked the skies" over America's Rhine. In the fall, it is breathtaking.

From Here to There
The other museum in this book that is nearest to the Gomez Mill House Museum is the **Trolley Museum** in Kingston. It is half an hour's drive north of Marlboro.

43

CAMP SHANKS/
"LAST STOP USA" MUSEUM

Orangeburg, Rockland County

$\mathcal{F}$or a little hamlet of thirty-five hundred people, Orangeburg sure has seen a lot of folks pass through it. 1,500,000 to be exact, from 1943 to 1945, many of them never to return.

The Rockland community, near the western shore of the Hudson River, was the home of Camp Shanks during World War II. Known as "Last Stop USA," the camp was the largest embarkation terminal for U.S. troops in World War II. It is estimated that as much as 75% of all the troops that comprised "Operation Overlord," which conducted the D-Day invasion of Europe, came through this tiny map dot.

"The camp is really remarkable," Jerry Donnellan, Director of the Rockland County Veterans Office and the museum's curator, told me. "Our museum shows a typical Army barracks, pretty much like what most of the soldiers who came through here would have seen. It's not much to look at, but it's real familiar to the old vets who come through here for a visit. It brings back a lot of bittersweet memories for them.

"Our story is one people either find hard to believe or have never heard of. The Army came into Orangeburg in September of 1942, and basically told most of the community they had two weeks to clear out. Once the evacuation was complete, the U.S. Army Corps of Engineers came through and leveled everything. In its place, they constructed 2,500 buildings between September and January. Three months! Today it takes that long to put a deck on your house," he observed.

The museum is housed in a weary-looking Quonset hut, draped with an American flag. These metal round-topped buildings were used by the permanent personnel at the camp. This included teachers, cooks, administrators, etc. The museum is in one of the last ones standing. Inside you are greeted by the attendants at the front desk, who are eager to answer any questions and to show you around. On the day of my visit, the front desk was manned by three World War II veterans. They had some great stories, and they all had a personal connection with Camp Shanks. The displays are indirectly lit, to give it a "sense of period," and the informational panels are comprehensive and compelling, both in text and photographs.

"Over half of our visitors are veterans and their families," Donnellan said.

From Orangeburg, the men would be taken by train (or would walk) to the giant piers along the Hudson River where transports would take them to Europe. For many soldiers, Orangeburg would be the last glimpse of a home they would never return to.

While Camp Shanks was in operation (it could hold 50,000 troops at one time), Hollywood celebrities and entertainers would bring their USO shows to entertain. Judy Garland, Benny Goodman, Frank Sinatra, Dinah Shore, Ethel Merman, Betty Grable, and Mickey Rooney all performed at Camp Shanks. Sgt. Joe Louis would train for his heavyweight fights while here. During his time at Camp Shanks, he was a familiar sight in the early morning fog, running the streets of Orangeburg.

Wow Factor

"We do get a lot of school kids coming through here, and it is funny. Those younger than, say, twelve think of it as just your average museum. Those older than that really do get it, though. They are engrossed in the stories, love the large sand table diorama of the camp showing it as it appeared during the war, and so on. But what is really amazing to me is how they react to the movie we show here," he said.

From 1942 to 1945, famed movie director Frank Capra completed seven war propaganda films for the American movie audience. The films are controversial today, but in the 1940s they were seen as a key component in revving up the fighting spirit of a country entering a war.

"The kids see this film, which uses politically incorrect language in it, as an unusual look back to a different time. The young teenagers really spend a lot more time watching this film than I thought they would (the movie loops over and over during the museum's open hours). It is very interesting to watch these kids' reaction to the whole Camp Shanks experience," Donnellan told me.

The Take-Away

The Camp Shanks Museum is an important piece in the historic puzzle that was World War II, and it tells its tale in a small, dignified way. The museum itself is hard to find, tucked away behind a school (there are signs to it, however). It looks a bit grim and "uncertain" on the outside, but the inside is extremely well done. My visit was greatly enhanced by the wonderful storytelling abilities of the volunteers at the front, all World War II veterans.

Military museums cover many chapters in our nation's history, both grand and small. This museum is among the smallest ones I encountered in my research for this book. Still, I would definitely recommend a visit to this old historic Quonset hut.

The Nuts and Bolts

Camp Shanks
"Last Stop USA" Museum
South Greenbush Road
Orangeburg, New York 10962
(845) 638-5419
No website.

- *Travel Suggestion*
  From the western terminus of the Tappan Zee Bridge (Nyack), travel south to Piermont. Orangeburg is five miles to the west of here. (Piermont was the river port where the ships would pick up the soldiers from Camp Shanks to take them to Europe and North Africa. A statue of a soldier waving good-bye to his buddies is found at the waterfront.)

- *Museum Hours*
  Memorial Day through Labor Day, Saturday and Sunday noon to 4 p.m.

- *Admission*
  Free

- *Number of Visitors Annually*
  2,000

Up around the Bend

In keeping with the theme of military museums, I would suggest you travel the thirty-five miles north out of Orangeburg (Palisades Parkway to US Route 9W) to New Windsor. The Purple Heart Museum is one of our state's newest, and it is the home of the largest database of Purple Heart winners in the country. The United State Military Academy at West Point is only twenty-five miles north of Camp Shanks. It has a full array of guided and self-guided tour availabilities.

From Here to There
The other museum in this book that is nearest to Camp Shanks is the **Purple Heart Museum**. It is located near New Windsor, thirty-five miles north of Orangeburg.

44

NATIONAL PURPLE HEART
HALL OF HONOR

Vails Gate, Orange County

Been there. Nick, too.

"*H*mmmm, are we a museum?" mused program director Peter Bedross-ian. "Good question.

"Although the word museum is not in our official title, I think every-body who comes through here thinks of us as a museum. What makes us different is our scope. Most museums focus on a finite timeline. A certain period, a certain battle, a certain period of natural history. Our timeline never ends, or at least won't end until wars cease."

The National Purple Heart Hall of Honor is one of New York's young-est historic sites, having opened on November 10, 2006.

"Our goal is collecting stories and preserving history. Nearly two mil-lion Purple Hearts have been awarded. The award itself has had an ever-morphing life, starting with the presentation of three Badges of Military Merit handed out by General George Washington on August 7, 1862. Since then, there have been changes in the qualifications for the award-ing of the badge, as well as to the name itself. After General MacArthur's order in 1932 rededicating the award by its new name, the Purple Heart, it was given for wounds received in combat as well as for meritorious service. Executive Order 9277, dated December 2, 1942, officially identi-fied the award as one given for wounds received in battle or injuries that caused death in combat as well as authorizing its awarding to all branches of service. This means there were many different types of recipients.

"Lt. Annie Fox was one of the first women to receive the Purple Heart. She was not wounded in combat, but rather was awarded it for her actions

as a nurse at Pearl Harbor," Bedrossian told me. "We have Civil War veterans, including the first African-American Purple Heart recipient, getting their medals in the 1930s, when these men were in their nineties. The stories are amazing."

The museum is situated right outside Newburgh and is co-located with Washington's New Windsor Cantonment Historic Site. This was the Continental Army's final encampment, and seven thousand soldiers in six hundred huts were placed here from 1782 to 1783."

"The two sites are complementary," said Bedrossian. "In the summer the Cantonment has interpretive programs in the buildings at the site, with volunteers dressed in period outfits telling the story of life in Washington's Army. Many of our visitors wander up to the cantonment site to enjoy the history there also."

The Purple Heart Hall of Honor encompasses several areas. Your experience here starts with an interesting fifteen-minute film telling of the Purple Heart as well as the New Windsor Cantonment. "It is called 'For Military Merit,' and it was made by ABC News for us," the program director explained.

Another section features three unusual-looking kiosks. The metal, odd-shaped cylinders allow you to sit inside for a private video presentation.

"They represent air (a plane's cockpit), sea (a ship's hull), and land (a bunker) based on the different texture of each kiosk. The individual presentations within describe how the soldiers got wounded and received their purple hearts, another tells how it changed their lives, and the last honors those who sacrificed their lives. The stories are quite vivid and moving," Bedrossian told me.

Wow Factor

"Again, I have to go back to what separates our facility from a typical museum. Unlike, for example, a museum of natural history where you could say a giant elephant was a wow factor, or a great statue in another museum was a standout, here it is just the whole aura of the place that really is unforgettable. We have an exhaustive database of Purple Heart recipients on record. Many times a veteran comes in and sees his name on the roll, unaware that a family member or comrade placed him on it. They are surprised. Kids see their grandfathers' names on the roll and are brought to tears," Bedrossian said. "The whole atmosphere is so inspiring that you just cannot help but saying 'wow!' to yourself as you walk through our halls.

"I am quite struck by the comments our visitors make to me when they depart. 'Thank you.' 'God Bless You.' 'We appreciate what you are doing here.' It is a feeling that is hard for me to describe. And for them also. Particularly for the veterans of those singularly nasty battles. I have met soldiers here who fought in the Battle of the Bulge. And Khe Sanh. And Iwo Jima. And the Frozen Chosin from the Korean War. These memories are painful for them, and you can tell that when they walk in. But almost to a man, when they leave the Hall of Honor they are inspired, optimistic, and almost relieved by their visit here. I am always honored to meet the guys who actually fought in the great battles I have read about in books. It is quite remarkable.

"I remember a couple of guys coming in here once. Nice guys, unassuming. One was Roger Donlon, and the other was his brother. Donlon was the first living Viet Nam veteran to receive the Medal of Honor. Both he and his brother were Purple Heart winners. These guys were living, breathing pieces of history. Just to talk to them was an unforgettable experience. They were awestruck by our facility.

"Another memory is Sgt. Ken Peck. He came here with his family. He was entitled to get the Purple Heart for wounds he received in Afghanistan. He never applied for it. Four years later he did, at his friend's insistence, and he came here to receive his award personally at the Purple Heart Hall of Honor. After the ceremony I congratulated Sgt. Peck. He said something I will never forget. 'I am merely the custodian of this award for those who can't be here.'"

The Take-Away

The first sense I got when I entered the Purple Heart Hall of Honor was one of reverence. The building is chapel-like in its serenity. The displays are gripping, the video presentations are all worth watching, and a sense of history permeates the air here. The buildings are modern and well lit, as befits one of the newest historic sites in New York State.

The historic cantonment site is just a country stroll up into the woods. It is fascinating on its own and totally appropriate as a companion to the Hall.

Plus, this place has a great gift shop! The inventory includes books, mugs, hats, shirts, art, car emblems and ribbons, medals and pins, war-themed toys, and jewelry. There is much to absorb in this tasteful military-themed shop.

Oh, and of course the "don't miss item" at the Purple Heart Hall of Honor is, well, an original Badge of Military Merit. The real one.

It was called The Badge of Military Merit at the time. Washington gave out three in 1783. The recipients were Sgt. William Brown, Sgt. Daniel Bissell, and Sgt. Elijah Churchill. Sgt. Churchill's family gave this more-than-two-century-old award to the Hall of Honor. You can see it on display here. It is a very small heart-shaped piece of purple cloth surrounded by delicate white lace.

Now that is history.

The Nuts and Bolts

The National Purple Heart Hall of Honor
374 Temple Road (Route 300)

Vails Gate, New York 12584
(845) 561-1761
www.thepurpleheart.com

• *Travel Suggestion*
Leave the New York State Thruway at Exit 17. Follow Route 300S toward Newburgh approximately four miles to the Hall of Honor (on your left).

• *Museum Hours*
Monday through Saturday 10 a.m. to 5 p.m.
Sunday 1 p.m. to 5 p.m.
Closed Holidays except Veterans Day, Memorial Day, Independence Day, and Presidents Day

• *Admission*
Individual visitors: free.
There is a $3.00 per person fee for large group tours.

• *Number of Visitors Annually*
Approximately 20,000

Up around the Bend
To continue on your "military themed" visit to the Hudson Valley, travel just ten miles south of Vails Gate to West Point Military Academy. The combination of West Point and the Purple Heart Hall of Honor makes for a fascinating daylong trip to this historic part of New York State.

Also Washington's headquarters in Newburgh (where he stayed from 1782 to 1783 and where he established the Badge of Military Merit, is six miles northeast of the Hall, and Knox's Headquarters is two miles East.

From Here to There
The other museum in this book that is nearest to the National Purple Heart Hall of Honor is the **Gomez Mill House Museum** in Marlboro.

OTHER MUSEUMS TO
EXPLORE IN REGION EIGHT

Cuddebackville: Neversink Valley Museum. "The mission of this museum is to preserve and document the history of the peoples and industry of the Neversink and Shawangunk valleys of the Catskill region. The museum is housed in several historic D&H Canal buildings." (845) 754-8870, www.neversinkmuseum.org.

Goshen: Harness Racing Museum and Hall of Fame. (845) 294-6330, www.harnessmuseum.com. "Dedicated to the support and promotion of the Standardbred industry, its history, and its tradition. From 1930 to 1956 harness racing's top event was run here at Good Time Park." (845) 294-6330, www.harnessmuseum.com.

Hudson: FASNY Museum of Firefighting. "Over three hundred years of firefighting history is on display here. More than ninety fire vehicles are also on the museum floor." (877) 347-3687, www.fasnyfiremuseum.com.

Monroe: Museum Village. "A living history museum committed to the exploration, interpretation, and preservation of 19th-century life." (845) 782-8247, www.museumvillage.org.

Poughkeepsie: Mid-Hudson Children's Museum. "More than 60,000 visitors come to enjoy this children's wonderland in the Hudson Valley. It is a totally hands-on, interactive play center for children, with many interesting exhibits. Check out the play-area model of the human heart. The grounds of the museum are beautifully situated on the banks of the Hudson River." (845) 471-0589, www.mchm.org.

Region Nine

CAPITAL DISTRICT/SARATOGA

Albany, Rensselaer, Schenectady, Saratoga, and Washington Counties

45

USS SLATER DESTROYER ESCORT HISTORICAL MUSEUM

Albany, Albany County

*T*his is perhaps one of the most unusual museums in Upstate New York, located in one of the most majestic settings you could imagine.

The USS *Slater* (DE 766) is the last of all of the 563 World War II–era destroyer escorts afloat in the U.S. It is moored in the Hudson River with the stunning skyline of New York's capital city as its backdrop.

"She is a beauty, isn't she?" said Tim Rizzuto, the museum's executive director.

Yes she is. All 306 feet and 1,200 tons of her. Her gleaming battleship gray contrasts starkly with the shimmering blue water of the Hudson. Her guns bristle out from all sides and her battle flags flap in the brisk northeast wind.

"We love this old ship," Rizzuto told me. "Untold hours went into restoring it to this first-class condition. People of all ages come on board and crawl all over it. We have guided tours, and many veterans, including those who actually served on the *Slater*, have come back to relive old memories here. They call it 'reliving their worst nightmares,' but you can tell there is a bit of nostalgia in it for each of them."

The ship is wide open to visitors. And what an amazing tour it is. Visitors can go down to the galley and see the kitchen set up just like it was in the war years. The sleeping quarters, the engine room, the officer's dining room, everything is available to see and touch.

"People really get a kick out of the shower facilities," Rizzuto told me. "The ship could make its own fresh water, but just a small amount. So the

two hundred men and the twelve officers all had to lather up in saltwater and then dive into a '60-second shower' to rinse off. Believe me, when the old vets see those showers again, they start to shiver all over," he laughed.

I asked him what the connection between the ship and Albany was.

"None, really. After the war, the ship began its travels all over the world and eventually ended up in the Greek navy. Greece decommissioned her in 1991, and she was tugged to New York, where she joined the Intrepid Sea-Air-Space Museum. When they decided to downsize, they started looking for a new, permanent home, and Albany was picked. The city has been a wonderful host to the *Slater,* and we believe that the *Slater* has been a wonderful addition to this great city."

A small visitors' center adjacent to the ship tells the story of the heroic destroyer escorts in the war years. An exciting video is aired showing these agile ships in action, protecting the Merchant Marine supply ships convoying across the oceans, defending their larger charges as well as locating and destroying enemy submarines.

"We see a lot of generational bonding go on here at the *Slater*. People expect us to be 'just' a museum. But we are a real ship, a time capsule of sorts. The older generation remembers it well, and the younger ones know of the ships and the war through movies. Still, no matter how many stories the kids hear, or how many pieces of information we give them, it all falls apart when we get them up on deck by the guns. They put on helmets and crawl into the gun turrets and start swiveling around in them. They love it, and no matter what anybody tells you, that is always a highlight for the younger ones," Rizzuto said with a smile.

Destroyer escorts were named for naval heroes. The *Slater* is named after Frank O. Slater, an Alabama native who was killed at the Battle of Guadalcanal.

The ship is moved twice a year. "The powers that be at the Port won't let us stay here over the winter because of the ice buildup. So they make us take her down a mile to Rensselaer, where we berth her at a commercial dock. I gotta tell you," he said, "on those two trips, down in the winter and back in the spring, everybody loves to come and watch this old ship sail down the Hudson (it is pulled by a tugboat). Just to see her free, out on the water again, well, you can bet that everybody brings a camera on those days."

Wow Factor

"Without a doubt the thing that everybody takes away from a tour of the *Slater* is the fact that living conditions on this ship were horrendous. The cramped quarters, the strict, rank-concise ladder of command, the limited amenities. Wow! All of that, and then imagine doing this, living here, working here in a Pacific squall where the ship is rising thirty-five feet on a wave only to slide all the way down the other side of it. And with the threat of a submarine or U-boat attack at any moment. It was scary. These guys were heroes," Rizzuto said.

The Take-Away

I think Tim Rizzuto nailed it when he talked about the ungodly living and working conditions. That is really what I (and everybody) take away from a visit to this museum. I'll never forget what Tim said to me: "These guys weren't even treated like prisoners in a federal prison. Each crewmember of the *Slater* was allotted just one-sixth of the amount of living space afforded an inmate in a U.S. prison."

Another strong impression I will always take away from this ship was the reverence shown to it by veterans and former crewmates. They clearly loved the *Slater* and gave a real piece of their life while serving on her. The connection is real, visceral. I could see it and hear it in the faces and voices of the old veterans chatting on the decks of the ship.

The wartime executive, Lt. Cmdr. Marcel J. Blancq, from New Orleans, left explicit directions that he was to be buried from the ship he commanded so bravely.

"Blancq's family brought his ashes here in 2002. We held a solemn ceremony right here on the fantail of the *Slater*, overlooking the skyline of Albany, and then quietly scattered his ashes into the Hudson River. He loved this ship," Rizzuto told me.

One other impression I got from my visit to the *Slater* was how wonderful the downtown area of Albany really is. The *Slater* is tied up near the base of slaloming State Street, which goes from the New York State Capitol to the Hudson River. Often, a replica of Henry Hudson's ship the *Half Moon* is anchored nearby. The Hudson is narrow here, and the green banks of the eastern shore are easily visible, making this a very pleasant place to spend an afternoon.

The Nuts and Bolts

The USS *Slater* Destroyer Escort Historical Museum
Broadway at Quay Street
Albany, New York 12202
(518) 431-1943
www.ussslater.org

• *Travel Suggestion*
The Albany waterfront runs directly behind the massive gothic, gargoyled State University of New York headquarters situated at the foot

of State Street. There you will find walkways, picnic areas, entertainment venues and, of course, the *Slater*.

• *Museum Hours*
Open Early April through late November (call for exact dates).
Wednesday through Sunday 10 a.m. to 4 p.m.
Open all major holidays except Easter, Christmas, and Thanksgiving.

• *Number of Visitors Annually*
15,000

Up around the Bend
Troy, one of Albany's great "sister cities," lies up and over the Hudson about seven miles away. Troy is a historic city with a rich and vibrant downtown area. There are many dining choices and a plethora of unique antique shops and specialty stores to while away the hours in. Be sure and include a visit to Oakwood Cemetery (50 101st Street) on your side trip to Troy. The city is known as "The Birthplace of Uncle Sam" and, well, Oakwood is the final resting place of Samuel Wilson, the "real Uncle Sam." The local Boy Scout troop raises and lowers an American flag at Uncle Sam's grave every day.

From Here to There
The other museum in this book that is nearest to the USS *Slater* Destroyer Escort Museum is the **Burden Iron Works Museum** in Troy. It is nine miles north of Albany.

46

NATIONAL BOTTLE MUSEUM

Ballston Spa, Saratoga County

*T*his unusual museum requires you to wander under the tutelage of a tour guide. If not (or unless you are a bottle collector), this museum is going to look just like "a whole store of empty bottles."

But, oh the history here.

"I knew nothing about bottles when I first started here fifteen years ago," Gary Moeller told me. He is the museum's director, and man, was I lucky to find him on my visit.

"Yes, there are a thousand stories in here," he chuckled.

We started our tour right at the front of the building, where we first met a colorful display of bottles each with the likeness of George Washington. They glistened in the autumn sun pouring through the front window of the museum.

"These are here to show you that really, anybody can be a bottle collector," he began. "The two larger ones on the top are originals, and will probably set you back a bit if you wanted to buy them. But the others are all reproductions of varying sizes, and many people collect them. They date from 1932 to 1976, and are readily found."

The museum is housed in a tall, deep 1901 storefront right on the busy Main Street of downtown Ballston Spa, a bustling community of about 6,000 residents located just five miles south of Saratoga Springs. The interior walls of this former hardware store tower above the visitor, all the way up to the 20-foot ceiling. And every inch of every wall is covered with glass bottles.

"We call this a permanent collection in open storage," Moeller told me. "These bottles are basically being stored, but they are on display for museum guests." Glass partitions cover the front of the collections. "We have more than 2,000 glass bottles in our collection," he said.

Many of the bottles are quite beautiful. Others are fairly plain and utilitarian.

"These are Wheaton Village collectibles," he said as he pointed to a large display of multi-hued commemorative bottles. "They are very popular items from the 1970s." I recognized the faces of General MacArthur, Abraham Lincoln, W.C. Fields, Robert F. Kennedy, and others on the fronts of the decanters.

A gaily colored display case in the front of the museum holds what Moeller called "whimsies."

"These are basically end-of-the-day products that glass blowers would create to show off their talents. As you can see, they could make almost anything," he told me as we peered into the case holding dipping spoons, glass walking sticks, church candlesnuffers, and more.

"All of these items are over a century old," he said.

Evidence of the art of glass making is everywhere in this crowded museum. The walls are filled with seltzer bottles, dairy milk bottles, commemorative bottles, and stoneware. The display of antique glass pharmacy bottles is interesting. The labels describe the contents on these old bottles as aids in curing everything from "consumption" to "female problems" to "wet armpits."

"Our oldest bottle dates back to 1710, and one of our most recent items dates back to our nation's bicentennial in 1976 (a 7-Up soft drink bottle with the Liberty Bell on it). There is also now a milk bottle from 2005 that was a commemorative bottle made for the National Association of Milk Bottle Collectors. So you see we have more than 250 years of bottle examples in our museum."

One of the most interesting collections at the museum is the many "poison bottles" on display.

"In the old days they really wanted to make sure that folks didn't get their hands on the poisons found in the house. So they made the bottles a deep cobalt blue, unlike any other bottle color. They printed DO NOT TAKE across the sides and even etched in hash marks on the glass so you could actually feel that you were picking up a bottle you shouldn't. Some of the rarest poison bottles are in the shape of skulls or caskets," he chuckled. Recently the museum had several of these on display. Creepy.

As I said, I was very glad to have Gary Moeller with me as a guide on the day I visited. He knew every bottle inside and out (almost literally).

Wow Factor

Moeller had no trouble picking out his wow factor at the bottle museum.

"Let me show you my favorite one," he said as we walked over to a display that carried a series of richly colored bottles from the 1800s.

"These are all stamped with the bottlers' names on them because they wanted to reuse them as many times as possible. And they didn't charge deposits on them. So they stamped them with their names or the names of their businesses on them so everybody would know whose bottle it was. I like this one best of all," he said as he picked up a bright blue bottle with bold, clear lettering on it.

"This guy really did not want anybody else to have his bottle so he stamped it in a most unusual way. It reads: 'THIS BOTTLE WAS STO-LEN FROM W.S. CHEYNEY.'"

The Take-Away

As I mentioned before, a guide is almost imperative when visiting this museum. And to their credit, the staff is extremely helpful and knowledge-able. The stories behind these bottles are just so rich and interesting that you simply do not want to miss any of the details.

The building also has a second floor, which is a handsome brick-walled gallery space that holds more bottles as well as exhibit space for local craftsmen and artists to show their paintings and crafts.

I must say I was surprised at how busy this little museum really was. During my 90-minute visit and tour with Mr. Moeller, at 2:00 p.m. on a Friday afternoon, the door never stopped opening and closing. Everybody was encouraged to sign the guest book, and just before I left I went to see the home places of the folks who came in during the short time I was there. The towns were Sheepshead Bay, Rochester, N.Y.; West Orange, N.J.; Albany, N.Y.; and Hartville, Ohio.

The most interesting section of the museum for me was the privy dig display. In the old days when people would have outhouses rather than indoor toilets, in the winter when they were unable to gather their garbage to burn they simply dumped much of it "down the two-holer." Including their glass bottles. A hundred years later, these privy grounds are among the richest hunting areas for old bottles.

"If you are a bottle collector and you come across an untouched privy pit, you have found paradise," Moeller told me. In fact, TV's Travel Channel sent a crew from their popular series "The Best Places to Find Cash and Treasures" to the museum, and they went on a privy pit hunt. A tape of the show is available for viewing in the museum. And yes, they did find several valuable bottles.

The Nuts and Bolts

The National Bottle Museum
76 Milton Avenue

Ballston Spa, New York 12020
(518) 885-7589
www.national bottlemuseum.org

• *Travel Suggestion*
Take the Ballston Spa/Malta exit (Exit 12) from the Northway (I-87).
Follow the signs. The museum is twenty miles north of Albany.

• *Museum Hours*
Monday to Friday 10 a.m. to 4 p.m.
Note: The museum sponsors one of the largest antique bottle shows in
the East every June. Visit the website for details.

• *Admission*
Free. (Donations are gladly accepted.)

• *Number of Visitors Annually*
3,000

Up around the Bend

Saratoga Springs is just five minutes north of Ballston Spa. This historic
village is one of Upstate's most popular tourist destinations. If you visit the
Bottle Museum in August, save yourself some time to head to the horse
races at Saratoga. They only race in the month of August, and it is a wonderful and fun way to spend the day.

From Here to There

The other museum in this book that is nearest to the Bottle Museum is
the **New York State Military Museum** in Saratoga Springs. It is five miles
north of Ballston Spa.

47

SLATE VALLEY MUSEUM

Granville, Washington County

"It has been an interesting year," remarked Kate Weller, executive director of the Slate Valley Museum.

On August 28, 2011, the usually calm and bucolic Mettowee River came raging out of its banks behind the museum with a force never before seen. "Yeah, thanks a lot, Irene," the good-natured Weller said. Hurricane Irene savaged many communities in Upstate New York and the damage here, along the border with Vermont, was among the most severe.

"Old timers have told me they have never seen anything like it," she said. "The damage was considerable to many structures along the river, the museum included. Thanks to God and an army of volunteers and supporters, almost our entire collection was saved."

Slate Valley is unique in the world. It runs twenty-five miles north and south of Granville, sashaying back and forth between New York and Vermont. The area is one of the richest slate regions in the world. "And Granville itself is unique in that we are the only place in the world where red slate can be found," she said proudly.

Hence the sign at the edge of town, reading "Welcome to Granville. The Colored Slate Capital of the World."

"We sure have plenty of the familiar gray slate, but look at what makes us so special," she told me as we walked down a line of glass display cases. "Greens, purples, reds, browns, and blacks. It's our own rainbow." These unique colored slates were and are in high demand by architects and contractors. "You won't find them anywhere but right here in the Slate Valley."

The Slate Valley Museum is a wonderful repository, a cornucopia of social and industrial nuances. "We try and focus our goals on three mainstays here: Industry, Community, and Technology," she told me.

All are represented in thoughtful and exciting displays. In the Industry section we learn about the actual mining of slate and the dangers inherent in it. "This was an era where safety rules and guidelines were basic at best and nonexistent at worst. The quarrymen worked long hours in a dangerous job. Many died in accidents and many others were injured. It was not an easy life," Weller said. This is all exhibited in archival photographs showing workers straddling huge slabs of slate, hanging on to a piece of chain, while dangling hundreds of feet above the quarry floor. The photos are gripping.

"As for the exhibit 'Heavy Lifting: A Historical and Technological History of Moving Slate from Quarry to Market,' we try and show the timeline, from the rudimentary methods of quarrying slate up through the many technological advances making the process both easier and safer."

It was the exhibit "The Dream and the Reality" that I found to have the most interesting story to tell. "The earliest quarry workers here were from Wales. The Irish, Italians, and Eastern Europeans were not far behind them," the director explained. "As you can see, our museum is located right on the river, and the small street behind us, Water Street, was home to quarrying families who emigrated from Poland, Slovakia, and other Eastern European countries in the late 1800s and early twentieth century. Local residents, in an effort to disparage new immigrants, called the street 'Hun Alley.'

"Although the tensions between the varying ethnic groups and the local residents were strong, the religions, cultures, foods, traditions, and social idiosyncrasies all blended together right out our back door. It was amazing," she said.

The room that holds the exhibit "The Dream and the Reality" is fascinating. Large photographs show early workers from Wales celebrating Christmas in the street. Italians can be seen marching in parades. Scattered around the display rooms are artifacts from another era. Old clothes, family Bibles, work tools, and precious heirlooms from the various countries are all on exhibit.

One large panel shows a crystal-clear 1914 photograph of a large group of Slovakians all dressed up in their native costumes celebrating Independence Day.

"There is a wonderful story about this old photo," Weller said as we walked over to it. "We know of a woman, now 95 years old, who lives in Florida. She is a friend of the museum. When she comes here, she always visits this photo. Believe it or not, her father is actually in it," Weller said softly. "And the story doesn't stop there. This woman was born right here at 17 Water Street. Exactly where we are standing today!"

One of the most impressive stops along our tour was the Quarryman's Shack. It is a replica of one of the shacks that sat atop a quarry and where workers would sort, split, and trim slate. The replica is sparsely adorned, much like it would have been a hundred years ago. Just an old picture on the wall, a small stove, and a calendar. In the center is a giant trimming machine.

"It is an original slate trimmer from 1910. There were hundreds of these shacks scattered across Slate Valley. Usually there would be two men in here. One would sort and split the slate and the other would trim it on the trimmer," she explained. Weller demonstrated the process. ("We do not let visitors try this, for obvious reasons.") She picked up a large, uneven piece of actual slate. She pumped away at the foot pedals until she was red-faced and the cylinder in the center of the machine was whirring nosily as it spun. Around and around it churned. When it reached the right velocity, she slammed a piece of slate into its jaws and "SNAP!" the piece was trimmed. She quickly turned the slate. "SNAP!" A second side was trimmed. She did this until all four sides were beveled. The velocity and power exhibited in this process was surprising. She showed me the finished piece. The remainders all went into a big pile of slate scraps.

"Ninety percent of all slate ended up being wasted. It is a fragile material, and you can see that if you were not precise in your techniques a lot of it ended up in the waste pile. There are hundreds of slate heaps all across Slate Valley. They are of no use to anyone, so they just remain there as signposts to the past. Almost every town around here has a heap."

It was an awesome demonstration.

Wow Factor

"Look at this," the director exclaimed as we rounded a corner and entered the center court of the museum.

My eyes widened at the sight.

Standing before me was the largest, meanest, most awesome dump truck I have ever seen. It was the size of a tank.

"This always gets everybody's attention," she laughed. "I just love this old truck. We have it here to show the changing technology of the slate industry. This 1950 Mack truck represents a significant milestone in the industry. Before these huge trucks came along, they relied on railroads and even horses. With these trucks, they could increase their heavy-lifting capacities. It was a major step forward."

The truck, adorned with the name of an old local quarry on the side, is a demonic, dynamic presence in the museum. It actually looks alive. And angry.

"Imagine in the early fifties what this area was like with hundreds of these monsters crawling all over the valley, kicking up slate dust and groaning under the weight of tons of slate," Weller said.

Imagine, indeed.

The Take-Away

This museum is very modern and beautiful. Not the least of its wonderful features is the structure that holds the museum. "Yes, isn't it magnificent? It is a New World Dutch barn originally located south of Albany and moved to its present location. We have had many people come and visit us just to marvel at our impressive building."

Impressive is an understatement. The interior soars a full three stories above the main floor. "See those beams up there?" Weller said as she pointed skyward. "They are all original, and some are more than two hundred years old."

The building is extremely well-lit and attractive inside. Of course, there is much slate in evidence in the construction materials. The floors are all made of local slate.

Jim Morris, a local craftsman, put down the large display floor. It is a 1,100-square-foot slate showroom floor made up of more than four thousand different pieces of local slate. The design evokes an Amish quilt-like pattern and the mosaic utilizes all seven of the different colored slates found in the area.

"It's funny. Slate made this valley what it is and slate saved this museum when the floods hit," Weller said. "Many other buildings in the area had to be completely gutted of the rotting infrastructure, moldy foundations, and weakened underpinnings after Hurricane Irene sent river water into the buildings. Not us. While we had some minor water damage, our slate pulled us through. We simply had to come in and wash it off."

Not to be missed is the full-length mural that covers the entire back wall of the museum. It was done in 1939 by WPA artist Martha Levy, whose pieces are also on display at the Smithsonian Institution.

Titled "Men Working in Slate Quarry," the painting has been called one of the finest examples of WPA work found in Upstate New York. The 25-foot-long, four-foot-tall mural depicts the steps, process, and timeline of mining slate. It is colorful, daring, muscular, and quite beautiful. It is a real showstopper, for sure.

The thirteen men depicted in this powerful painting were all local quarrymen with names like "Duck" Roberts, Robert "the big Welshman" Williams, and "Boss" Dickinson.

The Nuts and Bolts

Slate Valley Museum
17 Water Street
Granville, New York 12832
(518) 642-1417
www.slatevalleymuseum.org

• *Travel Suggestion*

Granville sits directly on the New York/Vermont line. The easiest way to get here is off the Northway (I-87). Take Exit 20 (Queensbury) and follow Route 149 east through the historic village of Fort Ann to Granville. From the Northway you are about forty minutes from the Slate Valley Museum.

• *Museum Hours*

Tuesday to Friday 1 p.m. to 5 p.m.
Saturday 10 a.m. to 4 p.m.
Closed Sunday and Monday
Open year round

• *Admission*

Adults: $5.00
Others (including slate company employees and their families): Free

• *Number of Visitors Annually*

5,000

Up around the Bend

A nice side trip for your visit to Granville would be a stop in Whitehall. This little community has a lot of history and a lot of charm. Known as

"The Birthplace of the American Navy" for its involvement in the Revolutionary War, Whitehall has several nice shops, cafes, and museums to explore and enjoy. Oh, and that giant castle-like building hanging off the mountain overlooking Whitehall? Yes, it is a castle. Take a ride up Potter's Terrace Road and see for yourself!

Whitehall is about fifteen miles northwest of Granville.

From Here to There

The other museum in this book that is nearest to The Slate Valley Museum is the **New York State Military Museum** in Saratoga Springs, sixty miles southwest of Granville.

48

NEW YORK STATE MILITARY MUSEUM

Saratoga Springs, Saratoga County

"*W*hen we started out here almost ten years ago, we still had painted lines on the floor for basketball games," Mike Aikey told me as we scanned the cavernous open space of the old Saratoga Armory.

The New York State Military Museum is an astounding collection of military artifacts and rotating exhibits ranging back to and through every war America ever fought. "Our collection is considered to be one of the best in the nation," Aikey said. "We are kind of the envy of other military museums. The collection spent most of its history at the New York State Capitol in Albany, and then it went to the Watervliet Arsenal, where it languished for several years. Finally, this armory became available and we grabbed it. Actually, it is perfect for us."

The old wooden floors of the armory gleam with a mirror finish and you can almost hear the echoes of the ghosts of young people from the past century playing a spirited game of pick-up ball here. And yet, despite the gargantuan size of the building, it comes off as rather small and intimate in a way.

"That is by design," the director told me. "We have approximately 10,000 square feet of exhibit space here to fill, so we simply "brought it all down" and forgot about the ceiling space. Visitors can walk among a series of maze-like partitions which take them on a time travel of sorts."

The museum has five core exhibits: the Revolutionary War, the Civil War gallery, World War I, World War II, and a nineteenth-century gallery featuring New York's militia and National Guard during the century. All are filled with interesting artifacts, photos, panels, and stories.

"We also have a revolving schedule of rotating exhibits," Aikey told me as we walked over to a 9/11 exhibit. "This section tries to tell the story, in a narrow focus, of what happened on September 11, 2001."

It is quite moving. There are twisted pieces of metal from the World Trade Center, pieces of emergency services equipment from that terrible day, and a series of photographs of the many "Help Me Find" posters which littered lower Manhattan by the thousands as rescue workers desperately tried to find any survivors. Several of these original handmade posters are on display.

"Many of these posters were put up at the Lexington Avenue Armory in New York City, the home of the Fighting 69th," Aiken said softly. "We have these on display because we are a military museum and we like to remind people, to tell them about the real cost of war."

One that gave me chills read: "Looking for Nolbert Salomon. Last seen on the forty-fourth floor helping others to get out." It was accompanied by a color photograph of a vibrant young office worker.

I told the director that this place felt like a shrine to our fighting forces through the years.

"Yes," he said. "Even for me, after all these years here, there are several emotional cues which really still get to me."

He showed me one of these emotional cues. It was in the World War II exhibit.

"Up there are two original Medals of Honor," he said, pointing to two shiny objects in the center of the display. "They were awarded to Sgt. Thomas Baker and Lt. Col. William O'Brien of the 105th U.S. Infantry. They were both National Guardsmen from Troy, N.Y., and knew each other. They were awarded their medals posthumously for an action which took place on Saipan. Baker and O'Brien were caught up in the largest banzai attack of the war, when 5,000 Japanese soldiers attacked two American battalions. Baker was seriously wounded but refused to be evacuated from the battlefield. The last soldier out gave Baker a pack of cigarettes and a pistol with eight rounds in it and propped him up against a telephone pole.

When they came back later they found him, dead, still leaning against the pole with an empty pistol in his hands and eight dead Japanese soldiers nearby. O'Brien was found on a Jeep, where he was last seen firing a .50 caliber machine gun to buy time for his men to fall back. Thirty dead enemy soldiers lay around the vehicle. On the day of the attack, an Army dentist (not a New Yorker) also picked up a rifle to gain time for his men to escape. All three of them, including the dentist, died in the same battle. It is the only time in World War II that three Medals of Honor were awarded to three different men from the same unit for the same battle," he told me.

The many display cases showcase a pageant of uniforms, from the plain to the fussy, worn by U.S. soldiers over the last two centuries. In its entirety, the museum tells a saga of courage, sacrifice, and inspiration.

"We have 2,000 battle flags, the largest collection in the country. We have thousands of personal items, from soldiers since the dawning of our nation. We have hundreds of weapons and artillery shells. The collection is really quite awesome."

I told Aikey that I could sense his deep, emotional attachment to this place. "It's true. I love this place. Just think of the history that came from here." He pointed to the big front doors of the armory. "Just imagine, hundreds of local boys marched out that front door and down to the train station during World War I. Twenty-five years later they did it all over again for World War II. Amazing," he said softly.

As the state started consolidating the military collections of the many armories around New York, Aikey was called into action. "The day after an armory was sold off or closed, I was there gathering up the military items to be brought here. These artifacts cannot speak or fend for themselves. That is our job.

"And not everything we have here comes from a fighting man," Aikey told me. He pointed to a typewriter. "It belonged to Ira Wolfert. You can see his name still stenciled across the top of it. He was one of the most famous wartime correspondents. In 1943, his reporting from the Battle of Guadalcanal won him the Pulitzer Prize. Very famous man.

"Sixty years ago or so his car breaks down while he is out for a drive. It catches on fire. A passerby stops and helps Wolfert put out the fire. To thank the stranger, Wolfert reached into his trunk and gave him his typewriter. Sixty years later a friend of the museum's from the Plattsburgh area called and asked us do we want this. I couldn't believe it," Aikey smiled as he scratched his head.

Heroes come in all shapes and forms.

Wow Factor

I could almost feel Aikey's pulse race as we walked over to a separate glass-walled room near the front. "You talk about a wow factor, look at this," he said.

In a glass case is the uniform of a Union Soldier from the Civil War. But not any ordinary soldier.

Elmer Ellsworth was one of the premier military trainers and drill-masters of the pre-war militia. He was born nearby in Malta and grew up in Mechanicville. He was young, handsome, dashing, and sharp; brilliant, some would say. And he was a close personal friend of President Lincoln's.

On May 24, 1861, within hours of Virginia seceding from the Union, Colonel Ellsworth marched his men by a huge Confederate flag flying from the top of a large hotel just across the Potomac from the Capitol. He crossed over to the Marshall Hotel, ascended the steps, took the flag down, and proceeded to come back downstairs. On the third floor, the hotel owner shot Ellsworth to death with a single shotgun blast to the chest.

Colonel Elmer Ellsworth was the first notable Union casualty of the Civil War.

"Of course, Lincoln was devastated at what happened to his young friend," Aikey told me, "Ellsworth was afforded one of the largest funerals ever given at the time. Thousands came out to pay tribute to the young soldier. And that is what makes this my personal wow factor," he said pointing to the uniform.

It is Ellsworth's. The one he was wearing when he was killed. The cloth is in excellent shape, still showing some shadings of blood from his mortal wound. You can see a quarter-sized hole torn in the uniform where the bullet struck Ellsworth almost directly in the heart. "He was dead before he hit the floor," Aikey told me. A bent copper button gives testimony to the velocity of the fatal blast.

"This is history," the director remarked. "Real history."

The Take-Away

This is an incredible museum. Spacious, well lit, easily accessible. The informational panels are descriptive and exciting. The collection is displayed beautifully in elegant cases. There is seemingly no end to the scope of what this museum holds.

I asked the director about this.

"It's true, he told me. "Literally every week another great surprise just walks in the front door."

I asked him for some recent examples.

"Well, just a couple of weeks ago a woman came in and gave us nearly two hundred letters written by a family member of hers during the Civil War, Captain Carlos Alvarez de la Mesa. A de la Mesa has fought heroically in almost every American War. He was of Spanish origin. The letters are written in Spanish and are a real treasure trove for us. We currently have engaged a Skidmore college student to translate these letters for us. Also, the son of Stuart Symington, the first Secretary of the Air Force and later a U.S. Senator from Missouri, recently donated a letter his dad had. It was written by the famous Father Francis P. Duffy, the most awarded chaplain in Army history."

The basement of the museum holds the Veterans Research Center. There, workstations are available for people doing family research. "We have thousands of pieces of paper down here, from enlistment papers to discharge forms. For tens of thousands of servicemen," he told me.

In other rooms you can see huge pieces of weaponry stored for cataloging and future display. Artillery shells, cannon, shoulder arms, and more. One odd-looking item got the best of my curiosity. It was a rusty, sinister-looking weapon. It had four barrels and sat on two beat-up old tires. I just had to ask.

"Yes, this is rare for sure," Aikey said. "It is an old 1950s-era Soviet anti-aircraft gun, a ZPU4, which was found in the deserts of Iraq."

The Nuts and Bolts
New York State Military Museum and Research Center
61 Lake Street
Saratoga Springs, New York 12866
(518) 581-5100
www.nysmm.org

• *Travel Suggestion*
From Albany, take Exit 13N off the Northway (I-87). Proceed to Route 9 and go about five miles to Lake Street. Make a right on Lake Street and go three blocks to the museum.

• *Museum Hours*
Tuesday to Saturday: 10 a.m. to 4 p.m.
Closed on Sundays, Mondays, and every New York State Holiday.
Note: Appointments are needed to use the Research Center.

• *Admission*
Free

• *Number of Visitors Annually*
   12,000

Up around the Bend

Saratoga Springs is a splendid little city about a half hour north of Albany. With a background as a Revolutionary War turning point and with a pedigree as one of our nation's ritziest and toniest small communities, there is a big chunk of eye candy on almost every corner in the "Spa City." Grand Victorian mansions with sweeping front porches and manicured lawns are the hallmark of the center city historic district. Try and plan your visit to the military museum in August. That is when the ponies run at the Saratoga Race Track, the oldest venue *of any sport in America*!

The racetrack is about six blocks from the museum.

From Here to There

The other museum in this book that is nearest to the New York State Military Museum is the **National Bottle Museum,** located five miles south of Saratoga Springs in Ballston Spa.

49

BURDEN IRON WORKS MUSEUM

Troy, Rensselaer County

*T*he Burden Iron Works Museum is housed in the former corporate headquarters of one of the largest and most significant industrial sites in New York. The building's architect was Robert Robertson. He was known as one of the premier designers of institutional buildings as well as grandiose churches and magnificent mansions.

The Burden Iron Works building is a little creepy. Not in an Alfred Hitchcock kind of creepy. But more in line with a Harry Potter kind of creepy.

"As you can see, we are still a work-in-progress," P. Thomas Carroll, executive director, told me as he slowly opened the massive front doors to the building. "We call ourselves the not-ready-for-prime-time museum."

The inside of the building must be seen to be believed. Its massive atrium-like center hallway is brightly lit by a large skylight. The surviving original architectural flourishes include gleaming solid cherry wood ceilings. The effect is quite stunning.

"You should have seen this place before we got to it," he said as he showed me a photograph of the same building, pre-conservation years, with its windows knocked out and its veneer well worn.

Now there is a great sense of regalness to this old office building. The office wasn't built until after Henry Burden had died, but all around it here in South Troy, Burden, one of America's most successful industrialists, plotted his long line of inventions, crafted out his intricate patents, and supervised (at one point) the more than 1,400 employees laboring in his nearly three-quarter-mile-long factory on the east bank of the Hudson River.

313

"You must remember that Troy was one of America's greatest cities at one time," Carroll explained. "We had it all here, and the businesses and industries of Troy were key to the growth of our young nation. In 1840, Troy was, per capita, the fourth wealthiest city in America. We had it all."

What the director meant by "having it all," as far as Henry Burden is concerned, was having an embarrassment of natural riches from which to create his heavy industries of the early- to mid-nineteenth century. "From right here where we are standing," Carroll told me, "we have a large escarpment in front of us and the mighty Hudson River just a few feet out our back door. Down that escarpment flowed many streams and waterfalls, all harnessed by water wheels that powered the machines here at the bottom. After the work was done, it was out the back door with the product, onto a ship, and down the Hudson to New York it went. It was the total package. Water for power and water for transportation."

Troy's luminous industrial past is well displayed at the Burden Iron Works Museum (which is under the umbrella of an organization known as the Hudson Mohawk Industrial Gateway). Troy was a leading maker of stoves, bells, detachable shirt collars and cuffs (at one point nearly ninety percent of all collars made in America were made in Troy, the "Collar City"), water valves (some used in the construction of the Panama Canal), fire hydrants, and agricultural equipment (Troy-Bilt rototillers).

"Troy was the Silicon Valley of the nineteenth century. If you wanted to go to a place in America where new things were being done, things that you couldn't find anywhere else in the world, you came to Troy," Carroll said.

For Henry Burden it was all about horseshoes and railroad spikes.

"The main source of power around here was the waterfall above the factory complex. At one time Burden had five water wheels operating in the ravine where his original plant was located. But they kept failing, or the wood kept rotting out in the buckets, or there were snags caused by debris. The story goes that Burden used to burden (pun intended) his wife, Helen, with repeated complaints about his unreliable water wheels when he would come home at night. Finally exasperated, she told him, 'Henry, you have so many problems with all your little water wheels. Why don't you close them all down and open up one big giant water wheel?'"

He did.

The Burden Water Wheel was constructed on the south side of the nearby Wynantskill just below the upper falls. Five stories tall, and with thirty-six giant buckets made out of Georgia Pine, it was the most powerful vertical water wheel in human history. Journalists came from all over the world to marvel at its heft and power. The editor of the *Knickerbocker Magazine* dubbed it "The Niagara of Water Wheels."

It is said that American engineer George Washington Gale Ferris, Jr., first got his idea for the amusement park ride now known as the "Ferris wheel" after viewing Burden's behemoth invention. The museum has a striking archival photograph of the water wheel while it was in operation (it is long gone now). But for a dramatic view of what this towering piece of machinery looked like, check out the large mural painted by artist Kevin Clark that covers an entire outdoor wall near the entrance to Troy from the Menands Bridge in the southern part of the city. Here, you will clearly see the amazing size of Burden's invention.

Burden was in the horseshoe manufacturing business, and a lot of power was needed to operate the heavy machinery used to bend and cut the iron. The water wheel did the trick. Burden's company was the leading manufacturer of horseshoes for more than fifty years, at one time making more than fifty million horseshoes a year (about one every second, *per machine*).

So proficient was Burden in this specialty that the Union Army gave him an exclusive no-bid contract to provide the overwhelming majority of all their horseshoes during the Civil War. The horseshoe orders were shipped out in one hundred pound wooden kegs stamped with Burden's (and Troy's) name on them. There are only two of these wooden kegs known to survive. They are both here at the museum.

The horseshoe business eventually declined (thank you very much, Mr. Ford, whose 1917 Fordson tractor led to a dramatic drop in the number of horses used on America's farms, which was where most horses were in those days) and went out of business in 1937. One of the final batch of horseshoes ever made here is still on display at the museum.

Burden also caught a wave with his invention of the first machine ever capable of manufacturing the hook-headed railroad spike. It was the perfect binder that the great, expanding railroads needed to keep their rails tight and intact. He made huge quantities of them right here on the banks of the Hudson River. His first large order was for ten tons of railroad spikes for the Long Island Railroad in 1836. The next large order was for one hundred tons of spikes for the Baltimore and Ohio Railroad in 1838.

Henry Burden, native of Scotland and a driving force in the Industrial Revolution, thus became one of the wealthiest men in America.

Because of horseshoes, railroad spikes, and the biggest water wheel the world had ever seen.

And all right here in Troy.

Wow Factor
"My own personal favorite is, alas, not one the general public can see, at least not yet," the director told me. "We have Henry Burden's actual 1835 patent for his horseshoe making machine. It was issued before patents were numbered and instead, the President of the United States signed each. Henry's patent is signed by President Andrew Jackson. Obviously, it

is far too valuable to have on display here. We hope in the future to create a reasonable facsimile for display purposes."

I asked Carroll what the average visitor here is most interested in.

"Believe it or not, it is the bells," he laughed. "We had four of the country's leading bell manufacturers here in Troy and nearby Watervliet. Between 1808 and 1951 more than 100,000 bells came out of them, including almost every famous bell in America. Look at this giant photograph," he said, sweeping his laser light up one wall. "This is known as the Centennial Bell. Since the Liberty Bell was cracked and unusable, they wanted a replica bell to be rung on the centennial of our independence. Meneely Bell Company got the order and made the bell. It was first struck at midnight July 4, 1876, and it still hangs in Independence Hall in Philadelphia.

"So you see, we have so many wow factors it is hard to pick just one. For the agricultural enthusiasts we have the oldest known surviving rototiller made in the New World (1938 model A1, serial number 21). The bell fanatics love the Centennial Bell.

"We have famous surveying equipment that was made in Troy also. In fact, the Apollo astronauts leveled their equipment on the Moon with little spirit levels made in Troy by Geier & Bluhm Company and containing little bubbles of Troy air inside them."

The Take-Away

The key to a visit to the Burden Iron Works Museum lies in the expert hands of P. Thomas Carroll, PhD. Tom was one of the most worthy museum guides I have encountered during the long journey in writing this book. Names, dates, obsolete occurrences (local, national *and worldwide*), as well as historical factoids flow as easily off of Tom's tongue as, well, as easily as the water of the Wynantskill used to flow off the bluff behind the museum. And, he is a great storyteller.

Tom is pretty much a "one man band" at the museum. It is lightly staffed and struggles for attendance and support. That is the down side. The up side is that virtually every reader of this book who visits the museum, after making the prerequisite phone call in advance, will be blessed with a personal tour from Tom himself.

It is clear he loves Troy, has an affinity for the industrial history of America, and has a deep, almost kin-like, relationship with a man he spends an awful lot of his time with, Henry Burden.

I loved this museum.

The Nuts and Bolts

The Burden Iron Works Museum
1 East Industrial Parkway
Troy, New York 12180
(518) 274-5267
www.hudsonmohawkgateway.org

• *Travel Suggestion*

From I-787 take Exit 7E onto Route 378E. Get in the left lane as you leave the bridge. Follow the double yellow lines in the middle of the road through two traffic lights. At the third traffic light, turn left on Main Street. Cross the railroad tracks and pass the concrete wall on your right. Turn right on East Industrial Parkway. The museum is the first building on the right, and its main entrance faces the railroad tracks.

• *Museum Hours*

Weekdays 10 a.m. to 6 p.m. Since there is minimal staff, you are advised to call ahead to let them know you are coming. Special tours can also be arranged in advance by phone for small groups.

• *Admission*

All visitors: $5.00 donation

• *Number of Visitors Annually*

1,500

Up around the Bend

A full weekend's worth of historic discoveries await the new visitor to Troy. For a beautiful side trip, just go a few blocks from the Burden Iron Works

Museum to 416 Third Street. Here you will find St. Joseph's Carmelite Church, built in 1848. On a bright sunlit day you will witness a sight rare these days. More than forty huge original Tiffany stained glass windows throughout the church throw off a dancing prism of bright blues, soft pastels, blood reds, and shimmering yellows. It is one of the largest collections of Tiffany windows in any church in America.

In fact, Downtown Troy holds a veritable treasure chest of Tiffany windows, decorations, and wonders. And yes, Tom Carroll has all the details. Be sure and ask him!

From Here to There

The other museum in this book that is nearest to the Burden Iron Works Museum is the **USS *Slater* Museum** in Albany. It is five miles south of Troy.

GRANT'S COTTAGE
Wilton, Saratoga County

*P*resident Ulysses S. Grant's Adirondack cottage has been a member of the New York State Association of Museums since 1995. It was here that the president, also one of the greatest generals in American history, spent the last four weeks of his life.

"Grant arrived here on June 16, 1885," Jonathan Duda, the museum director, told me. "He was in very bad shape when he got here. He had been diagnosed with throat cancer in New York City and came here in hopes that the cool, clean Adirondack air might aid in his recuperation. Sadly, he died here about a month later, on July 23, 1885. His last days were very grim."

Grant's Cottage is one of the most poignant places I have ever visited. It is just a small, unremarkable home set deep in the woods well off the beaten path. "Despite the ordinariness of this place, history really does come alive here," said Steve Trimm, one of the lead tour guides. "When you consider the huge importance of Grant, both as a president and as a Civil War hero, it is quite amazing that he spent his last days on earth right here in little Wilton."

Trimm and Duda took me on a two-hour private tour of the facility. Each room is appointed with actual items used by the Grant family. The whole house is much as it was when the Grants took residence in 1885. We entered the side door to the cottage and inspected the "sitting room."

"As many know, Mark Twain had contracted with President Grant to publish his memoirs," Trimm explained. "Grant was flat busted and going even deeper in debt when Mark Twain signed him to a very generous

contract for his life story. Grant literally raced against death to complete his memoirs, and in fact did so just three days before he died. Ultimately, the book was an enormous success (it is still in print) and the president's efforts left his wife and family debt-free and in fact quite wealthy," Trimm told me.

We looked around the room. It is dimly lit with sparse decorations and little furniture. "We can document that this is the very room that Grant and Twain would sit in and discuss the progress of the book," Trimm told me. The specter of two of the nineteenth century's largest personalities sitting in this unassuming room gave me goose bumps.

The next room is known as the "sick room." The story told here is unbelievable.

"This is the room that the general actually lived in up to the end. As I said, he was extremely ill," Trimm told me. "He could not sleep lying down so he pushed these two leather chairs together and used them for his bed and desk," he said as he pointed to the two large chairs in the center of the room. A cabinet stood near the chairs. Inside its glass panels you can see Grant's bedclothes, a bell he used to summon help (he was unable to talk because of his throat cancer), his brushes and beard comb, a top hat, and a blanket inscribed with his name on it. A tall glass jar sits on top of the cabinet. It is half filled with a clear liquid.

"Believe it or not, that is an actual bottle of cocaine mixed with water. Grant rinsed his throat with it several times a day to ease his pain. It was much fuller when he died and it has been sitting on that cabinet since 1885," Duda told me. "As you can see, it has evaporated about half its contents over the decades."

We then entered the main living area. It has two adjoining rooms and a large, ornate fireplace. "The owner of the house, Mr. Drexel (of the Philadelphia Drexels), installed the fireplace just for President Grant. Even though he arrived in June, Drexel had hoped the president would live through the autumn and would use the fireplace. He did not make it to autumn, of course," Duda said softly.

"The most poignant story of the house is told in this room," Steve Trimm told me. "On the day before he died, President Grant told his sons that his greatest wish was to spend a night sleeping in an actual bed. This was after weeks of sleeping fitfully upright in his chair. A bed was brought in from a nearby hotel and placed in the living room. President Grant was at last able to lie down on this bed to sleep on his final night on Earth. He died in the morning."

Like I said, poignant.

Wow Factor
There is a wow factor at every corner of this historic cottage. So among the three of us we were able to come up with three different thoughts.

"For me the whole wow factor has to be the authenticity of the place," director Duda began. "So many of our guests are just awestruck at the number of items we have that really belong here. Original furniture, original clothes, many items that belonged to the Grant family. The whole house is pretty much as it was on the day Grant died. Visitors, especially history buffs who have been to other restored homes of famous people, are literally speechless when observing the number of original items we have on display here."

As for tour guide Trimm, his wow factor was a specific item. "These little notes are what I find incredible," he told me as he pointed to some small handwritten notes and letters in a display case. "As I mentioned, Grant was unable to speak while here because of the advances of his throat cancer. So he wrote notes to communicate with his family and staff. They really are quite precious. Here is one that I particularly like," he said showing me a small note in Grant's own handwriting. It was a note to his son, Jesse, who lived with him here until the end. It said, "Tell Jesse to come down in fifteen minutes and play a hand of cards with me."

"So touching," Trimm whispered.

My own wow factor can be found in the main living area. After the president died, many large floral tributes arrived at the cottage. As odd as it sounds, they are still here! I especially liked the six-foot-tall floral depiction of the Gates of Heaven. It was sent by Leland Sanford, railroad tycoon, industrialist, and (at the time) U.S. Senator from California. It consists of thousands of tiny flowers, each one hand-dipped in wax to make them eternal. This floral tribute and others still stand as mute sentinels across the room from where Grant's deathbed is.

The Take-Away

This is a remarkable, historic, and sentimental place. I was almost overcome by the thoughts of the historic tableau that took place here for the four weeks in 1885 when President Grant was here. The weight of sadness is palpable in every room, and yet the downright history exhibited here is nothing short of startling. To think that Mark Twain came here, that many of the great "lions of the Civil War" came here to attend the funeral on the front porch (including General William T. Sherman), the whole nation being seized with the daily news of the legendary general's great fight against his final foe, the race to finish his final memoirs, his last hours, and more. All documented in a "time freeze" scenario as if the funeral train carrying Grant's body down the mountain had just departed. The story told at Grant's Cottage is one of great dignity and courage played out against the incredible beauty of one of New York State's most stunning natural settings.

The notion that only 3,000 visitors make the trek up Mount McGregor each year dismays me. I understand there are obstacles on your way here (more about that later), but the reward is well worth it.

Not the least of the reasons to come here is to visit the Eastern Overlook. This cleared promontory is a short walk through the woods down a path from the cottage. You exit the lush woods into a burst of wilderness wonderment. Here is where President Grant sat in a gazebo (now gone) on his last day. The view is awesome. With not a single tree or shrub blocking your view, you can see the towers of Albany's Empire Plaza (twenty five miles away), the rising Adirondacks (ten miles away), the Saratoga Battlefield and monument (twenty miles away), the foothills of the Catskill Mountains (fifty miles away) and, on a clear day, the Green Mountains of Vermont (sixty miles away).

I have witnessed and enjoyed many vistas throughout the Adirondack and North Country regions of New York.

None are better than this.

The Nuts and Bolts

> Grant's Cottage
> Mount McGregor Road
> Wilton, New York 12831
> (518) 584-4353
> www.GrantCottage.org

• *Travel Suggestion*

> From the Northway (I-87) take Exit 16 West on Ballard Road. Follow the signs to Grant's Cottage.
>
> Note: This is the tricky part. Grant's Cottage is actually on the grounds of a New York State Prison!
>
> Enter the grounds by checking in at the Mount McGregor Correctional Facility checkpoint. Tell them you are going to Grant's Cottage. They will write down your license plate and let you enter. You will follow the road along tall walls, razor concertina wire, and cellblocks. Eventually you will come to the Grant's Cottage Visitor Center on your left. Go in here and view an orientation film and visit the

gift shop. From this parking lot, you can walk up to the cottage as well as enter the woods to visit the Eastern Overlook.

- *Museum Hours*
  Memorial Day through Labor Day: Wednesday through Sunday 10:00 a.m. to 4:00 p.m.
  Labor Day through Columbus Day: Saturday and Sunday 10:00 a.m. to 4:00 p.m.

- *Admission*
  Adults: $5.00
  Seniors/Students: $4.00
  Under six: Free
  Special admission rates are available for large groups.

- *Number of Visitors Annually*
  3,000

Up around the Bend

The Battle of Saratoga was the turning point of the Revolutionary War. Since you get a glimpse of the sweeping battlefield from the Overlook, a trip to it seems almost natural. Guided tours are very interesting, the visitor's center is informative and features ever-changing exhibits, and the gift shop is stocked with enough toy soldiers, books, and videos to keep even the youngest visitor interested.

Be sure and visit the Saratoga Monument. This is the towering obelisk that can be seen by the eye from Grant's Cottage. There are four niches carved into the base of the monument. Each was to hold a life-sized statue of a great American military hero. One holds General Schuyler, another has General Gates in it, and yet another has famed rifleman, Colonel Daniel Morgan.

Curiously, the final niche is empty. It was here that Benedict Arnold's statue was to be placed. Obviously, historians and others had second thoughts.

From Here to There

The other museum in this book that is nearest to Grant's Cottage is the
N.Y.S. Military Museum in Saratoga Springs. It is eight miles south of
Wilton.

OTHER MUSEUMS TO
EXPLORE IN REGION NINE

Albany: New York State Museum. "Everything from early New York history to a large multi-room exhibit on the 9/11 terrorist attacks. This museum is free." (518) 474-5877, www/nysm.nysed.gov.

Albany: Irish-American Heritage Museum. "Preserves and tells the story of contributions of Irish-Americans and their culture in the U.S., and New York State in particular." (518) 432-6598, www.irishamericanheritage museum.org.

Albany: Albany Institute of History and Art. "The second oldest art museum in America. Robert Livingston, a signer of the Declaration of Independence, was its first president." (518) 463-4478, www.albanyinstitute .org.

Granville: Pember Museum of Natural History and Pember Nature Preserve. Granville. "One of the largest collections of mounted birds, mammals, and insects in the state. Provides invaluable learning experiences to hundreds of area schoolchildren as the only museum of its kind in the region." (518) 642-1515, www.pembermuseum.com.

Saratoga Springs: National Museum of Dance. "The only museum in the U.S. solely dedicated to dance." (518) 584-2225, www.dancemuseum .org.

Saratoga Springs: National Museum of Racing and Hall of Fame. "Museum is located across the street from the legendary Saratoga Race Course, the oldest organized sporting venue in the United States." (518) 584-0400, www.racingmuseum.org.

In Memoriam

The Walter Elwood Museum of the Mohawk Valley was one of my original fifty museums for this book. I include it now post-humously to pay tribute to its staff, as well as to illustrate the fragility of many of the smaller museums in Upstate New York. Everything you see in this chapter is a true reflection of my after-noon visit to it. Ann Peconie, executive director of the Walter Elwood Museum, was my guide. It was a bright, sunny July afternoon in 2011.

Three weeks after my visit, this museum was swallowed up by the Mohawk River, a victim of Hurricane Irene.

At this printing, the museum is hoping to rebuild.

51

WALTER ELWOOD MUSEUM OF THE MOHAWK VALLEY

Amsterdam, Montgomery County

*W*ho the heck was Walter Elwood and why did he collect so many weird things?

"Walter was a longtime educator and administrator in our Amsterdam School District. He had a penchant for world travel, and he collected anything and everything," Ann Peconie, executive director of the museum told me.

Boy did he ever!

As Ms. Peconie guided me through the cluttered rooms of this very impressive museum located on the banks of the Mohawk River, I thought, this is what an antique store looked like a hundred years ago!

"Walter was very interested in biology and natural history, which explains all the stuffed animals and the full skeleton hanging in the corner," she said. "But yes, he collected everything. And people liked him, so they gave him things. All kinds of things."

In one room we find old toys and trains and doll sets. In another, the "military room," we can observe Civil War relics, old uniforms, weapons, and art prints. It is the newest display room.

"In this room," Ms. Peconie pointed out with pride, "is the actual battle drum used by the then thirteen-year-old Henry Kingsley at the Battle of Gettysburg."

Another themed room is the library. "We have a collection of rare Amsterdam city directories that date as far back as 1870. They are invaluable to people doing research on the city's history," she told me.

331

Ms. Peconie is a wealth of fact and factoids. She was a totally charming guide through the maze of bric-a-brac. On one wall she showed me a series of autographed letters from and photos of past New York State governors. In the old-fashioned "Amsterdam Industry Room" she showed me how an old telegraph machine worked and actually played a march for me on a century-old Edison phonograph in the Victoria Parlor.

"I like to tell the kids who come through here that this is where all their fancy computer gadgets began. They have iPods to play their music; I play the Victrola for them. They have cell phones with them; I show them how to tap out a message on the teletype. It is all relative. I try and explain that this is really where 'it' all began. And you know what? They get 'it'!" she exclaimed.

Many historic paintings fill the walls of the center hall of the mansion. Among them are several by Amsterdam artist Mary van der Veer, who studied with James Whistler and exhibited at the Chicago World's Fair and the Paris Exposition.

And don't even get her started about the early television sets! One 1950s model actually pops out of a coffee table. Another is one of the earliest sets ever produced. "It was made right up the road in Schenectady by General Electric. It is so old that you have to watch the screen in a mirror because they hadn't figured how to invert the image yet to a monitor."

Sounds weird, doesn't it? Well, that was Walter Elwood.

Wow Factor

Ms. Peconie has plenty to choose from for a wow factor here, but when asked, she took me directly to the corner of the "Amsterdam History Room," directly off her office. Here she told me about an extraordinary lamp.

"This lamp is definitely one of a kind," she told me as she slowly twirled the top glass shade. "The lamp was hand-made in 1907 by Louis Comfort Tiffany, and each pane of the shade is an actual hand-colored glass slide of a nature photograph."

"How much is it worth?" I asked.

"Oh, my dear. We have no idea. It is just so rare and special," she said as we both stared at the glittering backlit panels of the photo slides.

The Take-Away

I liked this place a lot. As I mentioned, Ms. Peconie is a whirlwind of a tour guide and she really helped to liven up a rather old and stodgy collection. She made it exciting. Clearly, her favorite room is the "Natural History Room."

"Mr. Elwood eventually ran into a fascinating guy named Robert Frothingham, another nature lover and collector," Peconie says. "Many of the items here in the Natural History Room are from Frothingham's collection. The centerpiece is a huge stuffed walrus mounted on the front wall, with thirty-two-inch ivory tusks and all," she chuckled. Other marquee items are a Tyrannosaurus Rex dinosaur fossil footprint, a stuffed bald eagle (presumably from before they were an endangered species), and a basket made out of armadillo skin. It is all curious and really amazing (although the hollowed-out elephant's foot being used as an umbrella stand is a bit quirky).

The physical setting of the museum, the historic mansion known as Guy Park, is stunning. The home, built for a nephew of the legendary land agent and Indian emissary Sir William Johnson, sits on the banks of the

Mohawk River. It is always breezy here and the backdrop of the mansion, the river, and the mountains on the far side make for a place of beauty and tranquility.

History truly does live at the Walter Elwood Museum of Mohawk Valley History.

The Nuts and Bolts
The Walter Elwood Museum of the Mohawk Valley
366 West Main Street
Amsterdam, New York 12010
(518) 843-5151
www.walterelwoodmuseum.org

• *Donations*
Donations toward the relocation and rebuilding of the Walter Elwood Museum are greatly appreciated. (Video of the Hurricane Irene destruction of this museum can be found at the website.)

• *Number of Visitors Annually*
7,000

Up around the Bend
The city of Canajoharie lies just twenty miles west of Amsterdam. The Arkell Museum there is one of Upstate's best. Besides all the wonderful art pieces, you will also find a separate Beech-Nut Museum inside. This holds fascinating artifacts and historic memorabilia from the Beech-Nut Company, which made its headquarters here for over a century (the factory is now vacant). In downtown Canajoharie you will find one of the last three "dummy lights" in America. The traffic light is situated right in the middle of an intersection, rather than hanging high above it.

From Here to There
The other museum in this book that is nearest to the Walter Elwood Museum of the Mohawk Valley is the **Wildlife Sports and Education Museum** in Vails Mills. It is ten miles north of Amsterdam.

CHUCK D'IMPERIO is the author of several books about Upstate New York. His most recent title was *Monumental New York: A Guide to 30 Iconic Memorials in Upstate New York*, also published by Syracuse University Press. He is a longtime radio broadcaster (since 1989) with Townsquare Media in Oneonta, as well as a newspaper columnist. Chuck is married to Trish, an educator, and they are the parents of four children. They live, of course, in Upstate New York.